COMPLETE GUIDE TO
WINNING
KENO

ABOUT THE AUTHOR

David Cowles is recognized as the foremost authority in the world on the game of keno. He serves as a consultant for keno rooms in Las Vegas, Atlantic City, Nebraska, Montana, and other casinos around the country, helping them to form the proper odds, and make the payout schedules for their keno games.

Cowles is also the editor and publisher of the acclaimed *Keno Newsletter*, a publication read by casino executives and players, and he writes a keno column for the weekly, *Gaming Today*.

Cowles, who is an inventor and an attorney, currently resides in Las Vegas, where he keeps a constant pulse on the latest developments in Keno games.

COMPLETE GUIDE TO
WINNING KENO

David W. Cowles

CARDOZA PUBLISHING

Cardoza Publishing, publisher of **Gambling Research Institute** (GRI) books, is the foremost gaming publisher in the world with a library of more than 75 up-to-date and easy-to-read books and strategies. These authoritative works are written by the top experts in their fields and with more than 5,000,000 books in print, represent the best-selling and most popular gaming books anywhere.

Printing History

First Printing   April 1996
Second Printing   November 1997

Library of Congress Catalogue Card Number: 95-68285
ISBN: 0-940685-62-0

TABLE OF CONTENTS

CHAPTER   **PAGE**

FOREWORD
by
Michael Gaughan

In early 1973 I decided on a keno game. I took an area six feet from the back wall of the lounge and 30 feet in length. There was room for only four writers and a checker. The cocktail seating doubled as the keno lounge. My knowledge of keno was limited, so I wanted to see what everyone else did. I picked up every keno book in town and was amazed at how different the books were. Many were unclear and complicated as to rules, layouts and even the general information on how to play keno. I knew I could make a keno booklet simpler. It was then I discovered the difficulty in calculating keno percentages. It took anywhere from thirty minutes to an hour per ticket. For about a year the game did modestly well. Many times I thought about making some changes; but, because of the mental work involved, I was too lazy to do so.

About this time an unshaven, ill-dressed man approached me in the casino and tried to sell a book on keno. He had already been turned down by my keno manager. But, not wanting to offend any potential customer, I agreed to look at it. He said he wanted $100 or at least make an offer after I read it. I took the book to my office with no intention of buying it. However, later that afternoon, glancing through it, I quickly realized this person had spent an enormous amount of time preparing keno charts. I took out my percentage sheets and with some interpolation I checked to see if his calculations were right. What took me hours to do, I was now able to do in minutes. I could devise new and different keno tickets in no time at all using his schedules.

The next morning I gave him $200 for his book. He was extremely thankful and said that only two other managers in the entire town had bought his book and both had chiseled him down under the $100 asking price. His name was Ralph Schoup. He had spent months and months figuring hit frequencies on keno games. His book was a fabulous find and only a few had the foresight to buy it.

Ralph and I spent many hours together over the years discussing keno. He, himself was never a keno player, but a mathematician who loved to percentage keno tickets and develop new ways to play keno. He did calculations for 21 ball keno, 22 ball keno, 25 ball keno, jackpot specials, two game exactas, top and bottom tickets and high-low tickets. My book swelled to over a hundred pages. With the versatility of Schoup's book, the Royal Inn keno game became one of the most successful in town.

Finally after five years of friendship, Ralph died. I never got the chance to thank him. I had used his book in 1979 for the Barbary Coast and then again in 1986 for the Gold Coast. In 1991 the Gold Coast's major competition, the Palace Station, came up with a new keno booklet. In wanting to check their new payoffs, I discovered I had lost Ralph's book. And it was nowhere to be found.

Which leads me into why I am writing this foreword. Jim Abraham, my general manager at the Gold Coast arranged a meeting for me with a David Cowles. Jim informed me that he had developed a computer program for keno. I was skeptical, but being without my old book, I was open to anything. I went to David's office planning to spend half an hour. Three hours later, I left there thoroughly impressed. Where Ralph Schoup was a mathematician and did his calculations as a hobby, David Cowles was the ultimate keno player. He had analyzed every ticket of every game in town. He had everyone's keno book with any and all mistakes noted. He even knew what every casino's complimentaries were for their keno players. In fact, he knew more about Gold Coast keno than I did. When I bought his program, he asked me what kind of P.C. I had in my office. Embarrassed, I told him I did not have one. Within a week, I had a computer and a printer behind my desk, courtesy of Mr. Cowles. I can now redo my entire keno book in less than an hour and check the percentage of any ticket in seconds.

Since my first meeting with David, we have spent a great deal of time on keno. We have compared the advantages and disadvantages of low payout-high hit frequency tickets versus high payout-low hit frequency tickets. We have argued over the better ways of designing keno booklets and we have fought over house percentages. One of the reasons the Gold Coast keno lounge is number one in Las Vegas is David Cowles' undying devotion to keno and his advice and patience with me.

David's love for keno leads him to publish a monthly newsletter. This four to six page journal has become the gospel to all avid keno players. He praises those casinos with what he believes are fair tickets and he exposes those with rip-offs. Many an operator has changed his keno paybacks or in some cases even discontinued certain tickets because of his criticisms. One time he even embarrassed Caesars Palace into dropping their million dollar ticket because of the high hold. Some keno managers like him and some don't. The one thing I can truly say is that his numbers are never wrong.

Well, being the keno nut that he is, he has written this book. I have read it twice and can say that it is the most comprehensive dissertation on keno that I have ever read. There is knowledge for every level. He teaches the novice how to play and what to avoid, shows intermediates the better games to play and provides the experts the tools to percentage any keno ticket. No one other than David would have spent this much time and energy on a keno manifesto. It is truly a labor of love. Everything about keno is here.

ACKNOWLEDGEMENTS

This book could not have been written without the input, advice, and support of many people. I would like to single five of them out for their invaluable assistance in making this book as complete and accurate as possible. To these very special indi-viduals, I owe an enormous debt of thanks.

James K. Bopp has been employed in keno for more than thirty years. At this writing, he is keno manager of Binion's Horseshoe in Las Vegas. Prior to his keno career, he was an instructor of English at Loyola Academy in Chicago. Jim—as he prefers to be called— reviewed the completed manuscript and suggested numerous changes. Jim's viewpoint— based on his many years of experience from "behind the desk"—was instrumental in giving this book the proper perspective and balance. Jim also contributed a number of interesting anecdotes from the early days of keno.

Michael Gaughan is owner-operator of the Barbary Coast Hotel and Casino, Gold Coast Hotel and Casino, and McCarran Airport Slots, all in Las Vegas, Nevada; and, the Casino Queen Riverboat, East Saint Louis, Illinois. Mike (I am privileged to know him well enough to address him by his first name) is one of the very few casino owners who takes an active interest in his keno games, and he delights in personally creating new, exciting, liberal keno tickets for his casinos. Mike took time from his busy schedule to study the manuscript and contributed valuable suggestions. I am honored that he agreed to write the foreword to this book and grateful for the kind words expressed in that foreword.

Steve Harney worked hand-in-hand with me for nearly five years in preparing this book for publication. Without Steve's help, this book could not have been completed. He served as a sounding board for every chapter and worked with me every step of the way in its production. Steve prepared all of the charts and illustrations; he proofread; he edited; and he made countless recommendations. Additionally, Steve converted my computer program for calculating keno odds, which I had written in Wang Basic II language, into an easy-to-use program that will work on most any PC-type computer (see Chapter 35).

Terry R. Ridgway is a professor in the Department of Economics at the University of Nevada, Las Vegas (UNLV). I consulted with Terry on numerous occasions when I was stuck with a math problem. He gave generously of his time to review the entire manuscript and helped me make the formulas easier for the layperson to understand. Terry also supplied a majority of the language used in the chapter on the law of probabilities.

JJ Cowles, my wonderful wife, who patiently put up with the enormous amount of time I spent writing and editing. She never complained that I deferred hanging pictures in our home or didn't take her out to the movies often enough. Her continuous support and encouragement made the effort worthwhile.

Chapter 1

INTRODUCTION TO KENO

In addition to luck and playing strategy, it takes skill to be a consistent winner at most card games. Many good hands have been wasted by novice card players; an expert often wins despite a mediocre hand.

The card player constantly makes decisions based upon his knowledge and experience. In blackjack, each hand requires a decision: whether to split, stand, take a hit, double down, take "insurance," or (at some casinos) surrender. The poker player must determine which cards to hold and which to discard; whether to call, raise, or fold.

Poker, blackjack, baccarat, craps, roulette, and other table games can be very intimidating to newcomers to casino gaming. These games seem (and often are) complicated and difficult to master.

Inexperienced players don't like to display their ignorance of the games by making mistakes, nor do they want to risk their money on games they don't understand. It's no wonder that most first-time visitors to a casino shy away from the table games and, at least initially, stick with the slot machines.

But ... sooner or later, they'll discover keno.

Keno is easy to play - anyone can learn how in just a few minutes.

Keno requires no skill or experience - it's just a guessing game!

Keno's exciting - every game is a new opportunity to parlay a small bet into a huge payoff.

Keno has universal appeal - even those with the most modest gambling budget can enjoy keno. It doesn't take a large bankroll to play, but a lucky keno player can wind up with one!

Keno is relaxing - it's slow-paced and doesn't demand a lot of concentration. Most keno lounges are comfortable, and the cocktail waitresses always keep players well supplied with complimentary beverages.

Keno is a friendly game - it's easy to develop camaraderie with the other players, and many lifelong friendships have started in a keno lounge.

Keno is periods of slow play punctuated by moments of sheer ecstasy, when a player hits it *big* ... perhaps winning enough money to buy a TV, automobile, or even a new home!

Keno players need a lot of patience ... keno's a long shot game, so the wins—particularly big ones—can be exasperatingly far apart. A lot of people try the game, and, before really giving it a chance, move on to something else, saying "I never win anything at keno!"

Keno's fun, and it's convenient - the only game you can play in a casino's coffee shop, restaurant, or cocktail lounge.

Keno, however, is not as simple as it first appears—as you'll soon learn.

The surest way of making money at keno is to own a casino—but, even owning a casino won't guarantee that you'll show a profit a hundred percent of the time. As with any other business, from your gross receipts you'll have to deduct a lot of costs—payroll, rent, utilities, equipment, supplies, maintenance, advertising, taxes, and other operational expenses.

Can keno players ever beat the casino? In the long run, no.

Casinos will always win more than the aggregate of players. But, some players do win consistently, and some players do wind up winning enough to retire.

Keno has long had the reputation of being the game with the highest house percentage in the entire casino, except perhaps for the Big 6 (Wheel of Fortune). If this reputation is true, keno players have virtually no chance of coming out ahead of the game.

On the other hand, keno is one of the oldest casino games, and has a legion of devotees. Why would so many people keep playing a game that statistics say they cannot possibly beat?

The truth lies somewhere between the two extremes.

There are keno tickets with outlandishly high house percentages; others have PCs that are comparable to slots, roulette, and the table games. On occasion, some keno tickets actually have percentages in the players' favor!

In the following pages I'll show you how to recognize (and avoid) the rip-off tickets, and what to look for *before* you place your bet.

You'll learn how to write a basic keno ticket, how to write a way ticket, and more about alternate types of keno than you could have imagined existed.

You'll learn all about "winning numbers," how many numbers to mark, and how much money to bet. I'll teach you playing strategy and money management techniques.

In short, this book will show you how you can win more and lose less at keno. That is to say, you'll win more when you're winning, and lose less at all other times.

Chapter 2

HISTORY OF KENO

The game of keno was, some say, invented by Ken O'Leary, son of the woman whose cow kicked over the lantern that started the great Chicago fire.

Others place the origin of the game in Wisconsin, where it was supposedly played to raise money to support orphans in the town of Kenosha.

If you believe either of the above stories, give yourself a rating of 10 in gullibility. I just made them up.

In the year 1530 a game resembling keno, "La Lotto de Firenze," began in Florence and spread like wildfire throughout Renaissance Italy. Popularity continued through the centuries and the game evolved into the Italian National Lottery in 1870. Except for a few interruptions due to war, it's been played there ever since.

Although the first known public lottery is said to have been sponsored by Augustus Caesar to raise funds for repairing the city of Rome, it's more likely that "La Lotto de Firenze" was brought back to Italy by Marco Polo or one of the other early world travelers; for the game we now call keno originated in China and was operated as a national lottery more than a thousand years before the birth of Jesus.

Legend tells us that keno came about as a result of the "Canon of Change," written in 1130 B.C. by Chou Kung, son of the founder of the Kung Dynasty, and was used to finance construction of the Great Wall, one of the wonders of the world.

An Oriental figure, the "Yang and Yin," which symbolized creation, was the basis for the design of the keno ticket. The figure was divided into two sections. The upper section was considered feminine in nature and had to do with things heavenly and beautiful, while the lower section was masculine and pertained to things more earthly and devilish.

It didn't take long for Chinese entrepreneurs, seeing how much money the government was making on keno, to try to cut themselves in for a piece of the action. Naturally, the government outlawed these private games.

One version of keno was called "White Pigeon Ticket." The tickets were so named because of their illegal use. Professional gamblers, rather than risk arrest themselves, used carrier pigeons to send tickets and winnings between office and customer.

Keno was first introduced to America in the mid-19th century by the Chinese immigrants who came to the United States to help build railroads and work in the gold and silver mines. Thus, it was only natural that the game, played mostly by Chinese, was referred to as the "Chinese Lottery."

During the Great Depression, games similar to the Chinese Lottery were started by non-Chinese entrepreneurs in Montana. The game, which was then just called "lottery," appealed to people struggling to find ways to make ends meet in those trying times; it provided a chance to win a large amount of money for a very small investment.

Warren Nelson, then 23 years old, worked for a lottery game in Butte. In 1931 he opened his own game in Great Falls.

Gambling was against the law in Montana, and in Great Falls there was more or less continuous harassment by the police; Nelson's operation was shut down numerous times. Nevada, however, had legalized gambling (on March 20, 1931), so Warren put four or five men on a bus and moved his game to Reno. He opened Nevada's first keno game in the Palace Club in June, 1936.

Lotteries were still illegal in Nevada, and remain so to this day; but, "keno"—the old name for the game we now call bingo—was among the games that had been legalized by the Nevada gambling bill. So, with a quick change of nomenclature, the "Chinese Lottery" (no longer operated by Chinese) became legal.

To avoid confusion with the game of bingo—which, as I've pointed out, was called keno at that time—the lottery game was dubbed *race horse keno*. The names of race horses were written on the keno tickets, and each draw was called a *race*. The designa-tion stuck, and is still used today, although the practice of assigning the names of horses to the numbers has long been discarded.

As originally played, eighty numbers were written on slips of paper, and the papers tightly folded or inserted in small tubes. Each game, twenty of the numbers were drawn. The paper slips soon gave way to the use of small wooden balls, which were called *peas* by those in the business.

Then, while in California, Warren Nelson saw a carnival game at the Long Beach pier that used Ping-Pong balls dispensed from a wire cage to determine winners of merchandise prizes, such as kewpie dolls. He brought one of the cages and some balls back to Nevada, and the modern game of keno was born.

Joe Lyden, also from Montana, is given credit for opening the first keno game in Las Vegas, at the Fremont.

Another bit of vocabulary that remains from the early days of keno is the word *spots*, which refers to the numbers marked on a keno ticket.

Originally, all keno tickets were prepared by marking *spots* over the preprinted numbers with a brush and ink—the same technique used, traditionally, to write Chinese characters.

There are only a few places left where they still have a *brush game*, as most casinos have thrown away their brushes and inkwells and installed computerized keno writeup stations.

You can still play a brush game at Club Cal-Neva in Reno, which is owned by Warren Nelson—the same Warren Nelson who brought keno to Nevada. And, as of this writing, the Showboat in Las Vegas also has brush games. They order camel's-hair brushes direct from a company in Hong Kong in lots of several thousand at a time.

Instead of hand-prepared tickets, most customers now receive the product of a dot-matrix printer. It's interesting to note, however, that many of the computer printouts simulate the brush-and-ink spots of yesteryear, even though a check mark, *X*, or other symbol would serve the same purpose.

James K. Bopp, keno manager at Binion's Horseshoe, wrote me:

"I have eliminated the word *spot* from our pay booklets. I consider it an anachronism. The 'good ol' brush days' when both customer and writer spotted in tickets (sometimes with the skill of a proud calligrapher) are gone.

"To tell a newcomer to keno that a good ticket to play is a $1.00 6-spot is asking him to deal with an unknown that requires further explanation."

Bopp made a very good point, but I don't entirely agree with him.

The term *spot* might be new and perhaps confusing to a novice keno player, but I don't know of any other way to describe a "marked number on a keno ticket" as succinctly.

Keno has many other expressions that could also confound new players, such as *way tickets, flashboards, inside tickets, payoffs, blower, rabbit ears,* and *rates.*

Keno is not unique in having a lingo of its own. Every sport and industry has its own vocabulary, words which may seem strange to outsiders but which are an integral part of the endeavor.

The phrases *first seed, slam dunk, alley-oop,* and *fast break* mean a lot to college basketball fans, but are jibberish if one doesn't follow the game. Even *runs, hits,* and *errors,* words known to just about every American, are incomprehensible to people not familiar with baseball.

RAM, megabyte, and DOS require explanation to those not computer literate. Black's Law Dictionary has more than 1,500 pages devoted to words used by the legal profession. And so on.

The historical origin of the word *spot*, as used in keno, may be unknown by many of today's players, although brush-and-ink spots haven't quite gone the way of buggy whips and running boards. My conclusion is that the word *spot* is still very much a part of the game of keno, and likely to remain so for a long, long time.

If you would like to learn about the early history of keno in greater detail, read Wayne McClure's *Keno Winning Ways*, published by GBC Press, and available from Gamblers' Book Club in Las Vegas. McClure writes with authority; in addition to being an avid keno player, he dealt the game for many years in Reno and South Lake Tahoe and was an instructor to classes of student keno writers.

Keno Winning Ways thoroughly explains the origin of the game, with emphasis on the Chinese Lottery days, keno's introduction into Nevada, and its development into a fixture at most every Nevada casino.

McClure's book is a scholarly, comprehensive reference, with many interesting anecdotes about the pioneers of keno in Nevada. In it, he describes many variations of keno now all-but-forgotten. The book has numerous photos, as well as reproductions of pay tables and keno tickets from the thirties through the seventies, all of historical value.

Chapter 3

HOW TO PLAY KENO

Keno is a game of chance. Unlike card games, no skill of any kind is required.

Each game, twenty out of eighty numbered balls are drawn automatically from a wire cage or plastic bowl (sometimes called a *goose*). The selection is completely random, and which balls will be chosen is anybody's guess.

Choose the right ticket and mark the correct numbers, and you can win $50,000, $100,000, perhaps even a million dollars!

Keno is one of the simplest, easiest casino games to play—but, it can also be one of the most complex. This chapter deals only with the basics and teaches you how to play a straight keno ticket (sometimes referred to as a regular ticket). Way and combination tickets, catch-all and pay-any-catch tickets, top-and-bottom tickets, and the other myriad variations of keno are explained in subsequent chapters.

In the keno lounges, restaurant and bar areas, and wherever you can play keno, you'll find a number of keno supply items, yours for the taking.

These include keno paybooks or folders; pay cards that describe current "special" keno tickets; blank keno tickets; and, always, black crayons.

The keno paybooks, folders, and cards generally include a brief set of keno instructions, the casino's keno rules, a description of the tickets offered by the casino, and—most importantly—pay charts, which tell you how much money you can win.

The amount you can win varies; it's determined by the price and type of ticket you play, the amount of numbers you mark, and how many of your marked numbers are drawn. In general:

The more you bet, the more you can win.

The more numbers you mark, the higher the potential top prize—and the less likely it is that you will win it.

And, the more of your numbers that are drawn, the more money you will win.

There are exceptions to each of these generalities, as you'll learn in the following chapters.

Each keno ticket is printed with an 80-square grid. The numbers inside of each square correspond to the ones printed on the keno balls, which are numbered from 1 to 80.

Using a crayon and an unmarked keno ticket (keno blank), place a large X in each square that contains a number you want to play. You may mark from 1 to 15 numbers at most casinos. Many casinos also have a 20-number ticket, and a few casinos allow you to play 16–19, 32, or even 40 numbers.

In the space indicated on the ticket, usually the top right hand corner, write the amount you wish to wager. And, in the space indicated (usually in the right hand margin beneath the price), write the number of X's you marked on the ticket.

If you wish to play the ticket for more than one game, also write the number of consecutive games you wish to play and the total price of the ticket (price of one game multiplied by the number of games).

If you have any doubts about where to write these numbers, look at the examples in a keno paybook—or, ask any keno writer or runner.

If you're in the keno lounge, hand the ticket (sometimes called an *original* or *inside* ticket) to a keno writer, together

8-spot $1.00 regular keno ticket

1	2	3	4	5	6	7	8	9	10
11	✗	13	✗	15	✗	17	✗	19	20
21	22	23	24	25	26	27	28	29	30
31	32	33	34	35	36	37	38	39	40

41	42	43	44	45	46	47	48	49	50
51	52	53	54	✗	✗	57	58	59	60
61	62	63	64	✗	✗	67	68	69	70
71	72	73	74	75	76	77	78	79	80

1 00

8

with the amount of your wager. The keno writer will register your ticket and give you, in return, an authorized game ticket as a receipt for your bet.

The authorized game ticket (also referred to as a *duplicate, outside,* or *computer-generated* ticket) is prepared by computer at most casinos. It has all of the information you marked on the blank ticket, plus the numbers of the games you will be playing. A keno ticket is good only for the game or games indicated on the ticket.

Check the ticket for mistakes! If the keno writer made an error, and you don't get it corrected before the start of the game, the numbers on the authorized game ticket will be the ones upon which you will be paid, not the numbers you marked on the blank ticket.

If you're in a restaurant or bar area, give your ticket and amount of your bet to a keno runner. You can always recognize keno runners; most are female, wear distinctive uniforms, and call out "Keno!" as they make their rounds. The keno runner will take your bet to a keno writer and bring the authorized game ticket back to you.

Keno runners are for the players' convenience only. You are not placing your bet when you give your ticket and money to a keno runner—the keno runner will place it for you at the keno counter. Therefore, if you use the services of a keno runner, and she does not get to the keno lounge in time to turn in your ticket for the next game to be played—which sometimes happens—the casino is not responsible. Tickets carried by runners are not valid wagers until accepted at the keno counter. If your ticket was turned in too late for the current game, and your numbers are drawn, you won't get paid.

To help avoid other players' tickets from being picked up too late for the current draw, keno runners are instructed not to wait if your ticket is not ready to go when she passes by your table.

During the game, as each ball is drawn, its matching number is lit up on keno flashboards located throughout the casino and restaurant areas. In addition, the selected numbers are usually announced over a loudspeaker system in the keno lounge area.

Watch one of the flashboards to find out how many of the numbers on your ticket are drawn. The amount of numbers needed to win depends upon the type of ticket played and how many numbers you marked.

If you're a winner, take the ticket to a keno writer and collect your prize. But hurry! Most casinos require you to cash in winning keno tickets *before the start of the next game*. If you try to collect your money a couple of games later, there's a possibility that you won't get paid.

Perhaps that's one reason why a keno game is also called a *race*. If you're on the other side of the casino, it could be a race for you to get to the keno desk before the next draw begins!

If you're playing in a restaurant or bar area, give the ticket to a keno runner. She'll pay you immediately if the amount is small; if you've won a large amount, she'll have to get your winnings and bring them to you.

In Nevada, when you play multi-race keno for two to twenty games you must remain in a gaming area while all games are played. With some exceptions—see chapter 28, "Multi-game keno tickets"—you can't collect your winnings until the last game on your ticket has been called, but you must present the ticket for payment prior to the start of the next game. You can't be early, but don't be late! You might not be paid.

At casinos offering 21–1,000 game multi-game tickets, you need not remain on the premises and you have up to a year after the last game is played to go back to the casino and collect what you've won.

New games are played about every five minutes. You may play as many tickets on each game as you wish. There's never a limit to how much you can bet, only a limit on how much you can win. Be sure to read chapter 10, "Watch that aggregate limit!"

Chapter 4

HOUSE PERCENTAGES

Keno players expend a tremendous amount of energy trying to figure out the numbers that will make them a winner—how many spots to play, which numbers to mark, how much money to bet, and their chances of catching a sufficient number of spots to win.

Sad to say, the vast majority of keno players pay little or no attention to the only numbers that ultimately count—the *house percentages*. They don't understand house percentages, and therefore fail to appreciate their importance.

The *odds* of winning any keno game are computed from the number of keno balls in the wire cage or blower, the number of balls drawn each game, and the number of spots marked on the keno ticket.

The *house percentage* of a keno ticket—*PC* for short—is a number derived from the odds, the ticket price, and the casino's payoffs for that ticket. Multiplied by the keno department *handle* (total of all bets), it's the amount of profit that the casino will average over a period of time.

The operating word here is *average*. One big hit can throw the casino's win percentages askew for days, weeks, or even longer, but, over an extended period of time, the theoretical average will match the actual figures with great precision.

A house percentage of 25% does *not* mean that for every $100 bet the players will get back $75 and the casino will keep $25—although in the long run this is precisely what will happen!

Throughout this book you'll see one recurring theme. To win more and lose less at keno, never play tickets with high house percentages. The PC is what ultimately determines whether you'll be a keno winner or loser. The lower the PC, the more money you'll make when you're on a winning streak—and, the less you'll lose when you're not. It's as simple as that!

The percentages are in the house's favor on *all* casino games; but, of course, you already know that. The question is, just how much *do* they favor the casino?

By law, no slot machine in Nevada can have a house percentage in excess of 25%, except for a few older machines that were grandfathered in when the regulation was passed. Actually, the average PC on most slots is nowhere near the 25% maximum.

The PC on dollar slot machines is as low as 2.6%.

Some video poker machines have a PC that's actually about .6% in the players' favor, with perfect play; that is, playing the maximum number of coins, playing each hand according to the expected value of the first five cards dealt, and never making any mistakes.

Casinos earn a lot of money on these machines despite the negative house percentage. Nobody plays perfectly all of the time; inexperience, lack of knowledge, overindulgence, and exhaustion all take their toll. Casinos can bank on the fact that the actual payback of a video poker machine will be about two points less than the machine's optimum payback.

Most roulette bets have a house percentage of 5.26%; craps, .08% to 1.41%.

The median keno house percentage is 25–30%, depending on the type of ticket and number of spots marked.

If keno has such a high house advantage compared with other games of chance, why play keno at all? There's a very good reason. With keno, you have the chance of winning big for a very small bet!

A $10,000 blackjack wager pays back $15,000 maximum; but, a mere one dollar keno bet can make you $15,000 richer ... or more! The house edge is lower on keno than on any state lottery, and you can be right there in the middle of all the action when you play!

Casinos need to maintain a larger house percentage on keno than on their other games because it costs more to run keno than the other games.

Keno is labor-intensive. The casino needs to have a large number of keno writers, runners, supervisors, etc. on the payroll. Keno also takes up quite a bit of valuable floor space.

Keno is slow-paced, and the typical bet is small. In the same length of time it takes a slot player to run $100 through a slot machine (winning for the casino, on the average, about $2.60), a keno player playing one $1.00 ticket at a time provides the casino with an average win of 25 to 30 cents—and, that's about what it costs the casino to write a keno ticket.

Gaming is a business just like any other. Each business, and that includes casinos, must take in enough money to cover expenses and overhead (think of their electricity bills!) and give the owners a fair return on their investment. If the keno department doesn't show a decent profit, it would be prudent for management to tear out the keno lounge and install more slot machines.

The casino is a business, and you, the keno player, are their customer. So, why not do what you would do with any other company? You wouldn't order a new car without shopping for the best deal. You wouldn't buy a suit of clothes or a television if you knew you could get the same merchandise down the street for a fraction of the price.

Why, then, would you want to play keno at a casino that, when you win, pays you less—sometimes a *lot* less—than another casino a few blocks away? If you want to win more (and who doesn't?) you'll always play keno where the payoffs are better—

and this means where the house percentages are less. Play where your business is appreciated, and not where you're likely to get ripped off!

What? You thought that keno house percentages are standard everywhere, so it doesn't make any difference where you play keno or which tickets you play? Let me enlighten you.

The biggest mistake made by most keno players—even those who've played the game for years—is to assume that all keno payoffs are about the same. It's an easy assumption to make, because blackjack, roulette, and craps payoffs are (with a few exceptions) identical at all casinos. These players naively believe that they will win (or lose) the same amount of money no matter where they play, which type of ticket they choose, how many numbers they select, how much they bet, or how many games they play on a single ticket.

This couldn't be further from the truth! People place keno bets they would never think of making if they realized how widely the house percentages range in keno and if they were cognizant of how much difference the PCs make in determining whether they will make money or lose money.

Some keno tickets are quite liberal. And, at times, a few even have house percentages in the players' favor! If you know the house percentages, you'll know which tickets to play. Armed with this knowledge, if you have a little luck, you can be a big winner!

But, beware! Many keno tickets have fiercely high house percentages. These tickets can only be described as "sucker bets," for they provide virtually no chance at all for players to come out ahead. It's no wonder that casinos keep their keno house percentages a closely guarded secret!

In New Jersey, no keno ticket may hold more than thirty percent. But, as of this writing, the Nevada Gaming Control Board has failed to regulate keno house percentages. Nevada casinos are free to get as much as the market will bear on keno, and most of them do. Now you know why keno has the reputation of being the worst game in the casino!

It's not just the smaller grind joints you have to be wary of; I've found rip-off keno tickets at some of the most prestigious Las Vegas Strip casinos. One ticket offered by a world-famous resort was discontinued after I exposed it in *Keno Newsletter*; it had an outrageous house percentage of 94.3895%!

Other casinos, both large and small, have quite modest house percentages on some of their keno tickets—as low as 3.4275%, a figure that's quite competitive with the house edge of other casino games.

If the cost of bread varied from store to store as much as the house percentages in keno vary from ticket to ticket and casino to casino, you could pay as little as $1.22 or as much as $47.20 for the same loaf! When you play keno, it definitely pays to comparison shop!

At some casinos, you'll win $50,000 when you catch all numbers on an 8-spot $1.00 keno ticket. Others pay much less—$30,000, $28,000, $25,000, $22,000, $20,000—and at one place, all you'll get is $18,000! Are you beginning to get the picture?

Southern Nevada casinos have 25 different 8-spot keno ticket prices—from 40¢ to $100—with a total of 183 payoff schedules. For *all* 1–20 number keno tickets there are more than 3,000 payoff schedules!

Confusing? Of course it is. That's the way the casinos want it. By having many different ticket prices, conflicting payoff schedules, and so-called "special" games, casinos make it impossible for the average player to know which tickets to play - the winners - and which to avoid like the plague - the losers.

You might assume that to find the best keno tickets all you would need to do would be to study the paybooks from every casino and play only the tickets that provide the highest payoffs — but, that would be a monumental mistake. The worst house percentage I ever encountered was on a ticket that promised a million dollar payoff! You must convert the payoffs into house percentages, so that you take both the ticket price and the odds into consideration.

The casinos will never reveal their keno PCs; but, with the help of a pocket calculator, you can figure them yourself ... right in the keno lounge. I'll teach you how later in this book, so you can play to win, instead of just to make the casinos richer!

While you can compute the house percentages for one casino's tickets without too much effort, in order to find the best keno tickets in the state it would be necessary for you to gather and analyze all of the keno paybooks from every casino. That would take months of work; and, as soon as you finished, it would be time to start all over again, because casinos make frequent changes to their payoff schedules.

Casinos are likely to modify their keno payoffs whenever there's a change in ownership or gaming management, or whenever a keno manager makes an effort to be more competitive with neighboring casinos or tries to achieve a higher bottom line for his department. The casinos with the best (or worst) tickets today might not have the best (or worst) tickets tomorrow. If a casino has made any paybook changes since the last time you analyzed their keno tickets, make sure that you recompute the PCs before you take your wallet out of your pocket or purse!

All of the research required doesn't leave much time left for actually playing the game, but it's absolutely necessary if you want to locate the very best keno tickets available ... the ones with low house percentages ... the ones which will give you the opportunity to win more and lose less! And, it makes a lot more sense for you to spend some time determining house percentages than to waste it in a futile attempt to determine which numbers will be called.

In order to provide *Keno Newsletter* subscribers with the latest data on keno, my staff monitors every southern Nevada keno lounge at least once every ninety days and computer analyzes *all* of the keno payoff schedules from every southern Nevada casino's keno paybooks. Then, monthly, I report on the most liberal tickets ... the **winners**... and expose the tight tickets ... the **losers**.

Remember ... the *smart* keno players are the *educated* keno players. These people never play keno haphazardly. They find out the house percentages of keno tickets *before* they place their bets, and won't waste their money on tickets with PCs that are too high.

No Sharp Instruments, Please

If you don't have to be crazy to play keno, why is it that they only allow you to mark your keno tickets with a crayon?

Chapter 5

HOW TO
WIN MORE AND LOSE LESS

To win more and lose less at keno, always play the tickets with the lowest house percentages. The following examples should make the reasons for this crystal-clear.

The lower the house percentage, the more you will win when you win.

First, let's hypothesize that you're starting with a bankroll of $500, and that you've decided to play a 5-spot $1.00 catch-all ticket.

According to probability theory, there will be only one winner of this type game for every 1,550 losers (on the average). If you play a total of 500 games and *don't* win, it doesn't make any difference what the house percentage is. You've lost $500, and for you, the house percentage is effectively 100%.

But, let's assume that you're lucky, and catch all of your numbers once in the 500 game set. If the ticket has a payoff of $1,000 (35.5075% PC), you've made a profit of $500. However, if the ticket has a $1,250 payoff (19.3844% PC), you've made a profit of $750. Choosing the ticket with the lower house percentage increases your winnings by $250!

Before you state that the amount of profit is obvious, and that you don't need to know house percentages in order to make a valid comparison of keno tickets, let me set the record straight.

It's true that when catch-all tickets have the same number of spots marked and the same price (amount of bet), it's easy to determine which is the better ticket. Just compare the payoffs!

It's not so easy to compare catch-all tickets having a different number of spots marked or a different required wager, but most people can still do it—either in their head, or with the help of a pocket calculator.

Most keno tickets are *not* catch-all tickets, however, but have minor payoffs (for catching less than the total number of spots marked) in addition to the top prize. The *only* way to make a valid comparison of non-catch-all tickets is to look to the house percentages.

The lower the house percentage, the less you will lose when you lose.

For this example, let's assume that you're playing a regular (not catch-all) 5-spot ticket. This time you're starting with a bankroll of $1,000, and you're going to play it all at $1.00 per game.

According to probability theory, if you play a ticket with a 30% house advantage you'll wind up with $700 in your pocket (on the average)—but, if you play a ticket with a PC of 20%, you'll have $800 left. You'll lose $100 less by playing the one with the lower house percentage!

The lower the house percentage, the more games you can play before you run out of money.

After you've run your starting bankroll through once, you can take your profit (or loss) and go home. However, you may decide that you want to parlay your winnings or try to recoup your losses.

In the first example, you won enough on the ticket with the lower house percentage to buy 1,250 more tickets, but you can play only 1,000 more games with what you won on the ticket with the higher PC.

In the second example, the 20% ticket returned enough money to buy 800 more tickets, but the 30% ticket provided you with sufficient funds for only 700 more tickets. One of the additional tickets you're able to buy might just happen to beat the law of probabilities and be a big winner!

Put the money in your pocket, not in the casino's till.

For every $1,000 played, a one point reduction in the house percentage puts an extra $10.00 in your pocket, when you're winning. Conversely, for every $1,000 played, a one point increase in the house percentage puts another $10.00 in the casino's till, if you're losing.

Summing it up: The *true* cost of playing keno is not the ticket price, it's the house percentage. The lower the house percentage, the more games you can play before your bankroll is exhausted. The more games you play, the more chances you have of beating the odds and catching a big winner.

Please bear in mind that the results of the examples in this chapter are based on probabilities and long-term averages. What actually happens when you play on any given session may be quite different from the expected norm.

AVERAGE NUMBER OF $1.00 KENO GAMES THAT CAN BE PLAYED WITH A $1,000 BANKROLL	
HOUSE PERCENTAGE	GAMES
50%	2,000
35%	2,857
30%	3,333
25%	4,000
20%	5,000
15%	6,666
10%	10,000
Important: The above figures are based on *long-term averages*, and will not parallel any single playing session.	

Chapter 6

MAX & MORRIS

The sole purpose of this chapter is to illustrate once again just how vitally important it is to find keno tickets with the lowest house percentages possible. I really want to get this message across to you early in the book, so that you'll keep it in mind while reading the subsequent chapters!

My hypothetical friends Max and Morris decided to play keno. They agreed that each would go to a different casino, and each would play a 6-spot $1.00 catch-all ticket until he won the jackpot.

"I'm going to Casino A," stated Max. "They've got a really comfortable keno lounge, and the cocktail waitresses never let your glass get empty."

"They have lower house percentages at Casino B," Morris observed. "That's where I'm taking my money."

Max and Morris, being otherwise unemployed, spent their days and nights in the casino of their choice for the next several months. Neither one was about to give up, but the odds of catching all six numbers were formidable - 1 in 7,753.

As luck would have it, neither Max nor Morris caught all six numbers in the first 7,753 games. The law of large numbers had let them down.

"You see," Max derided Morris, "your theory about house percentages didn't mean a thing. Each of us lost $7,753. The house made 100%, we made zip."

Not one to be put down so easily, Morris convinced Max to keep on trying.

"OK," agreed Max, "but I'm still going where the drinks flow freely."

Fortune smiled on them, and by a strange coincidence, after playing 247 more games, both Max and Morris caught all six spots.

If you've been following the numbers, you know that by this time each of the boys had wagered a total of $8,000.

Casino A, where they plied Max with drinks, paid $5,000 for the 6-spot catch-all. The ticket computed to a house percentage of 35.5075%.

Morris got $6,000 for his win; Casino B's house percentage for the ticket was 22.6090%.

"You see," said Morris, "you're $3,000 in the hole, but I'm only down $2,000. I've lost less because my ticket had a lower PC."

"Let's try again," Max urged. "I still don't think the house percentage makes any difference. You either win or you lose."

By an even stranger coincidence (possible only in a fictional story such as this) each of our heroes caught all six numbers again, after playing exactly 2,800 more games.

"Now are you convinced that I was right?" prodded Morris. "I'm $3,200 ahead for the series, and you're only $2,200 ahead. I told you that I'd win more by playing the ticket with the lower house percentage, and I did!

"Moreover, on the entire 10,800 games we played, you lost $800, but I made a net profit of $1,200!"

I can almost hear you now. "Your story fails to make a point. Anyone can see that you're better off playing a catch-all ticket that pays $6,000 instead of one that pays $5,000." And, of course, you're right.

So, tell me which of the following 8-spot tickets has the

lowest house percentage:

CATCH	TICKET A $1.00	TICKET B $1.40	TICKET C $2.00	TICKET D $1.50	TICKET E $1.75	TICKET F $1.00
4	—	—	—	1.50	—	—
5	5.00	7.00	10.00	6.00	6.00	—
6	40.00	110.00	180.00	60.00	100.00	—
7	2,000.00	3,000.00	4,000.00	3,750.00	5,000.00	—
8	50,000.00	30,000.00	30,000.00	37,500.00	40,000.00	100,000.00

If the price and number of spots are the same, it's perfectly obvious which catch-all ticket is the best bet. But, unless you know the house percentages, you can't compare tickets with a different number of spots marked, different types of games, or different rates.

Here's the answer you've been waiting for: Ticket D is the best bet, followed closely by ticket E. Ticket F is a rip-off ticket that was heavily touted by a major Las Vegas Strip casino.

Don't be too upset if you guessed wrong. When comparing keno tickets with different prices and multiple payoffs, it's easy to be deceived. Without a computer I wouldn't have been able to determine which one had the lowest house percentage, either.

Ticket A — 27.5625%
Ticket B — 28.5577%
Ticket C — 30.9388%
Ticket D — 24.0838%
Ticket E — 24.4235%
Ticket F — 56.5434%

Chapter 7

BINGO!

Players new to casino gaming often confuse keno with bingo —and, with good reason. *Keno* was the original name for the game we now call *bingo!*

To a casual observer, the games are strikingly similar. In both games, numbered Ping-Pong type balls are randomly drawn from a blower or cage mechanism. Then, the selected numbers are **called** (announced) and displayed on an illuminated **flashboard**.

There, however, the similarities end.

Keno is played with eighty balls, numbered from one to eighty.

Seventy-five balls are used in bingo. In addition to the numbers, each bingo ball is imprinted with a letter. Balls numbered 1–15 have the letter *B;* balls numbered 16–30, the letter *I;* the letter *N* is on balls numbered 31–45; balls 46–60 have the letter *G;* and, *O* is on balls with the numbers 61–75. Together, the letters spell out the word *bingo.*

In keno, *you* select the numbers you want to play, and mark them on a blank *keno ticket.* In bingo, you have no choice—the numbers are pre-printed on the bingo cards or papers.

Exactly twenty numbers are drawn in every game of keno. In bingo, numbers are called until there's a winner—whether it takes four numbers or all 75.

If you don't know whether or not you've won a keno game, any keno writer or runner will be glad to check your ticket.

You're on your own when you play bingo. If you failed to cover one or more numbers when they were called—a very common occurrence—you could be a winner and not know it.

Now, here's the biggest difference.

In bingo, no matter how many people are playing, there is just *one winner per game*. (In case of ties, the winners must split the prize.)

With keno, *every* player can be a winner!

Chapter 8

KENO VS. LOTTO

Keno and Lotto are both long shot games, the attraction being the possibility of a small wager winning a large amount. Both are games of chance, not skill. Players select numbers on which to bet, and numbers are randomly drawn. The more numbers you "catch," the more you can win.

There is only one thing that keeps keno from being a lottery: the name of the game. "Lotteries" are illegal in Nevada.

Keno players select 1 to 20 numbers from a pool of eighty numbers. (A few keno tickets require marking more than twenty numbers.) Twenty numbers are drawn each game.

Most Lotto games require players to choose exactly six numbers, from 1 to 53 (6/53 Lotto) or from 1 to 49 (6/49 Lotto). Only seven numbers are drawn, which includes a "bonus" number.

The California State Lottery payoffs are adjusted, in a manner similar to the parimutuel payoffs in horse racing, so as to maintain a constant 50% payback to players. This is the equivalent of a 50% house percentage in keno—one which virtually all keno players would deem to be outrageous.

Lotto payoffs are low because 34% of the money taken in is earmarked for the California educational system. The cost of running the lottery accounts for another 11%, and 5% is paid as a commission to the retailers who sell lottery tickets.

Compare the Lotto payoffs to keno games with similar odds, and you'll quickly learn that you can win more money on keno—except for the top Lotto prizes, for which there are very, very few (but well publicized) winners.

A Lotto catch of 3-out-of-6 pays $5.00. The odds of catching 3-out-of-3 in keno are almost identical (1 in 72)—yet catching 3/3 on a $1.00 keno ticket pays $42.00 at most casinos!

It's easier to catch six numbers out of seven in keno (1 in 1,366) than 4-out-of-6 in Lotto. You'll catch 11-out-of-15 keno spots more often (1 in 81,021) than you'll get 5-out-of-6 Lotto numbers. And, it's nearly 17 times easier (1 in 230,115) to catch 8-out-of-8 in keno than it is to catch five Lotto numbers plus the bonus number.

I never object to the odds against winning a long shot game (unless they are patently absurd)—provided that those who do win, however few, are awarded prizes commensurate with the odds and the amount of their bet. In any long shot game there are always many losers and few winners. That's the chance you take when you play, and that's the thrill when you become a big winner.

What bothers me about the California State Lottery (and similar lotteries in other states) is that only 50% of the bets go back to the winners in the form of prizes. This makes Lotto a sucker game, in my opinion.

When you want to win more and lose less play keno—not Lotto!

And remember, while you're playing keno, the friendly, attractive cocktail waitresses will make sure that you never get thirsty. You won't even get a free Slurpee when you buy lottery tickets at 7-Eleven!

THE ODDS OF WINNING THE CALIFORNIA STATE LOTTERY

	6/49 GAME	6/53 GAME
Any of 6 winning numbers	1 in 13,983,816	1 in 22,957,480
5 of 6, plus bonus number	1 in 2,330,636	1 in 3,826,247
5 of 6 winning numbers	1 in 55,941	1 in 83,179
4 of 6 winning numbers	1 in 1,032	1 in 1,416
3 of 6 winning numbers	1 in 56	1 in 71

Chapter 9

KENO FLASHBOARDS

Keno flashboards are a familiar sight in casinos. They're located on the walls of keno lounges, restaurants, bars, and gaming areas.

A *keno flashboard* - sometimes called a *keno display board* - is an electric sign that measures about five feet in height and width, and looks like a big keno ticket. It has eighty numbered squares, one for each of the numbers printed on the keno balls.

Light bulbs behind a flashboard's front panel are turned on or off to display the current game number, the status of the game, and the numbers of the drawn balls.

When keno personnel are getting ready to start a new draw, and will accept no additional bets, they light up the word *closed* on the flashboards, and turn off the lamps that illuminated the previous game's called numbers.

Then, when the new draw begins, as each keno ball is ejected from the plastic bowl or wire cage into the *rabbit ears,* the number printed on the ball is (usually) announced over a public address system in the keno lounge.

At the same time, the lamp behind the appropriate numbered square is switched on, so that wherever you may be in the casino, as the keno game progresses you can look at a flashboard to compare the numbers drawn with those you marked on your keno tickets.

The keno game is over; twenty numbers have been called. If you'd caught just one or two more numbers you would have been a big winner. You throw your keno ticket away and finish your lunch.

Perhaps—just perhaps—you *did* win! It's quite possible that the flashboard has one or more burned-out light bulbs—the very same lamps that light up the numbers you needed to catch to turn your losing ticket into a winner!

Light bulbs *do* burn out, and it could be hours, or even days, before a maintenance man discovers the problem and corrects it.

Flashboards in the keno lounge area are usually kept in good order, but there's a high chance that flashboards in other parts of the casino have one or more lamps burned out. Make it a habit to count the illuminated numbers on the flashboard after every keno game. If less than twenty numbers are lit, something is wrong! Check your ticket against a different flashboard.

And please, when you find a keno flashboard that isn't working properly, tell the keno manager or casino manager. You'll not only be helping the casino, you'll be doing other keno players a big favor as well.

Some casinos now have electronic keno flashboards. These new flashboards use a series of LED's to indicate called numbers, thereby eliminating entirely the problems caused by burned-out bulbs.

Electronic flashboards often display very creative, animated graphics and tantalizing messages between games.

Now that you know all about keno flashboards, I'll let you in on a little known fact that's printed in just about every casino's keno booklet. *Casinos don't pay according to the numbers that light up on the flashboards!* They pay only according to the numbers printed on the drawn balls.

This may sound contradictory, but it really isn't. The keno caller might have made a mistake.

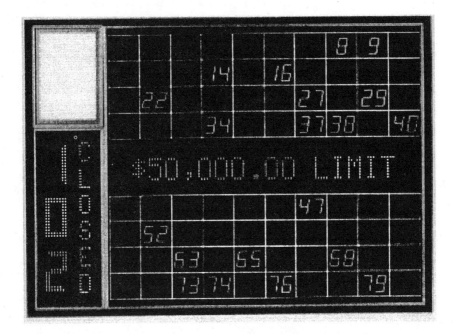

No, keno callers don't make mistakes very often. And, there's always a second pair of eyes watching, double-checking the caller. Yet, on rare occasion, a wrong number gets called and/or illuminated on the flashboards. Ask any keno department employee.

This type of mistake could work against you two ways. First, you might believe that you have a winning ticket, only to be disappointed to learn of the mistake when you go to the keno counter to collect your payoff.

Worse, you might think that your ticket was a loser, and throw it away without checking further.

So, whenever catching one more number could really make a difference, go up to the keno counter and look at every ball in the rabbit ears. With normal eyesight you should be able to see each number clearly, even if the balls are ten or twelve feet away. Make sure that each number in the rabbit ears is illuminated on the flashboard!

If you do catch a mistake, let the keno manager know immediately—before the balls are dropped back into the blower or cage. It just could be that you've won more than you first thought!

There are still other ways you can find out if you won, even if you don't look at a flashboard at all.

You can ask for a *draw sheet* after each game. Draw sheets are keno blanks that have punched-out holes to indicate the called numbers. If you're playing a lot of different keno tickets at one time, it's often easier to compare your tickets with the draw sheets than it is to refer to the flashboards. Just hold a draw sheet over your keno ticket and count the number of spots that show through the holes.

If the casino's keno department is computerized, as most of them now are, you can wait in line and have a keno writer check the computer to see if you're a winner. This is a good practice, especially if you have a complex way ticket, or are playing multi-race keno and weren't paying attention when some of the games were called.

But remember... the draw sheets, and even the data in the computer, could be wrong. If you think you may have a winning ticket, but the keno writer or keno runner says you don't, ask to speak to the shift supervisor or keno manager. After all, it's your money we're talking about.

Chapter 10

WATCH THAT AGGREGATE LIMIT!

Most novice keno players are confused by the statement printed in every keno paybook that reads something like this: "$50,000 limit to aggregate players each game."

The **aggregate limit** is the total amount a casino will pay out on any one keno game *to all winners of that game combined.*

If the total of the combined payoffs to all winners on any given game exceeds the casino's aggregate limit, the payoffs are prorated—and this always means *reduced*—so that the total amount paid out to the **aggregate** of players (all players combined) equals the casino's maximum limit.

For example, if the aggregate limit is $50,000, and there are holders of winning tickets totaling $80,000—two winners of $30,000 and one of $20,000—each of the $30,000 winners will get paid $18,750, and the $20,000 winner will get $12,500.

If this policy doesn't seem very fair, that's because it isn't. The casinos never limit the number of keno bets that they'll accept for each game! From a practical standpoint, however, the chances of more than one player getting a big winner on any one game are minuscule.

Ostensibly, the Nevada Gaming Commission set the maximum aggregate limit to protect *players* from the possibility that an undercapitalized casino might be unable to make all of the promised payoffs, in the event that there were multiple winners of large amounts in one game.

If that sounds like rationalization, that's because it is. Bear in mind that the regulation served an additional purpose. It put a ceiling on the casino's exposure, and protected the *casino* against the unlikely instance of several players happening to hit a big payoff at the same time.

Times change. Most casinos are now owned by or are themselves large, publicly-held corporations, so some of the safeguards instituted decades ago—whether to protect the players or to protect the casinos—are no longer necessary.

The maximum aggregate payoff was limited to $25,000 for many years. Because of inflation, it was subsequently raised to $50,000.

In 1989 the Nevada Gaming Commission abolished the legal barriers that limited the amount of money a casino was allowed to pay to keno winners each game, thus putting an end to the artificial cap on keno payoffs. Casinos are now free to set their own maximum per-game keno payoffs.

Some casinos still maintain the $50,000 aggregate limit. Others have increased it to $100,000 per game, and a few are now at a million dollars.

Don't get shortchanged by the aggregate limit!

Many casinos' keno paybooks not only show the payoffs for their basic rate tickets, such as $1.00, they also list the payoffs for multiples of that rate, such as $3.00 and $5.00. The casinos obviously want to stimulate you into betting more money on each ticket.

If you don't read and understand the paybooks, you're in danger of being shortchanged by the casino's maximum aggregate limit. The top payoffs for many tickets (7–15 spots in particular) don't always triple when you play for $3.00 instead of $1.00, and a $5.00 ticket doesn't necessarily pay five times the amount you might win on a $1.00 ticket.

For example, many casinos pay $25,000 for catching eight numbers on an 8-spot $1.00 ticket. If you play the same ticket for $2.00, you'll win $50,000 when you catch eight spots. But ... if the casino has a maximum aggregate limit of $50,000, no matter how much more you bet, the most you can win is $50,000!

To avoid getting shortchanged by the aggregate limit, if you're going to bet more than the basic rate always make certain that the top payoffs for your ticket are in proper proportion to the payoffs for the minimum price ticket.

Players can also get shortchanged by the aggregate limit when there are two or more winning tickets in the same game, and the combined payoffs exceed the casino's maximum aggregate limit.

This situation is rare, but when it does occur, it's usually because two players have identical tickets! No, it isn't a strange and mysterious coincidence when two keno tickets in one game are marked with the same numbers. The players are related to each other, and are playing numbers that represent ages, birthdays, anniversaries, or other important dates common to both of them.

When playing keno with your spouse, always let each other know what numbers are being played. If both of you unknowingly prepare duplicate keno tickets, and win, the combined payoffs might exceed the casino's aggregate limit, and you'll get shortchanged!

Chapter 11

HOW MANY NUMBERS TO MARK

Keno is unique among casino games. With keno, it's possible to win a lot of money for a small wager—except on 1- and 2-spot tickets.

The odds of catching the marked number on a 1-spot ticket are 1 in 4. The usual payoff for a dollar bet is $3.00, with a house percentage of 25% on the ticket.

The odds of catching two numbers on a 2-spot ticket are 1 in 16.63. At most casinos, the payoff for a $1.00 bet is $12.00, resulting in a PC of 27.8481%.

Even with exceedingly good luck you'll never get rich on these tickets; the potential payoffs are too low. With normal luck, they'll exhaust your bankroll in record time.

Compare the 1—and 2-spot keno ticket payoffs and house percentages with the payoffs and PCs on roulette. American roulette (with 0 and 00 slots on the wheel) has a house percentage of 5.2632%—except for the five-number bet, which is 7.8947%.

Play twelve numbers (dozens or columns), and, for your dollar bet, you can win $3.00—the same prize as on the 1-spot keno bet. On roulette, however, your chances of winning are considerably better; the odds are 1 in 3.1667.

Play one number in roulette, and, when you win, the payoff

will be three times as much as it would be on a 2-spot keno ticket—yet the odds of 1 in 38 are only 2.28 times greater than on the keno wager.

If you want to win more and lose less, avoid 1- and 2-spot keno tickets (and 1-spot and 2-spot ways on way tickets), unless you should happen to find bets with a house percentage lower than 5.2632%.

Instead, if you want to play a game of chance with a payoff-to-wager ratio of 36 for 1 or less, go to the roulette table. You may not make a fortune, but your money will definitely last longer.

Catching all of your numbers becomes increasingly difficult with each additional number that you mark. Depending upon how much business they do, most casinos will have an 8-out-of-8 winner every couple of months, and a winner of 9-out-of-9 about once a year. A winner of 10/10 or 11/11 would make the newspaper headlines. I've never talked with a keno manager or keno writer who's ever heard of a player catching 12-out-of-12.

No matter how enticing the prize may be, never, *never* get seduced into making a keno bet if the odds against you are so great that it's a virtual impossibility to win.

I won't play a keno ticket that has odds higher than 1 in 250,000, and that's stretching it, so that I can include the 8-spot progressive jackpot tickets.

Unless you're willing to go to a lot of trouble comparing payoffs for the various catches with the odds of catching the required number of spots, you'll be better off marking no more than eight numbers.

On the other hand, if the payoffs for catching less than all of your numbers meet with your approval, go right ahead and mark as many spots as you wish.

Don't misconstrue what I'm saying. There's nothing wrong in playing a 12-spot or 15-spot or even a 20-spot ticket, as long as you realize that you have only two chances of catching all the numbers: slim, and none.

So there you have it. You'll want to play at least three

numbers, in order to get a decent payoff, but not more than eight, if you hope to win the top prize.

ODDS OF CATCHING ALL NUMBERS	
SPOTS	EXPECTANCY
1	1 in 4
2	1 in 17
3	1 in 72
4	1 in 326
5	1 in 1,551
6	1 in 7,753
7	1 in 40,979
8	1 in 230,115
9	1 in 1,380,688
10	1 in 8,911,711
11	1 in 62,381,978
12	1 in 478,261,833

SPOTS MARKED	THE MAXIMUM NUMBER OF SPOTS THAT CAN BE CAUGHT WITH ODDS OF LESS THAN					
	1 IN 100	1 IN 500	1 IN 2,500	1 IN 10,000	1 IN 50,000	1 IN 250,000
1	1	–	–	–	–	–
2	2	–	–	–	–	–
3	3	–	–	–	–	–
4	3	4	–	–	–	–
5	4	4	5	–	–	–
6	4	4	5	6	–	–
7	4	5	6	6	7	–
8	5	6	6	7	7	8
9	5	6	7	7	8	8
10	6	6	7	8	8	9
11	6	7	8	8	9	9
12	6	7	8	8	9	10
13	7	8	8	9	10	10
14	7	8	9	9	10	10
15	7	8	9	10	10	10
20	9	10	11	11	11	13

Chapter 12

PICKING WINNING NUMBERS

Every keno player has a favorite set of numbers, or a sure-fire technique for selecting the numbers that he or she believes will result in big winners.

One of the most popular methods of picking keno numbers is to use numbers that have a personal meaning, such as ages, birthdays, or anniversaries. These can be of you and your spouse, children, grandchildren, dogs, elected officials, whatever. For the most part, this tends to put the numbers on the top half of the keno ticket, and explains why a majority of winning keno tickets have most, or all, of the numbers marked on the upper half.

Another popular method is the "repeater" system, which theorizes that numbers that have been called will be called; hopefully, in the very, very near future. To help the players who subscribe to this theory, some casinos provide folders in which drawn numbers can be logged.

Every casino will give you *draw sheets* - keno tickets with all of the called numbers from a given keno game punched out. Just ask any keno writer for them. Some players keep draw sheets for years, and maintain a running record of called numbers. For these players, it doesn't seem to matter which casino the draw sheets are from.

Don't waste your time trying to analyze draw sheets for numbers that have been called in previous games. It's absolutely impossible to forecast winning numbers based upon this useless information; as a means of determining potential winning numbers, draw sheets aren't worth the holes in the paper.

The "repeater system" might have some validity, if—and only if—some of the keno balls have become cracked,

Draw sheet

GAME 124

1	●	●	●	5	6	7	●	9	10
11	12	13	14	15	16	17	18	19	20
21	22	●	24	25	26	27	28	29	30
●	32	33	34	●	36	37	38	39	40

41	42	43	●	45	46	47	48	49	●
51	52	●	54	55	●	57	58	59	●
61	62	63	64	●	●	67	●	69	●
71	●	●	74	75	76	●	78	79	●

dented, or surreptitiously filled with liquid. However, the casinos check the balls often and replace them regularly, so last week's most frequently drawn numbers won't help you a bit.

Some people select numbers that *haven't* been called in the last several games, believing that it's their "turn" to come up.

Other players—particularly those who favor video keno—don't worry about the actual numbers, but play the game with elaborate (and usually symmetrical) patterns.

I've seen players spell out their names, one letter per ticket. This technique usually results in playing a lot of tickets with 13, 14, or 15 spots.

Some players insist that all selected numbers on their tickets must (or must not) touch every other selected number. I don't know if touching diagonally—only at the corners—counts.

Others close their eyes and mark their tickets at random. This process leads to spilled drinks and clothes smudged by black crayons, but I know of one instance where a variation of this method worked.

Jose Castillo, a busboy in the Gold Coast's Monterey Room restaurant, was having dinner with his bride of two weeks in the restaurant where he was employed. Jose decided to try his luck at keno; and, never having played before, he devised his own unique system.

Flipping the crayon in the air, he marked the numbers on his keno ticket wherever the crayon landed. On his very first keno game, he won a progressive jackpot of $98,714.20.

Some of the more exotic systems for selecting keno numbers incorporate phases of the moon, ESP, hunches, bank balances, automobile odometer readings, and numbers that won last week's state lottery (any state will do).

No matter what your own personal superstitions happen to be, go right ahead and *play those numbers!* It doesn't make *any* difference at all which numbers you play ... *they're all winners!*

It's a matter of fact that each uncalled number has an equal chance to be the next number called. Before the first ball has been drawn, every ball has 1 chance in 80 of being selected. After the first ball has been called, each remaining ball in the cage or blower has 1 chance in 79 of being the next one out. Then, each ball has 1 chance in 78. And so on, until twenty numbers have been chosen.

Over an extended period of time—for instance, a billion games—*every* number will be called *an equal number of times.* And, over an extended period of time, *every* pattern of spots will come up in *every* possible position on the board. It's like the old story about putting a monkey in front of a typewriter and teaching him to press the keys. Sooner or later, he'll type all of the works of Shakespeare, the Bible, and everything else that's ever been written.

If you have difficulty making up your mind about which numbers to mark on your keno ticket, the casinos have a solution for you. Just tell the keno writer how many numbers you want to play, say "quick-pick," and the computer will select the numbers at random and print your ticket. If you can't decide how *many* numbers to play, you've really got an indecision problem. (The numbers that the computer picks for you do *not* have a greater or lesser chance of being called than numbers you choose yourself.)

So, select your numbers by any method you prefer, with the knowledge that *sooner* or *later* there'll be a keno game when each and every one of the numbers you've chosen will be called. If you've got a ticket for that game, you'll be a big winner!

On those occasions when your numbers stay in the bowl, remember this: You selected all the right numbers, you just didn't play them at the right time. As with most things in life, in keno, timing is everything!

And finally ... if anyone ever attempts to sell you some magic formula for picking winning numbers, just ask that person, "If you're so smart, why aren't you rich?"

JJ's System

Experience has taught me that a meal anticipated is always a meal enjoyed, so I called home before leaving the office to ask my wife, JJ, what she was preparing for dinner.

"I'm making reservations," was her facetious reply. "I've been busy all day and didn't have time to shop, and I couldn't find anything in the freezer to thaw."

It wasn't until we were settled behind a tureen of steamed clams in the Gold Coast's Mediterranean Room that the real reason JJ wanted to dine out that evening became evident.

"I've got some 'lucky numbers' I want to try on keno," she announced.

I asked her where she had obtained the "lucky numbers," but she successfully sidestepped our conversation into another direction, and I didn't get the desired answer.

Sure enough, JJ's keno tickets won, and won handsomely. It was then that she finally disclosed that she had found the "lucky" numbers while browsing through the National Enquirer at the checkout stand in our neighborhood supermarket. As she offered to split her winnings with me, I mentally forgave her for the small fib about not having had time to shop. It seemed the right thing to do.

The next morning, while I was having coffee, JJ suddenly yelped "O-MY-GOSH!" I reacted by nearly scalding myself. She had just discovered that the numbers played the previous evening were *not* the ones found in the Enquirer. She'd read the wrong side of a memo to herself; her "lucky keno numbers" turned out to be the catalog number of an item she intended to order from Neiman Marcus.

Naturally, we had to make a return trip to the Gold Coast that evening to try out the National Enquirer recommendation. Yes, she won on those numbers also, while matched spots on my tickets were few and far between.

Near Misses

A few weeks before he passed away, Morris Shenker, former owner of the Dunes Hotel & Casino, told me an old Yiddish expression: "Man plans, and God laughs." Perhaps nowhere is this more true than in the game of keno.

Example 1: I had been playing numbers 1 though 7 on one of the Gold Coast's video keno machines, and had won several $5.25 jackpots for my 25¢ bets. However, numbers 8 and 9 kept showing, so I added them, hoping to catch seven spots out of nine for a win of $83.75.

Almost immediately, I did hit the 7-out-of-9, but was a little dismayed to find that if I *hadn't* added the two additional spots I would have caught 6-out-of-7, for a payoff of $100!

As I was somewhat ahead, I increased my bets to 50¢, and caught another 7/9 for $167.50. This time, however - despite the good payoff - I was extremely distressed. If I hadn't added numbers 8 and 9, I would have caught 7-out-of-7, for a payoff of $3,500!

I was now several hundred dollars to the good, so I increased my wagers to $1.00 per game.

"I'll add number 10," I thought, "and perhaps catch eight out of ten numbers for a win of $1,000."

I hit 6/10 several times, and even 7/10, which pays $142 for a dollar bet.

Then, on a "hunch," I erased the top row, and changed my numbers to 1 through 5 and 11 through 15, another 10-spot.

On the very next game, *all numbers in the top row popped in!* I won $5.00, for catching 5/10. If I hadn't changed my numbers, I would have won $10,000! If I had remained with the 9-spot, I would have caught 9/9, which also pays $10,000. And, if I had kept the original seven spots I started with, I would have won $7,000 by catching 7/7.

Nothing went right after that, and within a couple of hours the casino regained all of the money I had won.

Example 2: I was trying for the Gold Coast's progressive keno jackpot, which required catching 8/8 on a $2.00 ticket. At the time, the jackpot was over $130,000. However, catching 6/8 paid $200 and 7/8 paid $4,000, which are certainly not payoffs to sneeze at.

For several weeks I'd been playing the same numbers on a 6-way 8-spot ticket—one group consisting of 7, 8, 9, 17, 18, and 19, and with numbers 6, 10, 16, and 20 as Kings .

However, on a "hunch," this particular night I shifted the bottom row over two columns, so that I was now playing 7, 8, 9, 15, 16, and 17, with 6, 10, 14, and 18 for Kings.

On the second game, I watched in shock as the numbers appeared on the flashboard. If I had been playing my regular numbers, I would have caught 7/8 for $4,000; instead, I had an $8.00 payoff for catching 5/8.

So what did I do? Of course you know. I switched back to my "regular" numbers.

So then what happened? Of course you know again. I watched the flashboard in disbelief. I won another $8.00, but if I had kept the numbers I'd started out with that evening, I would have caught (on one game) three 6/8's and three 5/8's for a total of $624. And, a couple of games later, I would have caught 6/8 for another $200.

Too late, I realized that I had failed to follow my own advice.

All of your numbers are going to come up, sooner or later. You may (if you're lucky) be playing them when they do. But ... never, *never* change from your regularly played numbers or change the number of spots marked, unless you won't be upset when all of the numbers on the ticket you *had* been playing light up on the flashboard.

Perhaps your "hunches" are better than mine. If you want to play a hunch, by all means do so—you might regret it if you don't! But ... keep on playing the ticket you started with as well! Who knows? Perhaps you'll win on both tickets!

One Ball Short of a Keno Game

The numbered Ping-Pong balls used in keno are made from two hollow plastic hemispheres glued or welded together. They're reasonably sturdy, despite their light weight and fragile appearance, but do get a lot of use and abuse bouncing around in the keno cages or blowers used to mix the balls.

Therefore, a couple of times each week casinos replace all of the balls in their cage or blower, usually on the graveyard shift in the wee hours of the morning when business is at its nadir. They inspect the removed balls for dents, nicks, and cracks, then clean and wax the balls and put them aside in a safe place until the next time the cage is due to be changed.

A lot of precautions are taken to make certain that exactly eighty balls get put back into the cage or blower—each ball bearing a number from one to eighty, with no duplicates or missing numbers. But, when human beings or things mechanical are involved, problems have a way of cropping up.

I've heard of several instances when a keno ball cracked in half at the seam, and each half nested itself to another ball. More than one keno employee was astounded to see what was thought, at first glance, to be a single ball with two different numbers marked on it!

Which brings us to the mystery of Ball Number 29.

The graveyard keno supervisor at a popular Las Vegas casino had replaced the balls in their wire cage, as scheduled. Later that morning a customer remarked to the keno manager, "I've been playing keno for hours, and Number 29 never has come up. I don't think you have a Number 29 ball in the cage! Where is it, in your pocket?"

Such an assertion strained credulity, but, to satisfy the customer, the keno manager dutifully checked all of the balls in the cage before the next game started. Sure enough, Number 29 was missing.

It wasn't in the rack where the replacement balls were stored. It wasn't on the floor. It wasn't split in two and mated to other balls. No fragments of a ball were found around the wire cage. Number 29 had just disappeared into thin air.

Of course, the problem was immediately corrected. The keno manager made things right with the customer who noticed the missing ball and reported the incident to the Gaming Control Board. The original Ball Number 29 was never again seen.

If a ball can disappear from a keno game once, it's probably happened before and will inevitably happen again. What you need to know is how such an event will affect your chances of winning.

When you mark the number of a missing ball on your keno ticket, it'll always be a disaster. You obviously can't catch all of your spots, and your chances of winning a large amount are considerably lessened.

But ... it's really pretty unlikely that, by chance, you would mark your ticket with the number of a missing ball. If you play an 8-spot ticket, nine times out of ten you won't mark the missing number; there's only one chance in twenty that you'll mark a missing ball's number on a 4-spot ticket.

Unless by happenstance you've X'd the number of a missing ball on your ticket, you have a substantially better chance of winning a game played with 79 balls instead of eighty.

With the higher expectancy of winning a game played with just 79 balls, the house percentages of keno tickets change by a number of points ... in the players' favor! The amount the PCs go down depends upon the number of marked spots and the payoff schedule for the ticket played.

ODDS OF CATCHING ALL NUMBERS		
NUMBERS MARKED	80 BALLS IN CAGE	79 BALLS IN CAGE
4	1 : 326	1 : 310
6	1 : 7,753	1 : 7,171
8	1 : 230,115	1 : 207,103
10	1 : 8,911,711	1 : 7,797,747

And ... when you play keno tickets which have extremely low house percentages, such as Gold Coast's high-roller tickets, a missing ball can even change the house percentages into player percentages!

HOUSE PERCENTAGES HYPOTHETICAL CATCH-ALL GAMES		
SPOTS	80 BALLS IN CAGE	79 BALLS IN CAGE
4	25.0%	21.0548%
6	25.0%	18.9190%
8	25.0%	16.6667%

By now you should be convinced that all numbers have an equal chance to be drawn, in each and every game, and that it makes no sense at all to keep a record of which numbers were (or were not) selected in prior games. Both theories that require maintaining this information—i.e., the *numbers that have been called will be called again in the immediate future* (repeater) theory and the *numbers that haven't been drawn recently are "overdue" and will be drawn soon* theory—are just uninformed, inane foolishness.

However ... a missing ball can *never* be drawn, so if you do check the draw sheets or record the draws, you might someday learn that another keno ball has vanished. Perhaps it'll even be Number 29.

If you ever reach the conclusion that the casino is

HOUSE PERCENTAGES OF GOLD COAST'S $100 HIGH-ROLLER KENO TICKETS		
SPOTS	80 BALLS IN CAGE	79 BALLS IN CAGE
3	2.8724%	– .6715%
4	3.5031%	– .4502%
6	3.2746%	– 2.3080%
8	4.0793%	– 3.3736%
10	4.3935%	– 3.4469%

playing "one ball short of a keno game," there are two mutually exclusive courses of action you can take:

You can notify the keno manager immediately of your discovery. If you're wrong, he'll think you're some kind of a kook. If you're right, he'll thank you profusely and, after the initial shock wears off, he might even give you a dinner comp as a reward.

Or, you can remain silent and take advantage of your knowledge that the house percentages will be lower on all of your keno tickets (played without the missing number, of course) ... until someone else notices that a ball is missing.

Chapter 13

HOW MUCH TO BET

The keno paybooks, folders, and cards that the casinos place in their keno lounge and restaurant areas list the various *rates* they offer, such as 70¢, $1.00, and $1.50. Additionally, the paybooks usually show a few multiples of the basic rates, such as $1.40, $3.00, and $5.00.

You don't have to limit your bets to the amounts shown in the keno folders. You can wager *any* amount, as long as it's a multiple of one of the basic rates. You can play a keno ticket for $100, or even $1,000, if you so desire.

If you decide to bet more than the basic rate, watch out for the aggregate limit! If you can win $40,000 with a $2.00 ticket, you won't necessarily get $400,000 for a $20.00 wager. Your payoff will be limited to the casino's maximum aggregate payoff per game.

You can readily see the folly of increasing your bet beyond the point where the maximum payoffs stop getting proportionally bigger; all you're doing is donating money to the casino, if you should be a big winner.

One keno manager with many years of experience recommends that players bet as much as they can afford on each ticket, playing as few numbers as possible. I call this the "bigger bets" strategy.

If you heed his advice you'll win fairly often, and occasionally leave the casino with a profit. After all, it's easier to catch two spots out of two or three spots out of three than it is to catch six numbers out of six.

The problem with the "bigger bets" strategy is that, at most casinos, you can't really win big. When you win, it'll be just enough to tease you. If you play a ticket for $10.00, catching 2/2 pays about $120; catching 3/3 pays about $420.

And, please bear in mind that at $10.00 per ticket you can go through a lot of money in a very short time if luck isn't with you.

If larger bets don't bother you, and you'll be satisfied with payoffs of a few hundred dollars, then you probably shouldn't be playing keno. For the same amount of money wagered you can win more at roulette, because the house percentage on roulette is much lower than on most keno tickets—a mere 5.26%.

Never forget that keno is a long shot game. Even with the best of luck you won't win as often as you will at other casino games, but when you *do* win, there's nothing in the casino that can touch the high payoff-to-bet ratio that keno offers.

Generally, I prefer the "maximum games" strategy. Rather than putting all of your eggs in one basket, so to speak, you play as many *games* as you can afford, on tickets with a moderate amount of numbers marked; no fewer than three spots, and no more than eight spots.

When playing by this method, you'll usually wager the basic rate, whether it's 70¢, $1.00, $2.00, or some other amount.

There are three advantages to the "maximum games" strategy:

First, when you're not having good luck, your money will last longer. Perhaps it will even last long enough for your luck to change!

Second, when you have moderate luck, in most instances you'll win as much or more than you would have won if you'd played according to the "bigger bets" concept.

Third, when luck is in your corner and you catch all of your marked numbers, you'll go home a big winner!

Whether you choose to use the "bigger bets" or the "maximum games" strategy, never violate the following "good sense" rules:

When you play a ticket that has a progressive jackpot, *always* make sure that your bet is large enough to entitle you to the jackpot, if you happen to catch enough numbers to qualify for it.

Always bet the amount that makes the house percentage as low as possible. At some casinos, on some tickets, the house percentages drop dramatically when you increase your bets from $1.00 to $2.00, or from $2.00 to $3.00.

A few casinos now have high-roller tickets ($10.00 to $100.00) that are not just multiples of their regular rates, but separate rates with extremely low house percentages. If you've got the wherewithal to play these tickets, they can be the best bets in the whole casino!

The Less You Bet, the More You Lose When You Win!

My wife and I were dining in the coffee shop of one of our favorite Las Vegas casinos. As is our usual practice, we played keno during dinner. The progressive jackpot had climbed to over $135,000, which meant that the house percentage on 8-spot $2.00 tickets was down to about 7.5%. With those numbers, keno was no longer entertainment, it was serious business.

We both played 8-spot $2.00 tickets, with some 4-spot $1.00 ways thrown in for good measure. However, luck wasn't with us that night; we couldn't even catch two numbers out of four.

My wife, who is more into the Deuces Wild video poker machines than she is keno, was curious about the 190-way $19.00 tickets that were being promoted on the keno flashboard's moving message sign. I informed her that playing the $19.00 ticket wouldn't qualify her for the 8-spot progressive jackpot, because she would be playing for only 10¢ per way.

"If you want to be able to win the jackpot," I explained, "you'll have to play each way for $2.00—a total price per ticket of $380.

Let's pretend that we're playing the 190-way ticket for $2.00 a way, using the most common ticket marking for that type of ticket—that is, ten vertical 4-spot groups on the top half of the ticket and ten vertical 4-spot groups on the bottom half of the ticket—and you'll see how this type of ticket works."

On paper, we won about $230 on each of the next two games, which resulted in a hypothetical loss of about $150 per game, after deducting what the ticket would have cost.

The third game, one group of four numbers on our ticket came in solid, and three numbers were caught on another 4-spot group. Had we actually been playing, we would have won about $3,800, after paying for the $380 ticket.

Several following games we also had catches of 7/8 (twice on one ticket!), and, by the time we finished dessert and coffee, our net imaginary winnings on the 190-way $380 tickets totaled over $15,000!

After dinner, we sat down to the Deuces Wild machines, which were located near the keno lounge. Almost immediately, I caught four deuces, for a win of $250.

While the machine was dumping quarters into the tray, I walked over to the keno cage and marked a ticket for five 190-way games, at 10¢ per way—a total ticket price of $95. Tickets costing $380 were out of my league ... at least, on that particular night.

The very first game, two solid 4-spots came up. The 8-out-of-8 paid $2,500 on my 10¢-per-way ticket. On the five games I won a total of more than $2,600, for a net profit in excess of $2,500.

But ... if I had played the ticket for $2.00 per way instead of a dime, I would have won the progressive jackpot of more than $135,000!

The moral of this true story, of course, is nothing ventured, *nothing gained*. Who knows when, if ever, I'll catch 8-out-of-8 again? The odds of success are just 1 in 230,115. However, I will keep trying ... even if it's only at 10¢ per way.

Chapter 14

CHOOSING THE RIGHT KENO TICKET

Casinos offer many different variations of keno, each with its own peculiarities, advantages, and disadvantages. Choosing the right rate and type of ticket can help you win more and lose less.

Regular (Straight) Keno

Regular keno is the standard game played most frequently. Usually, you can mark one to 15 spots on regular keno, although a few casinos allow you to mark up to a maximum of twelve numbers, or have other restrictions.

Almost every Las Vegas casino offers regular keno at the $1.00 rate, except for some of the casinos located on the Strip, where the minimum is now $2.00 per ticket. A number of casinos also offer regular keno at 70¢ or $1.40 per game - a carryover from the "old days" when a popular keno rate was 35¢. Look at what inflation has done, even to keno!

You can always play a keno ticket for any multiple of the basic rate, such as $3.00, $5.00, or even $100.00 - but before you make a big keno wager, be sure to read chapter 10, "Watch that aggregate limit!"

You can usually play regular keno at a fractional rate on a way ticket, sometimes for as little as 10¢ per way. At a few casinos, if you play the required number of games on one multi-race ticket, you can play them at a fractional rate, perhaps for as little as a dime each.

Many people prefer regular keno. It's uncomplicated, and if they catch some, but not all of their numbers, they'll still win, perhaps enough to carry them through until they get lucky and hit a "big one."

Regular keno starts paying off when you catch about half of your numbers. For example, if you've marked eight spots and catch four numbers, you're likely to get back the amount of your bet. The more of your numbers that are called, the higher the payoff will be. Catching all marked numbers pays the most.

Even though the *cost* of playing a regular keno ticket might be the same at several casinos, the *payoffs* can be very different! To win more and lose less, always choose the ticket with the lowest house percentage.

Alternate Keno

In addition to regular keno, casinos usually offer a number of other types of keno tickets. Casinos often call these alternate tickets *specials*, although they may or may not be better wagers than their regular rate tickets.

If a casino doesn't indicate that a rate is "special," or use some other designation to distinguish it from their regular keno, there are a number of clues that will enable you to determine if you're playing an alternate ticket.

First, as you've learned, at most casinos you can mark from one to 15 spots on regular keno. Alternate rates are usually (but not always) more limited in scope. For instance, the casino may allow you to mark a minimum of four and a maximum of seven numbers on one of their alternate rates; another alternate ticket might require you to mark exactly eight numbers.

Second, refer to the payoff booklet furnished by the casino. There will be obvious differences between the payoffs of regular tickets and alternate tickets. Catch-all tickets, for instance, have one pay only - when you catch *all* of your marked numbers.

Third, the price of an alternate ticket will usually be different from the regular rate tickets. If the regular tickets cost $1.00 to play, the alternate tickets might cost $1.50, $1.75, or some other uneven amount.

There's an important reason why casinos often set their alternate tickets at a rate that's different from their regular tickets, to make certain that there's no possibility of a misunderstanding about which rate is being played, in order to avoid potential arguments with the players about how much they should be paid when they win.

It's very important to follow the paybook instructions precisely when you play an alternate rate. For instance, a casino may have an alternate ticket that costs $2.00 to play, and the paybook instructions state that you must mark your keno ticket "JS," for Jackpot Special.

If you fail to mark your ticket, and you win, you won't be awarded the Jackpot Special payoff; instead, you'll get a payoff based on the casino's regular $1.00 rate, prorated for the amount of your bet.

Always check your ticket before the start of the draw. Make certain that the keno writer entered the information correctly, and that the ticket you've received - whether printed by computer or marked by hand - is for the type of ticket you intended to play.

The following chapters describe in detail most of the alternate tickets currently in vogue.

Chapter 15

CATCH-ALL KENO

Most casinos feature a few *catch-all* (sometimes called *one pay*) keno tickets; in order to win, you must catch *all* of your selected numbers.

The advantage of catch-all tickets is that (dollar for dollar wagered) the top payoffs are usually much higher than the top payoffs on regular (straight) keno with the same number of spots marked.

The disadvantage is that, unlike regular keno, you won't have the smaller pays when you catch some, but not all, of your numbers. These minor payoffs serve an important purpose; they can provide you with money to play with until you hit the "big one."

The odds against winning catch-all keno increase dramatically with every additional number that you mark. For this reason, if you like the concept of catch-all keno, you'll probably want to mark a maximum of five or six numbers.

Let's examine a 6-spot catch-all ticket and see how it compares with regular keno.

One casino has a 6-spot $2.00 catch-all ticket that pays $11,000 when you catch all six numbers; you lose your bet if you don't catch all six spots. The house percentage on this ticket is 29.0583%.

A $2.00 regular 6-spot ticket with a similar house percentage would pay $3,000 for catching all six numbers—$8,000 less. However, you don't need to catch all six spots to win. You would win $2.00 for catching 3-out-of-6, $8.00 for catching 4/6, or $175 for catching 5/6.

Here's what the real gamble is when you play catch-all keno: *You're betting that you'll catch all of your numbers before you've wagered as much as the potential payoff.*

The odds of catching six numbers out of six are 1 in 7,753. You can readily see that if it took 7,753 games (at $2.00 per game) in order to win $11,000, you would lose $4,506 for every 7,753 games played—not a very palatable situation.

But, that's not how the numbers crunch. While you can precisely determine *what* your chances are for winning, you never know *when* you're going to win. You could win on the very first game played ... or the 27th ... or the 3,740th. You could catch 6-out-of-6 several times during a session of 7,753 games ... or, not at all.

Always remember: No matter how many games you play, the odds are exactly the same for each and every game played. Even if you've played 7,752 games, your chances of winning the next game are still 1 in 7,753!

If you play the 6-spot $2.00 catch-all ticket described above, you'll make money if you catch your numbers in the first 5,499 games played. On the other hand, if you play a 6-spot $1.25 catch-all ticket at another casino, where the prize is a mere $2,500, you'll have to win in the first 1,999 games played in order to come out ahead.

Comparing tickets with different prices and different payoffs is difficult. The house percentage is the common denominator. To find the best ticket, just look for the one with the lowest house percentage! (The $1.25 ticket mentioned above has an outrageous PC of 74.2030%.)

The lower the PC, the more you'll get paid in proportion to the amount of your bet when you win. Further, the lower the PC, the more games you can play before winning, and still realize a profit.

Few people have the patience, tenacity, and time - not to mention money - to sit through thousands of losing games, waiting for one big winner. If you possess these attributes, or if your luck has been great and you just want to chance a very long shot, perhaps catch-all keno will appeal to you.

Chapter 16

THE "PAY-ANY-CATCH" GIMMICK

After extensive contemplation, I've concluded that the best way to explain "pay-any-catch" tickets is to reprint the following article, which I published in *Keno Newsletter* in January, 1990:

The "Pay-Any-Catch" Gimmick

Many casinos now have one or more "pay-any-catch" tickets. The gimmick is that no matter how many of your selected numbers are called, even if you don't catch any numbers at all, you'll always get *something* back; therefore, you'll never feel like a loser.

Cat Schelling, the keno manager of Lady Luck Casino in downtown Las Vegas, wrote us concerning our recent analysis of one of the Lady Luck's "pay-any-catch" keno ticket:

"You show our 5-spot special (Any Catch) having a PC of 33.4504. I've enclosed the printout from our Keno Oddsmaker showing this

LADY LUCK 5-SPOT $1.00 PAY-ANY-CATCH TICKET		
Indicated house percentage: 25.0878%		
CATCH	PAYS	NET WIN
0 spots	.25	− .75
1 spot	.25	− .75
2 spots	.25	− .75
3 spots	1.00	.00
4 spots	15.00	14.00
5 spots	400.00	399.00

hold to be only 25.1%. You may want to check your figures to see which of us is correct. Thank you for your attention to this discrepancy."

Thanks to *you* for writing us, Cat. I'd been planning to prepare an article on "pay-any-catch" tickets for quite some time; your letter prompted me to end my procrastination, and to spend a little more time at the word processor and a little less time in the keno lounges.

I personally put the Lady Luck's 5-spot "pay-any-catch" ticket through our computer, and Cat was right!, our computer indicated a house percentage of just 25.0878%! (We compute PCs to four decimal places for greater accuracy.)

When I asked our computer expert, Izzy, why I didn't arrive at the same house percentage that we recently published, he dismissed my question curtly with a cryptic, "Figures lie and liars figure."

In further search for an answer to this dilemma, I turned to our resident prevaricators, Manny, Moe, and Vladimir.

"Fellas," I requested, "I'd like you to use your creativity with numbers and devise a pay-any-catch keno ticket with a *lower* house percentage than the Lady Luck's 5-spot ticket, but with *exactly the same net win amounts*." (The net win is the amount of each payoff *less* the amount of the bet.)

"Easy," Manny responded, almost too quickly. "Just add $1.00 to the Lady Luck's ticket price and to each of their 5-spot ticket's payoffs. The computer will show a PC of 12.5439%, and the net wins will remain the same."

MANNY'S 5-SPOT $2.00 PAY-ANY-CATCH TICKET		
Indicated house percentage: 12.5439%		
CATCH	PAYS	NET WIN
0 spots	1.25	− .75
1 spot	1.25	− .75
2 spots	1.25	− .75
3 spots	2.00	.00
4 spots	16.00	14.00
5 spots	401.00	399.00

Manny was on target. The PC was exactly what he predicted, and the net win amounts didn't change.

"Manny didn't go far enough," Moe interjected. "Instead of adding $1.00 to the ticket price and each of the payoffs, add $9.00, and you'll get a house percentage of just 2.5088%!

MOE'S 5-SPOT $10.00 PAY-ANY-CATCH TICKET		
Indicated house percentage: 2.5088%		
CATCH	PAYS	NET WIN
0 spots	9.25	− .75
1 spot	9.25	− .75
2 spots	9.25	− .75
3 spots	10.00	.00
4 spots	24.00	14.00
5 spots	409.00	399.00

"I think I'll copyright this payoff schedule. Maybe I can sell it to Bob Stupak. He's always looking for a new schtick to offer his customers at Vegas World.

"I can see his advertising now! 'Out of this world keno payoffs! Our 5-spot pay-any-catch ticket returns more than 97.4%! We guarantee you'll win a minimum of $9.25 *every game* ... no matter how many numbers you catch!'"

"Why bother with Stupak?" Vladimir admonished Moe. "We can sell my high-roller version to Caesars Palace! Just add $99.00 to the Lady Luck's ticket price and each of the payoffs, and you'll get a PC of .2509%! That's a lower hold than on craps, 21, or any of the table games.

VLADIMIR'S 5-SPOT $100.00 PAY-ANY-CATCH TICKET		
Indicated house percentage: .2509%		
CATCH	PAYS	NET WIN
0 spots	99.25	− .75
1 spot	99.25	− .75
2 spots	99.25	− .75
3 spots	100.00	.00
4 spots	114.00	14.00
5 spots	499.00	399.00

"Caesars can shut down most of their casino, and switch all of their players to keno. Perhaps they'll even change their million-dollar payoff keno ticket ... you know, the one with the astronomical house percentage!"

Izzy had been listening to us with thinly disguised amusement. "Forget it," he chimed in. "You've been feeding the wrong data into the computer. Remember, it's garbage in, garbage out.

"In order to determine the *true* house percentage on pay-any-catch tickets, you've got to pierce the *pay-any-catch fictions.*

"The first fiction is that you'll win more frequently on pay-any-catch tickets because they pay every time - whether you catch all of your numbers, some of them, or none of them. Let's see how this works out.

"The lowest payoffs on pay-any-catch tickets are always less than the amount of the bet. In the Lady Luck example, catching 0, 1, or 2 numbers pays 25¢. After deducting the $1.00 ticket price, you have a *net win* of minus 75¢ ... and, a negative net win is a *loss*!

"When you catch three numbers you break even. Even though the ticket *pays* any catch, you have to hit four or five spots in order to show a *net profit* on the wager.

"So you see, the phrase *pay-any-catch* is just a gimmick. You don't really *win* unless you come out ahead ... don't let 'em fool you!

"On many 5-spot regular keno tickets you'll come out ahead when you catch three spots or more. And, on regular tickets where you merely break even when you catch three numbers, you'll find that the payoffs for catching four or five spots are usually much higher than on the pay-any-catch tickets.

"Knowing this, it should be obvious that you win more often on regular keno than on pay-any-catch tickets ... and, I've just pierced the first pay-any-catch fiction.

"Now I'll address the second pay-any-catch fiction," Izzy lectured. "Proponents of this fiction would like you to believe that you're actually *winning* the minimum payoffs. I'll show you that you're not.

"Unless you lose your keno ticket or just don't feel it's worth standing in line to get a quarter back, you're always going to get paid at least the 25¢ *minimum payoff*—it's a sure thing!

"Since you're not gambling that you'll get the minimum payoff, you're not winning it ... you're just getting a refund.

"You might compare the minimum payoff with a 'cents off' supermarket coupon that reduces the price of a can of beans. Whether you turn in the coupon at the checkstand, or mail it to the manufacturer for a refund, the net effect is the same ... the coupon lowers your cost of beans.

"The minimum payoff amount is like the second supermarket coupon example. Your money is paid back after the game is over, instead of being deducted from the amount you pay for your keno ticket.

"The Lady Luck ticket costs $1.00 to play, and if you don't catch three spots or more the casino is going to refund 25¢ of your bet. Thus, you know that to try for the catch 3, 4, or 5 pays, each ticket is going to cost you 75¢ net.

"Once you see through the fictions, computing pay-any-catch tickets to show the true house percentage is easy," Izzy informed us. "All you have to do is deduct the minimum payoff from the ticket price and from each of the payoffs before you run the numbers through your computer.

"So, when you recalculate the Lady Luck's $1.00 pay-any-catch ticket as a 75¢ ticket and reduce all of the pays 25¢ - note that the net wins remain the same - the computer proves that the *true* PC is 33.4504% ... the same figure we printed in *Keno Newsletter*," Izzy concluded.

IZZY'S ANSWER		
LADY LUCK 5-SPOT $1.00 PAY-ANY-CATCH TICKET RECALCULATED AS A 75¢ STRAIGHT TICKET		
Indicated house percentage: 33.4504%		
CATCH	PAYS	NET WIN
0 spots	.00	− .75
1 spot	.00	− .75
2 spots	.00	− .75
3 spots	.75	.00
4 spots	14.75	14.00
5 spots	399.75	399.00

Well, Cat, I certainly learned something from Izzy and the boys. They've convinced me that the house percentage we published was correct.

* * * * *

Bill Holmes, formerly keno manager of the Western Village Inn & Casino in Sparks, Nevada, wrote me concerning the article on "pay-any-catch" tickets:

"Are (pay-any-catch) tickets gimmick tickets? Yes, but the gimmick is not the one that Izzy thinks it is. These tickets are not designed to make you think that you are winning more often (no one is that stupid). They are designed solely to get you up to the keno counter one more time, in the hopes that you will replay your ticket.

"It is thought by some keno managers that a player with just a little pay on a ticket will be more likely to replay it. There might be some validity to this view (witness the popularity of the 20-spot) but "pay-any-catch" tickets have never been particularly popular with the keno playing public, even though they have been tried by many keno games."

I responded editorially in *Keno Newsletter* to Bill's comments, as follows:

"You're absolutely right about the motivation of casinos in offering pay-any-catch tickets. On the other hand, I'm sure you'll agree that - because of the high cost of the labor to write a keno ticket - most casinos today would like to see players up to the keno counter *less* often, if it doesn't hurt their business.

"Casinos want all the business they can get, but there are more creative ways of achieving this goal than the gimmick pay-any-catch ticket. One such way is the multi-race keno ticket. Everyone benefits. The casino cuts down the expense of writing tickets. Players don't have to stand in line as often, and when they do, the lines are shorter. A few casinos even give multi-race players a real incentive to play multi-race keno by offering higher payoffs on these games!"

* * * * *

Some keno managers apparently don't understand the difference between *indicated* house percentages and *true* house percentages, and fail to realize that the PCs of pay-any-catch tickets cannot be computed in the same manner as other keno tickets.

As a result, the true house percentages of pay-any-catch tickets are invariably much higher than the PCs of other tickets in the same casino. Smart keno players won't play tickets with high house percentages. 'Nuf said.

Footnote: My prognosis about the advantages of multi-race keno was correct; see chapter 28, "Multi-game keno tickets." Oh, yes. Caesars dropped the million-dollar payoff keno ticket with the astronomical house percentage after the above article was published in *Keno Newsletter*!

Chapter 17

HIGH-END TICKETS

The pay scales for some keno tickets enable you to win *more often*. Others are structured so that *when* you win, you'll win *more money*.

The latter type of keno tickets are called **high-end** tickets. When you catch most or all of your selected numbers on a high-end ticket, the payoffs are greater. Correspondingly, when you catch fewer numbers, you'll win less, or not at all.

To make it easy for you to understand the effect of the various types of payoffs, I've devised some hypothetical 7-spot $1.00 tickets. The house percentages on these examples are all about the same—29.7% to 29.8%.

According to the law of large numbers, each of these tickets will return a little more than $7,000 to players—and the casino will get to keep a little less than $3,000—for every $10,000 wagered.

Look at Ticket A, and you can readily see why I stated that the examples are hypothetical. No casino would be so brazen as to

TICKET A – $1.00		
CATCH	PAYS	TOTAL PAYOFFS 10,000 GAMES
0	.00	.00
1	.80	2,521.54
2	.80	2,613.23
3	.80	1,399.95
4	.80	417.53
5	.80	69.11
6	.80	5.86
7	.80	.20
TOTAL PAYOFFS		**7,027.42**

offer—and no player would be so foolish as to play—a keno ticket with a payoff schedule such as this.

Ticket A will have lots of "winners." As long as you catch at least one number, you'll get an 80¢ payoff. But, as the ticket costs $1.00, you're going to lose 20¢ each time you "win"—and the entire $1.00 when you don't!

Note the "Total payoffs / 10,000 games" column. Most of the prize money will be paid out to those players who catch two numbers; winners who catch one spot come in a close second. For every $10,000 bet, the casino can expect to pay only 20¢ to winners who hit all seven numbers. This is definitely a *low end* ticket!

Nonetheless, the PC of Ticket A is 29.7259%—and that's close to the median house percentage for all 7-spot keno tickets in Nevada. So, if you're going to make any money on keno, you're going to have to find a better payoff schedule than this one.

The ultimate high-end keno ticket is the catch-all ticket. To win, you must catch *all* of your selected numbers. Ticket B is a 7-spot $1.00 catch-all ticket with a house percentage of 29.8427%.

Ticket B looks a lot better, doesn't it? For a $1.00 wager, you can win $28,750! But ... why do the payoffs only total $7,015.73 for every 10,000 games played?

It's because there won't be a winner every 10,000 games! On the average—according to probability theory—all seven spots will be caught but once each 40,979 games!

Sure, you could be the lucky one, but isn't it just a little bit more likely that you'll be among the 40,978 losers?

TICKET B – $1.00		
CATCH	PAYS	TOTAL PAYOFFS 10,000 GAMES
0	.00	.00
1	.00	.00
2	.00	.00
3	.00	.00
4	.00	.00
5	.00	.00
6	.00	.00
7	28,750.00	7,015.73
TOTAL PAYOFFS		7,015.73

When you play catch-all keno, you have but one objective: to catch all of your numbers before you've bet as much money as you'll collect if you win.

In the Ticket B example, if you win in the first 28,749 games played, you've made money. If it takes more than 28,750 games to catch all seven of your numbers, you've lost money.

Few people have the patience (or the financial wherewithal) to stick with 7-spot catch-all keno until they've won. If you want the higher payoffs that most catch-all tickets offer, but don't want to have to invest a small fortune, pick no more than five or six numbers. The fewer spots you mark, the more you increase your chances of winning before you run out of money.

The odds of catching all of your numbers are as follows:

3 numbers marked	1 in 72
4 numbers marked	1 in 326
5 numbers marked	1 in 1,551
6 numbers marked	1 in 7,753
7 numbers marked	1 in 40,979
8 numbers marked	1 in 230,115

Now that we've looked at both extremes, let's review another fictional payoff schedule. The payoffs of Ticket C compute to a 29.8365% PC; again, about the average for a 7-spot ticket.

On this ticket, you'll receive a small payoff (less than the amount of your bet) when you catch three numbers. Catch four numbers or more, and you've made a profit.

The most that you can win is $5,700—by catching all seven numbers. This is considerably less than the $28,750 you can win in the 7-spot catch-all Ticket B—yet the odds of catching 7-out-of-7 are exactly the same for both tickets!

TICKET C – $1.00		
CATCH	PAYS	TOTAL PAYOFFS 10,000 GAMES
0	.00	.00
1	.00	.00
2	.00	.00
3	.80	1,399.95
4	2.70	1,409.16
5	16.50	1,425.35
6	190.00	1,390.95
7	5,700.00	1,390.95
TOTAL PAYOFFS		7,016.36

As the prize increases in value, the number of winners of that prize decreases. There will be more 80¢ winners than $2.70 winners; more $2.70 winners than $16.50 winners; more $16.50 winners than $190 winners; and, more $190 winners than $5,700 winners.

Our hypothetical Ticket C was structured so that the total amount of money paid out would be evenly distributed among the winners of each category. You won't find this with actual tickets; they invariably favor catching some spots more than others. You'll see this in Ticket D.

At last, we're going to look at high-end keno. Ticket D has a house percentage of 29.7694%.

The minor payoffs (for catching fewer numbers) are eliminated on high-end tickets, so more of your numbers will have to be drawn in order for you to win—but when you do win, you'll win more money.

Catching seven spots on a high-end ticket doesn't pay as much as it does on a catch-all ticket, but it pays more than a regular keno ticket.

TICKET D – $1.00		
CATCH	PAYS	TOTAL PAYOFFS 10,000 GAMES
0	.00	.00
1	.00	.00
2	.00	.00
3	.00	.00
4	.00	.00
5	20.00	1,727.70
6	390.00	2,855.10
7	10,000.00	2,440.26
TOTAL PAYOFFS		7,023.06

Compare Tickets C and D. Notice how much more money Ticket D pays to winners of 5/7, 6/7, and 7/7 catches! Ticket D could be made even more high-end by eliminating the 5/7 payoff and increasing the 6/7 and 7/7 payoffs.

Most keno games with progressive jackpots are high-end. Progressive tickets that don't start out high-end can wind up that way if the jackpot gets big enough.

The following chart shows some of the ways the payoffs of an 8-spot $1.00 keno ticket can be structured. Each pay scale provides for a virtually identical house percentage—in this example, approximately 25.5%.

You'll win something—even if it's just the amount of your

bet—one time in three on the low-end ticket; once each ten games on the regular pay scale ticket; and one time every 48 games on the high-end ticket (on the average).

PAY SCALES FOR DIFFERENT TYPES OF 8-SPOT $1.00 KENO TICKETS						
CATCH	CATCH ZERO	ALL-OR NOTHING	LOW END	REGULAR	HIGH END	CATCH ALL
0	8.45	8.00	—	—	—	—
1-2	—	—	—	—	—	—
3	—	—	1.00	—	—	—
4	—	—	2.00	1.00	—	—
5	—	—	4.00	5.00	2.50	—
6	—	—	38.00	75.00	80.00	—
7	—	—	1,000.00	2,000.00	2,500.00	—
8	—	8,888.00	10,000.00	16,888.00	25,000.00	171,400.00
HOUSE PC	25.4150	25.5246	25.5149	25.5180	25.5127	25.5154
ODDS OF WINNING	1 IN 11	1 IN 11	1 IN 3	1 IN 10	1 IN 48	1 IN 230,115

In the past, keno was sometimes called *racehorse keno*. Even today, a keno *game* is often referred to as a keno *race*.

Perhaps the name was chosen with good reason. Playing catch-all keno is like betting on a long shot horse to win; high-end keno is like betting the horse to place; and regular keno can be compared to putting money on the horse to show. The bigger the gamble, the more you can win if luck is going your way!

I like high-end keno tickets. You'll win less often, but when you do win you'll get more money than you would on other types of tickets.

Never select more than eight numbers on high-end tickets. The more numbers you mark, the more difficult it becomes to catch most or all of them. If you want to play nine spots or more, look for tickets that have most of the payoffs in the middle range.

How can you determine which tickets are high-end? The casinos don't make it easy for you, because of their different ticket prices and payoffs.

To determine which of two keno tickets is high-end (both with the same number of spots and similar house percentages), divide each ticket's top payoff by the cost of the ticket (amount of bet). The ticket with the higher quotient is probably high-end.

Another way to identify a high-end ticket is to see which one requires you to catch more spots in order to get any payoff at all. Most likely, that ticket is high-end.

Some casinos' regular rate tickets are high-end. It's more usual, though, for a casino to label their high-end tickets as "specials." Watch out! "Specials" often have higher house percentages than the same casino's regular rate tickets.

A final reminder. When you play keno, always determine a ticket's house percentage before you lay down your money. If the PC is too high, it doesn't matter whether a ticket is high-end or not—you don't want to play it!

Chapter 18

20-SPOT TICKETS

Virtually every casino now offers 20-spot keno tickets. They can cost as little as $1 or as much as $10 to play, though most casinos require a bet of $5 when you mark twenty numbers. The payoffs mentioned in this chapter are predicated on a $5 wager and are typical for Las Vegas casinos.

Casinos promise big top prizes on their 20-spot tickets. Catch all twenty of your marked numbers and you'll win from $50,000 to a million dollars, depending upon the casino.

You can still win big, say the casinos, even if some of your numbers aren't drawn. If just 15 of your twenty numbers are called, you'll win $25,000. Most casinos pay $37,500–50,000 if you catch 16 spots, and $50,000 or more when you match 17–19 numbers.

With potential payoffs like these, no wonder 20-spot keno has become so popular!

And, winning appears to be so easy! On the typical 20-spot ticket, there are 18 ways to win, only three ways to lose (when you catch 4, 5, or 6 spots).

But ... according to the law of probabilities, you'll catch 4, 5 or 6 spots, and thus lose, 62.8487% of the time.

When you catch 2, 3, or 7 numbers, the casino will refund the amount of your bet. Catch 1 or 8 spots and you'll be paid $10.

You'll catch 1, 2, 3, 7, or 8 spots 34.9303% of the time, enabling you to break even or have a net win of $5—certainly nothing to write home about.

If you don't catch any numbers at all, you'll win $500. Catching nine spots pays $25; ten spots, $50, eleven spots, $200; and twelve spots, $1,000. You have a 2.2201% chance of winning one of these amounts.

This leaves you with a .0009% chance of winning more than $1,000—once every 110,595 games, to be precise.

I'll now compare the 20-spot ticket with a few other keno tickets, using the payoffs from a popular downtown Las Vegas casino in the examples.

Catch 13 numbers on the 20-spot ticket, and you'll win $5,000. But, if you bet the same $5 on a 7-spot ticket, and catch all seven numbers, you'll win $30,000.

Based upon these payoffs, you might conclude that it's six times harder to catch 7/7 than it is to catch 13/20. Not so! It's almost three times easier! The odds of catching 13-out-of-20 are 1 in 118,085, but the odds of catching 7-out-of-7 are only 1 in 40,979.

Catching 14/20 pays $12,500. Instead, play an 8-spot ticket for just $1, and when you catch eight numbers, you'll win $25,000! The odds of catching 14/20 are 1 in 1,821,882; the chances of catching 8/8 are 1 in 230,115. In other words, it's about eight times easier to win $25,000 on the 8-spot *one* dollar ticket than it is to win $12,500 on the 20-spot *five* dollar ticket!

Players of 20-spot keno greatly overestimate their chances of winning. Even when they know the odds, they have difficulty conceptualizing them. I'll give a few comparisons that should help clarify what the numbers really mean.

Let's start by finding out what it would take to catch 15 numbers out of twenty. If you play at the rate of one game per minute, 60 minutes an hour, 24 hours a day, seven days a week, 52 weeks per year, the odds of 1 in 41,751,454 mandate that you'll able to catch 15 spots out of twenty selected numbers once every 79 years, 4-1/2 months.

Just imagine ... an entire lifetime of playing keno around-the-clock at a cost of $300 per hour ... and the odds are that you'll win $25,000 only one time!

To catch 16 out of twenty numbers in keno, you're facing odds of 1 in 1,496,372,111. That's nearly one and a half billion—slightly less than the number of *inches* around the earth, at the equator.

Catching 17 out of twenty numbers requires beating odds of 1 in 90.6 billion (give or take twenty or thirty million). This is roughly equal to the number of *seconds* in 3,000 years!

To get 18 out of twenty spots, you're bucking odds of 1 in 10.5 trillion. That's about the number of *inches* to the sun *and back!*

Still think you can hit it big on the 20-spot ticket? To get 19 out of your twenty marked numbers, your chances are 1 in 2.9 *quadrillion*. That's 29 with 14 zeroes following!

And, to catch 20-out-of-20, you've got just one chance in 3,535,316,140,000,000,000. That's *3.5 quintillion!* I've had to round off to the nearest billion. When numbers get this large they're beyond the capacity of my computer.

If you do get 20-out-of-20, you'll win $50,000 to $1,000,000. A more appropriate payoff for winning a game with odds this high might be the states of California, Arizona, and New Mexico. What the heck, they should throw in Oregon and Washington, for good measure.

20-SPOT $5.00 KENO

CATCH	PAYOFF	PAYOFF/$10,000
0	500.00	1,185.71
1	10.00	231.36
2	5.00	497.14
3	5.00	1,248.64
4	———	.00
5	———	.00
6	———	.00
7	5.00	1,132.95
8	10.00	997.24
9	25.00	814.07
10	50.00	394.01
11	200.00	280.93
12	1,000.00	182.34
13	5,000.00	84.68
14	12,500.00	13.72
15	25,000.00	1.20
16	37,500.00	.05
17	50,000.00	.00
18	50,000.00	.00
19	50,000.00	.00
20	50,000.00	.00

The payoffs listed above are typical for a 20-spot $5.00 ticket, but payoffs do vary from one casino to another.

The payoffs/$10,000 column indicates, by the number of spots caught, the average amount of money a casino expects to pay to winners for every $10,000 in bets placed, according to the law of probabilities.

This ticket has a house percentage of 29.3596%.

Chapter 19

TOP / BOTTOM KENO

It's known by different names at different casinos - *top-and bottom, top-or-bottom, up-and-down, left-and-right, left-or-right, and side-to-side*. There are only three actual variations of this alternate keno ticket, and you can't necessarily tell the type of ticket you're playing from the name that the casino calls it.

Version 1 is properly called top-*or*-bottom keno.

To play, you don't mark any numbers. Just guess which half of the board will have most of the called numbers, and bet on that half.

If eleven numbers or more are called on your half of the ticket, you win. This ticket usually pays 2-to-1, and has a house percentage of 20.3243%.

Version 2 of top-or-bottom is a little different. You still indicate whether you want to bet on the top or bottom half of the ticket, and you'll still win when you catch eleven or more numbers.

Here's the difference: In Version 2, you'll get merely your wager back (or even less!) if you catch only eleven spots. But ... the more hits you have, the more money you'll win. If you're lucky enough to catch all twenty numbers on your half of the ticket, you can walk away with a prize of as much as $50,000.

Version 3 is a top-*and*-bottom ticket, although it's erroneously called top-*or*-bottom by some casinos. You don't mark any num-bers at all. If you catch seven numbers or less, or 13 numbers or more, on *either* the top or bottom half of the ticket, you win. The more (or fewer) numbers you catch, the higher your prize will be.

With several exceptions, the top/bottom tickets cost $5.00. Many casinos will allow you to play the left or right side of the ticket instead of the top or bottom half, if you prefer to do so.

$5 RATE TOP / BOTTOM KENO				
TYPICAL PAYOFFS AT LAS VEGAS CASINOS				
SPOTS CAUGHT	VERSION 1 PAYS	VERSION 2 PAYS	VERSION 3 PAYS	PROBABILITIES PERCENTAGE
0	.00	.00	50,000.00	0.000003899
1	.00	.00	20,000.00	0.000148538
2	.00	.00	3,000.00	0.002501519
3	.00	.00	1,000.00	0.024797666
4	.00	.00	200.00	0.162476377
5	.00	.00	50.00	0.748691143
6	.00	.00	20.00	2.519633656
7	.00	.00	5.00	6.345744022
8	.00	.00	.00	12.153232971
9	.00	.00	.00	17.880618624
10	.00	.00	.00	20.324303169
11	10.00	2.50	.00	17.880618624
12	10.00	7.50	.00	12.153232971
13	10.00	12.50	5.00	6.345744022
14	10.00	25.00	20.00	2.519633656
15	10.00	50.00	50.00	0.748691143
16	10.00	100.00	200.00	0.162476377
17	10.00	750.00	1,000.00	0.024797666
18	10.00	2,500.00	3,000.00	0.002501519
19	10.00	12,500.00	20,000.00	0.000148538
20	10.00	50,000.00	50,000.00	0.000003899
HOUSE PC	20.3423%	28.2501%	24.9923%	

The probability of winning on a top / bottom ticket requiring a catch of 11 or more numbers is 39.8378%.

The probability of winning on a top / bottom ticket requiring a catch of 0–7 or 13–20 numbers is 19.6080%.

The probability of winning on a top / bottom ticket requiring a catch of 0–8 or 12–20 numbers is 43.9145%.

TOP-OR-BOTTOM TICKET
(TOP NUMBERS)

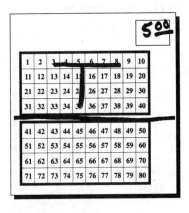

TOP-OR-BOTTOM TICKET
(BOTTOM NUMBERS)

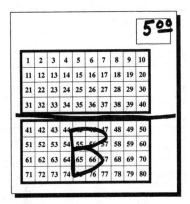

TOP-AND-BOTTOM TICKET

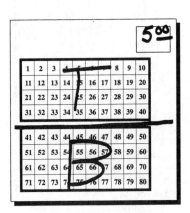

LEFT-AND-RIGHT TICKET

Chapter 20

HI-LOW KENO

The hi-low keno ticket (also called hi-lo or high-low) is offered by only a few casinos these days, and enthusiastically ignored by most players, but it's been around for a long time—so long, in fact, that there aren't very many keno managers left who still remember how hi-low keno works. It's safe to say that the majority of players who decide to try a hi-low ticket are betting in total ignorance.

To play high-low keno, you mark three groups of four numbers. Sounds like it might be a 3-way 4-spot, 3-way 8-spot, and 1-way 12-spot combination ticket, doesn't it?

Wrong. Hi-low keno is much more complex than that.

Payoffs are listed according to how many numbers you catch in each group; i.e., 3-3-2, 4-3-3, 2-2-1. The pay amounts don't seem to make any sense, until you recognize that a hi-low ticket is an 18-way 10-spot game.

Hi-low keno, according to oldtimers in the business, dates back to the days before casino gaming. It's said to be a variation of the ancient Chinese keno games, most of which required marking ten numbers.

Even the reason why the game is called hi-low is shrouded in mystery. The best explanation I've heard is that *hi-low* refers to a comparison of the game's payoffs with those of a 12-spot regular ticket.

For example, there are four possible ways of catching a total of seven numbers on a hi-low ticket: 3-2-2, 3-3-1, 4-2-1, and 4-3-0. Some of these catches pay higher and some pay lower than the payoff for catching seven numbers on a straight 12-spot ticket. Thus, hi-low.

In order to compute the house percentage on hi-low keno, you must determine what the payoffs are for *each way*. It's not an easy task, because the payoff schedules list only the total payoff for all 18 ways. To uncover the individual payoffs it's necessary to work the numbers backwards.

First, you need to know the breakdown of winning catches for each payoff group (4-3-2, 3-3-3, etc.). Here's a relatively simple (but time-consuming) method of accomplishing this task:

Total the hits on two of the three groups of four numbers, and treat the four numbers on the third group as if they were *kings* (individually circled numbers). This gives six possible ways of making a 10-spot.

Repeat the process twice more, each time using a different group of numbers as kings, and counting all of the hits in the other two groups.

An easier way to know the possible catches in an 18-way 10-spot game is to refer to the chart I've thoughtfully prepared for you. Note that a number of the possible catches aren't winners.

The second step in determining the PC of a hi-low ticket is to back into the payoffs. I'll use a typical $3.60 hi-low ticket as a model.

In this example, catching 4-4-4 pays $61,200. Refer to the

PAYOFFS OF A TYPICAL $3.60 HI-LOW TICKET				
NUMBERS CAUGHT		**PAYS**	**NUMBERS CAUGHT**	**PAYS**
5	2 - 2 - 1	2.00	8 3 - 3 - 2	508.00
	3 - 1 - 1	2.40	4 - 2 - 2	656.00
	3 - 2 - 0	2.80	4 - 3 - 1	804.00
	4 - 1 - 0	3.60	4 - 4 - 0	1,248.00
6	2 - 2 - 2	16.80	9 3 - 3 - 3	2,052.00
	3 - 2 - 1	20.00	4 - 3 - 2	2,280.00
	3 - 3 - 0	26.40	4 - 4 - 1	2,736.00
	4 - 1 - 1	26.40	10 4 - 3 - 3	6,000.00
	4 - 2 - 0	29.60	4 - 4 - 2	8,400.00
7	3 - 2 - 2	102.00	11 4 - 4 - 3	19,200.00
	3 - 3 - 1	122.40		
	4 - 2 - 1	142.80	12 4 - 4 - 4	61,200.00
	4 - 3 - 0	183.60		

chart at the end of this chapter and you'll learn that there are 18 ways to make 10/10 when all numbers in each group of four are drawn.

Thus, by dividing the $61,200 payoff by 18, we determine that the payoff for catching 10/10 one way is $3,400.

Catching 4-4-3 pays $19,200. A 4-4-3 catch has three ways of getting 10/10 and 15 ways to make 9/10.

Subtract the 10/10 payoffs ($3,400 x 3) from the total payoff of $19,200. This leaves a balance of $9,000. Divide the $9,000 by 15 (the number of ways to make 9/10), and we find out that the 9/10 payoff is $600.

Catching 4-4-2 pays $8,400. With a 4-4-2 catch, there's one 10/10 way, four 9/10 ways, and thirteen 8/10 ways.

From the $8,400 total payoff, subtract the payoffs we established above for the 10/10 and 9/10 ways ($3,400 x 1, and $600 x 4), and divide the balance of $2,600 by the number of ways of catching 8/10 (13). Thus, we learn that the payoff for catching 8/10 one way is $200.

I won't bore you with any more of the mathematics; by now you should get the drift of how to "back into" a hi-low payoff schedule. Once the payoff schedule has been established the house percentage can be computed in the usual manner.

If you encounter any problems in attempting to determine high-low payoffs, recheck your figures. It's easy to make a mistake, and, once made, an error will affect all of your subsequent calculations.

If the payoffs still don't seem to be quite right, there are other possible explanations. The person who originally devised the payoff schedule could have modified some of the payoffs to avoid having them end in odd cents, could have erred, or could have made other aberrations in the payoffs for reasons known only to him.

A printer's typographical error, never caught by the keno department, might be another reason for numbers that don't fit the perceived pattern.

There's one more thing that can throw a monkey wrench in your calculations—the aggregate limit. For example, all of the $3.60 hi-low payoffs at one casino are exactly twice those of their $1.80 ticket, except for the 4-4-4 payoff; it's only a third higher, due to the casino's aggregate limit of $50,000. Because of this, 10/10 pays more with catches of 4-4-3 or 4-4-2 than it does with a catch of 4-4-4.

When the 4-4-4 payoff is reduced because of the aggregate limit, it can't be used to compute the 10/10 payoff—and, you need to start with the 10/10 payoff in order to calculate the other payoffs. It's a "Catch 22" situation!

In this instance, since the $1.80 ticket isn't affected by the aggregate limit, just double the ways payoffs of the $1.80 ticket to get the ways payoffs for the $3.60 ticket. For all practical purposes the smaller 10/10 payoffs on the 4-4-4 catch can be ignored, although they do raise the house percentage slightly.

If the 4-4-4 payoff has been reduced because of the aggregate limit and you don't have a lower-priced ticket for comparison, you'll have to establish the 9/10 and 10/10 ways payoffs by trial-and-error. It's not an easy task, but it's not impossible.

You might begin with the casino's 10-spot regular rate "catch 9" and "catch 10" payoffs, and prorate them as if the regular ticket cost 1/18th the price of the hi-low ticket. That is, divide the regular rate 10-spot payoffs by the cost of the 10-spot ticket, multiply the quotients by the cost of the hi-low ticket, and divide those products by 18. The resultant figures should be close to the hi-low 9/10 and 10/10 payoffs, and in some instances, might be exactly the same.

On the other hand, the ways payoffs on a hi-low ticket may differ from the prorated payoffs of the casino's regular 10-spot ticket.

A case in point is the $3.60 hi-low ticket used as our "typical" example. At the casino that offers this ticket, the $2.00 regular 10-spot ticket payoffs (for each dollar wagered) are identical to the hi-low payoffs (per way) when five or six spots are caught; they're less, when seven or eight spots are caught; and more, when nine or ten spots are caught.

Hi-low keno payoffs (per way) compared with regular ticket payoffs		
CATCH	REGULAR	HI-LOW
0-4	—	—
5	2.00	2.00
6	20.00	20.00
7	132.00	140.00
8	960.00	1,000.00
9	3,800.00	3,000.00
10	25,000.00	17,000.00
PC	29.8820%	28.6308%

The above table compares payoffs (per way) of a typical hi-low keno ticket with the payoffs of the same casino's regular 10-spot ticket. Payoffs are prorated as if the wager per ticket or per way is $1.00.

Before playing hi-low keno, it's always a good idea to compare the house percentage with the casino's regular 10-spot ticket. Sometimes the hi-low ticket is the better bet, and sometimes it's the other way around.

HI-LOW KENO

ANALYSIS OF CATCHES ON AN 18-WAY 10-SPOT TICKET
– 3 GROUPS OF 4 NUMBERS MARKED –

TOTAL NUMBERS CAUGHT IN EACH GROUP	POSSIBLE WAYS		
4 - 4 - 4	18 - 10/10		
4 - 4 - 3	3 - 10/10	15 - 9/10	
4 - 4 - 2	1 - 10/10	4 - 9/10	13 - 8/10
4 - 4 - 1	3 - 9/10	3 - 8/10	12 - 7/10
4 - 4 - 0	6 - 8/10	12 - 6/10	
4 - 3 - 3	6 - 9/10	12 - 8/10	
4 - 3 - 2	1 - 9/10	7 - 8/10	10 - 7/10
4 - 3 - 1	3 - 8/10	6 - 7/10	9 - 6/10
4 - 3 - 0	6 - 7/10	3 - 6/10	9 - 5/10
4 - 2 - 2	2 - 8/10	8 - 7/10	8 - 6/10
4 - 2 - 1	4 - 7/10	7 - 6/10	7 - 5/10
4 - 2 - 0	7 - 6/10	4 - 5/10	7 - 4/10
4 - 1 - 1	6 - 6/10	6 - 5/10	6 - 4/10
4 - 1 - 0	9 - 5/10	3 - 4/10	6 - 3/10
4 - 0 - 0	12 - 4/10	6 - 2/10	
3 - 3 - 3	9 - 8/10	9 - 7/10	
3 - 3 - 2	1 - 8/10	10 - 7/10	7 - 6/10
3 - 3 - 1	3 - 7/10	9 - 6/10	6 - 5/10
3 - 3 - 0	6 - 6/10	6 - 5/10	6 - 4/10
3 - 2 - 2	2 - 7/10	11 - 6/10	5 - 5/10
3 - 2 - 1	4 - 6/10	10 - 5/10	4 - 4/10
3 - 2 - 0	7 - 5/10	7 - 4/10	4 - 3/10
3 - 1 - 1	6 - 5/10	9 - 4/10	3 - 3/10
3 - 1 - 0	9 - 4/10	6 - 3/10	3 - 2/10
3 - 0 - 0	12 - 3/10	3 - 2/10	3 - 1/10
2 - 2 - 2	3 - 6/10	12 - 5/10	3 - 4/10
2 - 2 - 1	5 - 5/10	11 - 4/10	2 - 3/10
2 - 2 - 0	8 - 4/10	8 - 3/10	2 - 2/10
2 - 1 - 1	7 - 4/10	10 - 3/10	1 - 2/10
2 - 1 - 0	10 - 3/10	7 - 2/10	1 - 1/10
2 - 0 - 0	13 - 2/10	4 - 1/10	1 - 0/10
1 - 1 - 1	9 - 3/10	9 - 2/10	
1 - 1 - 0	12 - 2/10	6 - 1/10	
1 - 0 - 0	15 - 1/10	3 - 0/10	
0 - 0 - 0	18 - 0/10		

Chapter 21

PROGRESSIVE JACKPOTS

Keno games with progressive jackpots, *progressive keno*, have become very popular with players, and for good reason.

They offer the possibility of winning a very large payoff for a small bet ... the same attraction that entices people to buy lottery tickets. The Flamingo Hilton has already paid a keno jackpot of nearly a half million dollars; but, unlike Lotto, the entire prize was paid in one lump sum.

The odds of winning a game with a given number of spots never change, but the house percentages for progressive keno change according to the size of the jackpot. As the jackpot grows, the PCs of the progressive tickets decrease. When the jackpot gets high enough, some of the tickets have negative house percentages. That is, the percentages are actually in the players' favor!

Casinos with progressive keno have electronic displays (usually incorporated into the flashboards) that proclaim how much money is currently in the jackpot.

The actual jackpot amount is the amount in excess of that figure to which the jackpot meter will be reset, after the jackpot has been won in its entirety; but, at most casinos, the jackpot meter reflects the total of both the actual jackpot amount and the base payoff.

Progressive jackpots—and this includes slot machine progressive jackpots—are the subject of a legal fiction that states that the money in the jackpots belongs to the players, not the casino. By law, casinos must set aside a reserve equal to the total of all of their progressive jackpots, to guarantee payment in the highly improbable circumstance that all jackpots are won at the same time.

The money set aside *must* be paid out to players, sooner or later; it's an inviolable fund, and the casino cannot just pocket it, even if they eliminate the tickets built around the jackpot. Once started, it isn't easy for a casino to drop a progressive jackpot program. They must wait until the jackpot is won, transfer the funds to a similar program, or set up special bonuses until all of the jackpot money is distributed to players.

Progressive keno was originally conceived as a way to circumvent the gaming regulations that limited the maximum aggregate keno payoffs. These regulations have been repealed and casinos are now free to set their own aggregate payoff limits, so it's no longer necessary for casinos to provide progressive keno in order to offer high payoffs. What's more, they can list big prizes in their paybooks without having to put money into a reserve account. As a result, some casinos have already dropped progressive keno tickets, and others will undoubtedly follow suit in the future.

The only thing that can be said with absolute certainty about progressive keno is that it has a jackpot that gets larger as time goes by. Each casino offering progressive keno has its own variations and rules; the lack of standardization has resulted in vast differences in progressive keno from casino to casino.

Some casinos pay all progressive keno winners the entire jackpot. Because these jackpots revert to the minimum base payoff each time there's a winner, there are wide swings in the PCs. At times, they're even in the players' favor!

At some casinos, most—if not all—of the progressive winners receive a mere fraction of the jackpot. The number of spots marked, the number of spots caught, and the amount of the bet determine the percentage of the jackpot that will be paid. At one casino, winners of 6/6 get 2% of the jackpot; 7/7 winners get just 5%. It takes a very difficult catch (9/9 or 10/10) to win the whole ball of wax.

Jackpots seldom bottom out on this type of progressive. Rather, they're chipped away at by the fractional jackpot payoffs, which more or less counterbalances the increases added to the jackpots as a result of play. Therefore, both the amount of the jackpot and the house percentages remain relatively stable.

At most casinos, on a basic rate ticket you'll need to mark and catch nine numbers or more in order to win the entire jackpot. If more than nine numbers are marked, you may be able to win the jackpot even when you don't catch them all; i.e., catching eleven numbers on a 12-spot ticket or 12, 13, or 14 numbers on a 15-spot ticket might entitle you to the jackpot—check the casino's paybooks.

The odds of catching 9-out-of-9 are 1 in 1,380,688; if more than nine numbers are marked, the odds are considerably greater. Understandably, progressive games that require a minimum catch of 9/9 in order to win the jackpot aren't hit very often—perhaps just once a year at the average casino. Jackpots at casinos with this type of progressive may climb to several hundred thousand dollars before someone scores.

One Las Vegas casino—the Gold Coast—has a $5.00 progressive keno ticket on which you need to mark and catch just eight spots in order to win the entire jackpot.

And what a jackpot! The minimum (the amount to which the meter is reset after the jackpot has been won) is a whopping $250,000! Moreover, the starting house percentage of the Gold Coast ticket is quite moderate, and gets even lower as the jackpot grows.

The chances of catching 8/8 are 1 in 230,115, and, therefore, someone wins the jackpot quite regularly—usually, every couple of months. (See chapter 44, "Lightning strikes again!")

A few casinos offer progressive keno tickets that pay the

jackpot when you mark six numbers and catch them all. Jackpots on 6-spot progressive tickets rarely exceed $15,000, for the relatively low odds of 1 in 7,753 guarantee frequent winners.

You can still win on most progressive keno tickets, even if you don't get enough hits to win the jackpot. Check the casino's paybook for the ticket you're playing to find out how many numbers you need to catch in order to get a payoff, and to learn how much the lesser payoffs will be.

There are four methods casinos use to build the progressive keno jackpot:

1. The keno jackpot is increased by a percentage—usually between 1% and 3%—of all keno bets placed at the casino. The keno computer keeps track of the bets placed and updates the jackpot meter after every game.

2. The keno jackpot is increased by a percentage—again, usually between 1% and 3%—of the total keno bets placed the preceding month (or some other time period), or by an arbitrary amount set by casino management. The amount to be added to the keno jackpot in a given month is spread over the month on a time basis. With this system, the jackpot meter is constantly being incremented, day and night, regardless of the volume of play.

3. The jackpot for a particular type of ticket (i.e., number of spots) is increased by a percentage of all of the wagers placed on that type of ticket only.

4. The jackpot is increased on a periodic basis by a fixed amount. Harrah's in Laughlin, Nevada featured a "progressive" 5-spot ticket for years. The "jackpot" started at $1,000, and was increased $20.00 each day until someone won it. (I've used the quotation marks to indicate that this is not progressive keno in the usual sense.)

As with all other types of keno, the house percentages on progressive keno differ from casino to casino. Some of the PCs are brutal, others are moderate. There is one very important difference on progressive keno. As the jackpots grow, the house percentages go down!

Because of the "players' money" fiction, casinos compute the house percentages on progressive tickets as if the jackpot had just been won; that is, at the base amount with no jackpot at all.

Players, however, should always figure the house percentages based upon the amount of money they can win at the time they place their bet. One keno manager calls this the "Man from Mars" concept. A Martian arrives on Earth, goes into a casino, makes one keno bet, and then gets back in his rocket ship and goes home. The only thing that matters to the Martian (and the only thing that should matter to you) is the house percentage at the time the bet is placed and the game is played.

Depending upon the number of spots marked, the initial house percentage, the size of the jackpot, and the casino's formula for determining what portion of the jackpot you'll receive, the reduction in the house percentage of a progressive keno ticket (as the jackpot grows) can be negligible or it can be substantial. The house percentage can actually get so low that it becomes a player percentage!

GOLD COAST 8-SPOT $5.00 PROGRESSIVE KENO TICKET	
CATCH	PAYS
4	5.00
5	25.00
6	450.00
7	7,500.00
8	★ JACKPOT
★ JACKPOT	HOUSE PC
250,000	15.6013
300,000	11.2557
350,000	6.9100
400,000	2.5644
429,505	0.0000
500,000	− 6.1270

According to probability theory, from the time the PC gets in the players' favor until the jackpot is won, the casino won't take in as much money on the progressive tickets (in total) as they will be paying out (all payoffs, including the jackpot) to the aggregate of players.

Keep an eye on the progressive jackpot meters! When the jackpots get big enough to change the house percentage of a keno ticket into a players' percentage, you may have found the best—albeit a long shot—bet in the entire casino!

Chapter 22

GIMMICK TICKETS

Tired of run-of-the-mill keno tickets? Looking for something different, keno with a "gimmick?"

Many keno managers are quite creative, and have introduced a number of innovative variations of keno. Some of their ideas have been well received by keno players, and, consequently, other casinos have been quick to copy them.

The 20-spot is a good example of a relatively new keno ticket that is now ubiquitous. I don't know where the ticket got started, but it was copied so precisely by some casinos that they also duplicated a mistake printed on the pay cards. Even today, some casinos tout their 20-spot ticket as having "17 ways to win"— although, as usually played, the 20-spot has 18 winning catches!

Other concepts have been duds, and are dropped by the casino without fanfare—usually, when the keno manager gets fired and is replaced by somebody new.

Still other gimmick keno tickets enjoy a degree of success at the casino where they were introduced, but, for one reason or another, haven't been picked up by others. Thus, gimmick tickets give a unique flavor to the keno program at the casinos where they can be played.

Bill Holmes, formerly keno manager at Western Village Inn

and Casino in Sparks, Nevada has to receive my vote as the most prolific creator of novel keno tickets.

Bill is extremely knowledgeable about the game of keno, and I've enjoyed numerous conversations with him—many of which centered on our disagreement about the correct way to compute the house percentages of pay-any-catch tickets.

His "bank shot" 20-spot ticket costs $7.00, which is $2.00 more than most casinos charge for a 20-spot ticket. It has a house percentage of 28.4211%, which is only a little less than the PC of a typical 20-spot ticket, but pays $50,000 for catching twelve or more spots! Compare this with most other 20-spot ($5.00) tickets, which pay $1,000 for catching 12/20, $5,000 for 13/20, $12,500 for 14/20, and $25,000 for 15/20.

It's about four times easier to catch twelve or more numbers out of twenty than it is to catch 7/7, and about 23 times easier than catching 8/8. The "bank shot" ticket provides a substantial payoff with appropriate odds of winning.

The "retrogressive" 5-spot catch-all ticket is another of Holmes's brainstorms. It's the opposite of progressive keno. Instead of a jackpot that goes up, the price of the ticket goes down (5¢ per week) until someone catches all five numbers.

Most casinos merely prorate their regular payoffs for way tickets, but the Western Village's "villager" way ticket has enhanced payoffs to make the wager more attractive.

Holmes also created the "line drive," a ticket which uses all eighty numbers, and pays when five or more of them appear on the board in a continuous, unbroken line, either vertically or horizontally.

"The edge," another gimmick ticket originated by Holmes, has payoffs predicated upon how many of the 32 numbers on the perimeter of a keno blank are drawn. This ticket has been copied by Caesars Palace and a few others. At Caesars, you can also bet on 32 inside numbers. See chapter 34, "Keno odds," for the odds and probability percentages for tickets marked with 32 spots.

What do you play when it seems like none of your numbers

are coming up? Some casinos offer catch-zero tickets, which pay only if you don't catch any of your marked numbers at all.

Your chances of getting a blank are fairly high. The odds are about 1 in 2.4 that you won't catch any numbers on a 3-spot ticket. You have to mark 15 numbers or more in order to face odds greater than 1 in 100 that none of your numbers will be drawn. Even with a 20-spot ticket, you won't catch any spots once every 843 games.

You have a good chance of winning when you play a catch-zero ticket; but, because of the low odds, payoffs are minimal. At some casinos the payoffs are so low and the house percentages so high on the catch-zero tickets that it would be charitable to call them rip-off tickets. You'll never get rich playing catch-zero keno!

Remember ... when your numbers haven't been coming up, they could be getting ready to all show up together on the *very next draw!* Or, perhaps not. Reread chapter 12, "Picking winning numbers."

Bobby Dean, keno manager at the Palace Station, has a clever gimmick for certain 1- through 4-spot tickets. When all marked numbers are caught, and one of them is the last ball drawn, the payoff is doubled. How do you know which was the last ball drawn? The light behind the last number drawn blinks on the Palace Station's keno flashboards.

Compute the house percentages of last-ball-drawn tickets exactly the same way you would figure the PCs of any other keno ticket—*except*—you have to use the *average* payoffs, not the payoffs listed in the casino's paybooks.

To determine average payoffs, when catching the last ball drawn results in a bonus prize, add to the *top prize* listed in the paybook: 5% of the bonus prize for a 1-spot ticket, 10% for a 2-spot bet, 15% for a 3-spot wager, 20% if four numbers are marked, and so on. Use all other payoffs exactly as they're listed in the keno paybooks—*don't* increase them.

The Peppermill (Mesquite, Nevada) had a different gimmick. When their 8-, 9-, or 10-number $5.00 "bonus keno" tickets were played for five consecutive multi-race games, the casino gave "free insurance." If there wasn't a win on the five-game series, they paid $25 in "keno money" (scrip) for the 8-spot tickets; $50 for 9-spot tickets; and $100 when ten numbers were played.

The chances of collecting on the insurance were:

Odds On Collecting On Insurance	
8-spot ticket	1 in 6.7343
9-spot ticket	1 in 12.7705
10-spot ticket	1 in 26.1457

When the expected "insurance" payments are included with the expected wins, the *indicated* house percentages drop dramatically (see the following chart). However, there's one more thing to consider.

It's a certainty that players would get *something* back on every five-game $25 multi-race ticket. If they didn't win one or more of the regular payoffs, they would collect the "insurance." At the very minimum, they got $3.00 back for each $25 wagered (for catching three numbers on just one of the five multi-race games).

Since players were *absolutely sure* that they would get a minimum of $3.00 back on every $25 wager, they were not actually winning $3.00, they were being repaid for a "temporary loan to the casino." Thus, the Peppermill's "bonus keno" multi-race ticket was a variation of a pay-any-catch ticket.

To determine the *true* house percentage of pay-any-catch keno, the first step is to deduct the minimum payback from the cost of the ticket and from each payoff. For a complete explanation of why this is necessary, reread chapter 16, "The 'pay-any-catch' gimmick."

The Peppermill's "bonus keno" is a little different from the usual pay-any-catch situation because of the multi-game feature. Therefore, it's necessary to deduct the *average* minimum payback ($3 ÷ 5 = 60¢) from the cost of each individual game and from each payoff.

When recomputed as pay-any-catch keno tickets, the true

house percentages of the Peppermill's "bonus keno" multi-game tickets were as follows:

	PEPPERMILL "BONUS KENO" HOUSE PERCENTAGES		
SPOTS	NO INSURANCE (SINGLE GAME)	WITH INSURANCE INDICATED PC	WITH INSURANCE TRUE PC
8	26.1405%	11.30%	17.17%
9	26.1898%	10.52%	17.39%
10	26.0033%	10.72%	18.70%

The Gold Coast Hotel and Casino offers a "keno exacta." The exacta is an add-on wager, similar to taking the odds in craps.

Here's how it works at the Gold Coast: Mark one to ten numbers, and play the ticket for two consecutive $1.00 rate games. Add 25¢ more to play the exacta, for a total of $2.25.

Whether you win the exacta or not, you'll still receive the normal game payoffs. When you catch the same amount of winning spots on both games, the combined payoff is increased to as much as $2,000,000.

House percentages of the exacta portion of the bet are quite low, from 7.4507% on the 2-spot ticket down to absolutely no house edge at all on the 1-spot ticket.

	GOLD COAST KENO EXACTA 6-SPOTS MARKED		
CATCH	1ST GAME PAYOFF	2ND GAME PAYOFF	EXACTA PAYOFF	TOTAL PAYOFF
3-3	1.00	1.00	3.00	5.00
4-4	5.00	5.00	115.00	125.00
5-5	75.00	75.00	9,850.00	10,000.00
6-6	2,000.00	2,000.00	246,000.00	250,000.00

To compute the odds of winning an exacta, merely square the one-game odds.

For example, the odds of catching three out of four numbers are 1 in 23.1225. To catch three out of four numbers on two consecutive games (the exacta), the odds are 1 in 534.65.

Once you've figured the odds for every possible catch, you can compute the house percentages on the exacta in the usual manner. Use the cost of the exacta as the ticket price, and the exacta portion of the payoffs, not the total payoffs.

Gold Coast's sister casino, the Barbary Coast, has a similar exacta program, also with low house percentages on the exacta. But beware ... there are a couple of "exacta" tickets at other casinos that are total rip-offs! Again, I remind you that you should *always* know the house percentage of a keno ticket *before* you place your bet!

Please bear in mind that by the time this book gets into print it's a certainty that some of the payoffs (and consequently, the house percentages) of the gimmick tickets detailed in this chapter will be changed, some of the tickets will be dropped, and new and improved gimmick tickets will be introduced.

Gimmick tickets can be fun to play. They provide a different twist to keno, and help keep the game fresh and exciting. Just remember ... if you want to win more and lose less, don't play *any* keno ticket unless it has a reasonable house percentage.

Chapter 23

COMBINATION, WAY, AND KING TICKETS MADE SIMPLE

You take your basic 6-spot or 8-spot ticket up to the keno desk. Everyone else seems to have groups of numbers or individual numbers circled on their tickets.

These people look like they know what they're doing. They often play several tickets at a time, and always seem to be collecting on their wagers. Suspecting that they've found a more profitable method of playing keno, you look through the casino's keno paybook, hoping to find an answer.

Yes, there you find illustrated examples of *way, combination,* and *king* tickets, but they look quite confusing, and any explanation of how and why to play them is minimal.

You find a statement, "Our friendly keno writers and runners will be happy to explain way tickets," or words to that effect. Now you know for a certainty that way and combination tickets are for the players with years of keno experience. There's so much to learn about these tickets that there isn't room in the paybooks to print adequate playing instructions!

You would like to take the casino up on its offer for help but the runners are always in a hurry, and you don't want to keep them from getting all of their keno tickets turned in on time. You're also hesitant to show your ignorance by asking a keno writer to give you a keno lesson, especially since there are several people behind you in line, all anxious to place their bets before the next draw starts.

Actually, these tickets are quite easy to understand. They're just a short-cut method for placing several different keno wagers on a single piece of paper. As usually played, each of the bets will have some common numbers.

Combination means that two or more groups of numbers, when put together, combine to form a larger group of numbers.

The term *way* refers to the number of ways you can win on one ticket; in other words, how many different wagers you're making on that ticket. Each way is a separate bet.

A *king* ticket has one or more numbers that are *individually circled*. That's the only thing that makes a king ticket different from a combination or way ticket.

For simplicity, let's refer to all of these as *way tickets.*

Now, let's look at some examples. For these examples we're going to bet $1.00 each *way.*

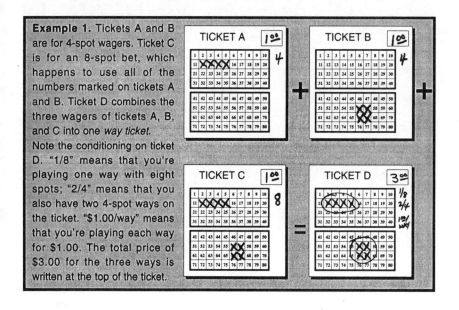

Example 1. Tickets A and B are for 4-spot wagers. Ticket C is for an 8-spot bet, which happens to use all of the numbers marked on tickets A and B. Ticket D combines the three wagers of tickets A, B, and C into one *way ticket.* Note the conditioning on ticket D. "1/8" means that you're playing one way with eight spots; "2/4" means that you also have two 4-spot ways on the ticket. "$1.00/way" means that you're playing each way for $1.00. The total price of $3.00 for the three ways is written at the top of the ticket.

Example 2. Ticket A is a regular 5-spot ticket. We've added a number to the five numbers marked on ticket A, to make Ticket B—a 6-spot ticket. Ticket C is a slightly different 6-spot ticket, which we made by adding a different additional number to the five numbers of ticket A. By using the five numbers of Ticket A, plus the numbers added on both Tickets B and C, we've created Ticket D, a 7-spot ticket. We can place all of these bets individually, by writing four separate keno tickets. Or, we

can combine them into one way ticket—see Ticket E. The individually circled numbers on this ticket are called *kings*. The payoffs for each way are computed individually. They're identical to the payoffs you would get if you wrote each way on a separate ticket.

In this example, if you catch all seven numbers on Ticket E you'll get paid the same amount as if you played tickets A, B, C, and D individually, and caught five numbers on Ticket A, six numbers on Tickets B and C, and seven numbers on ticket D.

Of course, you don't have to catch all of your numbers in order to win, unless you've chosen to play catch-all keno. You can win on *each* way, if you catch enough spots. Remember, payoffs are figured the same as if you played each way on a separate ticket.

Most casinos pay when you catch three or more spots on 5, 6, and 7 spot tickets. On this example, you'll get paid for every way on which you've caught three or more spots.

Example 3. Three groups of four numbers are marked on this ticket.

The possible combinations are: one way of playing twelve spots; three ways of playing eight spots; and three ways of playing four spots.

It isn't necessary for the circled numbers on way tickets to be contiguous. You must, however, be able to clearly indicate which numbers belong to each group.

-112-

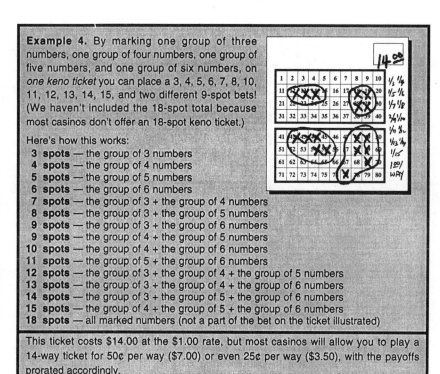

Example 4. By marking one group of three numbers, one group of four numbers, one group of five numbers, and one group of six numbers, on *one keno ticket* you can place a 3, 4, 5, 6, 7, 8, 10, 11, 12, 13, 14, 15, and two different 9-spot bets! (We haven't included the 18-spot total because most casinos don't offer an 18-spot keno ticket.)

Here's how this works:

3 **spots** — the group of 3 numbers
4 **spots** — the group of 4 numbers
5 **spots** — the group of 5 numbers
6 **spots** — the group of 6 numbers
7 **spots** — the group of 3 + the group of 4 numbers
8 **spots** — the group of 3 + the group of 5 numbers
9 **spots** — the group of 3 + the group of 6 numbers
9 **spots** — the group of 4 + the group of 5 numbers
10 **spots** — the group of 4 + the group of 6 numbers
11 **spots** — the group of 5 + the group of 6 numbers
12 **spots** — the group of 3 + the group of 4 + the group of 5 numbers
13 **spots** — the group of 3 + the group of 4 + the group of 6 numbers
14 **spots** — the group of 3 + the group of 5 + the group of 6 numbers
15 **spots** — the group of 4 + the group of 5 + the group of 6 numbers
18 **spots** — all marked numbers (not a part of the bet on the ticket illustrated)

This ticket costs $14.00 at the $1.00 rate, but most casinos will allow you to play a 14-way ticket for 50¢ per way ($7.00) or even 25¢ per way ($3.50), with the payoffs prorated accordingly.

There's practically no limit to the number of combinations you can make. If you run out of ideas, the keno folders are full of them (of course). Here are a few creative way tickets, all of which were suggested in the keno folders of various casinos.

THE BEGINNER

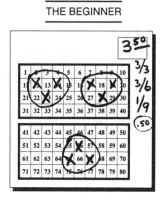

NATURAL SEVEN

THE KING

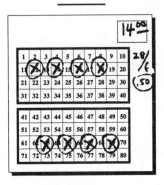

CORNERS COVERED

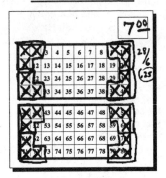

MICKEY MOUSE ?

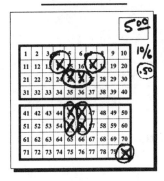

190 WAY BLACKOUT

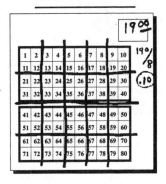

THE BUTTERFLY

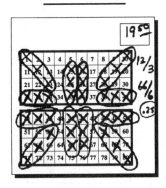

45 WAY 6-SPOT

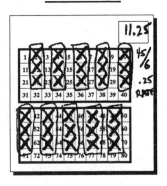

Chapter 24

CONDITIONING THE WAY TICKET

On each blank keno ticket there's an area (usually on the right or at the top) where you instruct the casino how you want to play the ticket. This is called *conditioning* the ticket.

Always condition way tickets, so that the casino will know which of the possible ways you want to bet and for how much money per way.

For instance, you might write a way ticket with three groups of four numbers.

When you play all of the seven ways possible on this ticket—one 12-spot, three 8-spots, and three 4-spots—the conditioning will look like example A.

EXAMPLE A

However, you may not want to play all of these ways. If you decide that you don't want to play the 12-spot, condition the ticket as in example B.

And, if you only want to play the three 8-spots, your conditioning should look like example C.

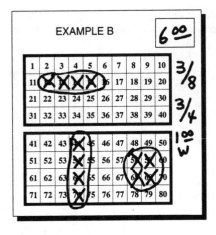 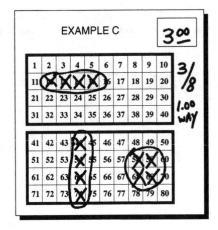

Fractional rate tickets. Most casinos allow you to play *each way* of a way ticket at a fraction of their straight (regular) ticket minimum price.

Each casino has its own rules, but, at the majority of casinos, you can play the $1.00 rate for 50¢ per way if the ticket has three or more ways; and, for 25¢ per way, if the ticket has ten ways or more.

At $1.00 per way, playing all possible ways on a 7-way ticket costs $7.00 per game. Played at half rate, or 50¢ per way, the ticket costs only $3.50. Of course, when you play at half rate all payoffs are also cut in half!

Split rate tickets. You don't need to bet the same amount of money on each group of ways. Example D shows how you might condition a 7-way split rate ticket.

Example D has a bet of $2.00 on the 12-spot portion of the ticket; 50¢ on each of the three 8-spot ways; and $1.00 on each of the three 4-spot ways. The total price of the ticket is $6.50. The payoffs for each way will be determined by the amount bet on the way, prorated to the regular rate payoffs.

Some keno players become very creative in conditioning way tickets; it's as if they're trying to create a puzzle for the keno writers to unscramble.

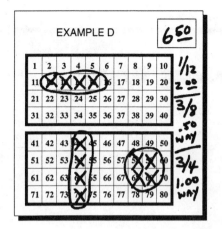

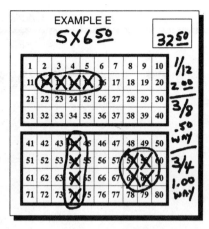

Multi-game keno. Most casinos allow you to play one ticket for two to twenty consecutive games, and a large number of casinos sell multi-game tickets for up to a thousand games. When playing multi-game keno you must also condition your ticket with the number of games you want to play and the total price of the ticket (the number of games multiplied by the cost of playing one game). See example E.

Chapter 25

LET ME COUNT THE WAYS ...

One popular way ticket is made by marking twelve numbers on a keno blank and then dividing the numbers into three groups of four (example A).

This ticket has three 4-spot ways and one 12-spot way. Also, there are three possible ways to combine the groups into sets of eight numbers.

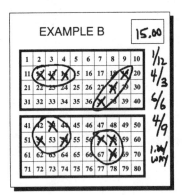

Another frequently played way ticket is also marked with twelve numbers, but the numbers are divided into four groups of three (example B).

In addition to one 12-spot way and four 3-spot ways, the groups combine to make six 6-spot ways and four 9-spot ways.

It's not too difficult to figure out how many ways there are on these simple tickets, but some way tickets are considerably more complex.

Many casinos offer a 190-way 8-spot ticket at 10¢ per way (example C).

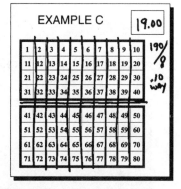

All eighty numbers on the keno ticket are utilized, by dividing the ticket into twenty groups of four numbers. How can you be certain that there are actually 190 ways that the groups combine into sets of eight numbers? Do you take the casino's word for it?

You don't have to, for there's a simple mathematical formula to figure the number of possible combinations.

First, divide the total number of spots in a way (W) by the number of spots in each group (S) to determine how many groups are needed (N) to make each way.

$$W \div S = N \qquad 8 \div 4 = 2$$

In the above example, there are four numbers in each group; thus, it takes two groups to make each 8-spot way.

Once you know how many groups are needed to make each way (N), use the following formula to determine the possible number of ways. G indicates the total number of groups; C, the number of possible ways.

$$\frac{G \times G\text{-}1 \ldots \times G\text{-}2 \times G\text{-}3, \text{etc.}}{N \times N\text{-}1 \ldots \times N\text{-}2 \times N\text{-}3, \text{etc.}} = C$$

Start the calculation with the total number of groups (G) and the number of groups needed for each way (N). Then, extend the calculation as far as necessary, by decreasing each subsequent G and N number by 1, until the last N number equals 1.

Using this formula, the twenty group 8-spot ticket is shown to have 190 ways.

$$\frac{20 \times 19}{2 \times 1} = 190$$

Example D is a ticket with twelve groups of two numbers. The possible combinations are as follows:

66 POSSIBLE 4-SPOT WAYS
Each way is made from two groups of two numbers.

$$\frac{12 \times 11}{2 \times 1} = 66$$

220 POSSIBLE 6-SPOT WAYS
Each way is made from three groups of two numbers.

$$\frac{12 \times 11 \times 10}{3 \times 2 \times 1} = 220$$

495 POSSIBLE 8-SPOT WAYS
Each way is made from four groups of two numbers.

$$\frac{12 \times 11 \times 10 \times 9}{4 \times 3 \times 2 \times 1} = 495$$

In addition, twelve groups of two numbers can be combined to make 10, 12, 14, 16, 18, and 20-spot ways.

If math isn't your strong suit, forget the formula and refer to the following chart. It lists the possible combinations for up to twenty groups total, and for ways comprised of two to seven same-size groups.

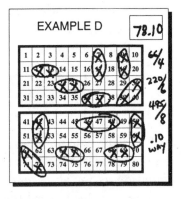

Find the total number of groups circled (G, in the formula) in the first column. Then, refer to the column for the number of groups needed to make a single way (N, in the formula).

Find the number of possible ways at the intersection of the two columns.

The numbers in the chart all relate in a most curious manner. Each number is equal to the sum of the number immediately above it plus the number in the column to the left of the number immediately above it.

TOTAL NUMBER OF GROUPS	NUMBER OF GROUPS NEEDED TO MAKE A WAY					
	2	3	4	5	6	7
1	0	0	0	0	0	0
2	1	0	0	0	0	0
3	3	1	0	0	0	0
4	6	4	1	0	0	0
5	10	10	5	1	0	0
6	15	20	15	6	1	0
7	21	35	35	21	7	1
8	28	56	70	56	28	8
9	36	84	126	126	84	36
10	45	120	210	252	210	120
11	55	165	330	462	462	330
12	66	220	495	792	924	792
13	78	286	715	1287	1716	1716
14	91	364	1001	2002	3003	3432
15	105	455	1365	3003	5005	6435
16	120	560	1820	4368	8008	11440
17	136	680	2380	6188	12376	19448
18	153	816	3060	8568	18564	31824
19	171	969	3876	11628	27132	50388
20	190	1140	4845	15504	38760	77520

Therefore, if you want to extend the chart, you can do so easily using only addition—no other mathematical skills are required!

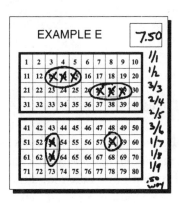

Not all way tickets are written with every group of equal size. Example E has two groups of three numbers, one group of two numbers, and a king (single number).

Even a simple ticket like this has the following possible ways:

1 / 1	2 / 4	1 / 7
1 / 2	2 / 5	1 / 8
3 / 3	3 / 6	1 / 9

You don't have to play all of the possible ways on a ticket. For instance, on this ticket, you might choose to play only the ways with 3, 4, 5, 6, and 8 numbers.

However, if you play the ways for any given number of spots, such as six, you must play *all* of the ways that total that number.

It isn't necessary to wager the same amount of money on all of the different ways played. You can write a split rate ticket, such as the example F ticket.

Most casinos allow you to play ways at a reduced rate. Typically, if the casino's straight ticket minimum bet is $1.00, you will be able to play three ways or more at 50¢ per way; ten ways or more at 25¢ per way; and fifty ways or more at 10¢ per way.

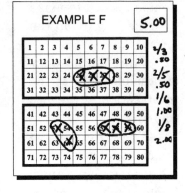

The minimum amount you can wager on a way differs from casino to casino, so be sure to check the rules in the casino's keno paybook before writing your ticket.

The Keno Book of Ways

Bill Holmes has written and published a very useful book, *The Keno Book of Ways*, which lists all of the possible way tickets that can be created when one to 16 total spots are marked. This reference work can save a lot of time for the keno player who wants to develop creative way tickets, and is invaluable for keno personnel, who encounter uncommon way tickets on a daily basis.

The Keno Book of Ways is available at Gamblers' Book Club in Las Vegas, and may be ordered by telephone.

Chapter 26

WHY PLAY WAY TICKETS?

There are two—*and only two*—valid reasons for playing way tickets ... convenience, and fractional rates.

Convenience. If you want to play more than one keno ticket at a time, *and* you want to play some common numbers on each ticket, it's more convenient for both you and the keno writer if you play a way ticket.

If this is what you want to do, fine. But ... bear this in mind. When you win $1,500 or more there can be a decided disadvantage to playing a way ticket instead of two (or more) straight tickets.

Let's assume that "Lucky" won $1,200 on a keno ticket. The same game, Lucky's wife played a slightly different ticket, and won $900.

If they had combined both tickets into one way ticket, the total amount of money won would have been the same; i.e., $2,100. However ... when a person wins a net of $1,500 or more on keno, the casino must prepare (and the player must sign) a W2-G form, which the casino submits to the Internal Revenue Service.

While I.R.S. regulations require *all* gambling winnings to be reported, preparation of the W2-G form is a nuisance for both the player and the casino. Read chapter 48, "Reporting winnings to the I.R.S.," for more details on this subject.

Fractional rates. Every casino has a minimum keno ticket price. To play three keno tickets at a casino that has a 70¢ minimum ticket will cost you $2.10.

By combining the three tickets into one way ticket you can usually play at a fractional rate, such as 35¢ per way—a total of $1.05.

Let's see how this works, using typical payoffs (which will differ somewhat from casino to casino):

If you've marked two groups of three numbers and catch a total of five spots, on a 70¢ rate way ticket played three ways (1/6, 2/3) at 35¢ per way ($1.05 total ticket cost) you'll win the following:

Catch 5 of 6 .... Win	30.00
Catch 3 of 3 .... Win	15.00
Catch 2 of 3 .... Win	.35
TOTAL WAY TICKET PAYOFF	45.35

Now, let's compare way ticket payoffs with straight ticket payoffs:

If you had played the same six numbers on a $1.05 straight ticket and caught five spots you would have won $90.00 instead of $45.35. If you were lucky enough to catch all six spots, the total payoff on the way ticket would be $580.00; on the straight ticket, $1,650.00.

Here's another example, again using typical payoffs: Play a 3-way ticket consisting of one 3-spot and one 4-spot group for 50¢ per way, at a total cost of $1.50. Let's assume that you catch six numbers—three in each group.

With the way ticket, you'll win $173.00. On a straight 7-spot ticket, played for $1.00 (50¢ less per game!), you'll win $300.00. But ... if you drop four quarters in a video keno machine and catch 6-out-of-7, you'll win $400.00!

If the only reason you want to play way tickets is the fractional rate—that is to say, you want to play for 25¢ or 50¢ per way—play video keno instead of live keno. With a few exceptions (detailed in other chapters), the house percentages on video keno are much, much lower!

When you do play a way ticket, don't fall into the trap of playing the 1- and 2-spot ways. These are seldom good bets; see chapter 11, "How many numbers to mark."

Way, combination, and king tickets can be fun, because you'll have a winning ticket much more often. But, who are you fooling? You would still have the same number of winners if you played each way as a separate straight (regular) ticket.

Sometimes Nothing Helps

I was dining at one of my favorite casino restaurants. Two men at the adjoining table were talking rather loudly, and I couldn't help eavesdropping on their conversation.

"My keno luck has really been terrible lately," one man said to his companion. "I decided to play all eighty numbers on a 190-way 8-spot ticket, and do you know what they did? They started calling *letters!*"

Chapter 27

SLOW, FAST, AND INSTANT BANKRUPTCY

One long-time keno writer not-quite-jokingly refers to three of the way tickets featured most often in keno paybooks as "slow bankruptcy," "fast bankruptcy," and "instant bankruptcy."

Slow bankruptcy is a ticket marked with three groups of two numbers. It has a total of seven ways—one 6-spot, three 4-spot, and three 2-spot ways. It costs $3.50 to play the ticket at 50¢ per way, $7.00 at $1.00 per way.

Fast bankruptcy has fifteen ways. The four groups of two numbers com-bine to make one 8-spot, four 6-spot, six 4-spot, and four 2-spot ways. When the ticket is played at 50¢ per way, it costs $7.50; played at $1.00 per way, the cost is $15.00.

Instant bankruptcy is also a ticket with fifteen ways. Its four groups of three numbers form one 12-spot, four 9-spot, six 6-spot, and four 3-spot ways. It also costs $7.50 to play at 50¢ per way; twice that at $1.00 per way.

Despite the keno writer's disparaging appellations for these

" SLOW BANKRUPTCY "

ONE 6-SPOT WAY
THREE 4-SPOT WAYS
THREE 2-SPOT WAYS

tickets (he probably doesn't like 2- and 3-spot ways any more than I do) they're favorites of many players. They provide a balance between small wins—which encourage players to keep on playing and help provide the funds to do so—and the infrequent big hits that every player dreams about.

A few casinos enhance some of the payoffs on their featured way tickets. These bonuses make the house percentage of the way ticket wager lower than when the same ways are played as separate tickets. Bonuses are usually added to the payoff for catching all of the numbers, and, in some instances, for catching no numbers.

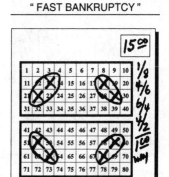

" FAST BANKRUPTCY "

ONE 8-SPOT WAY
FOUR 6-SPOT WAYS
SIX 4-SPOT WAYS
FOUR 2-SPOT WAYS

Your decision of whether or not to play any keno ticket should always be made with knowledge and acceptance of the house percentage; but, with these tickets, it's not so easy to determine just what the house percentage is.

Payoffs for featured way tickets are listed somewhat differently in the paybooks; the pays for each way are combined into one figure. To find out how much was won on any draw, count the numbers caught *in each group,* then look down the pay table for a match.

For example, a catch of "2-2-1-0" means that you've caught two numbers in two of the groups, one number in the third group, and no numbers in the fourth group.

When the payoffs of a way ticket are listed in this manner, before you can compute the house percentage you must dissect all of the "X-X-X-X" payoffs in order to determine the individual payoffs for every possible catch on each of the ways; after you have done that, you can use the individual payoffs to reconstruct the pay schedules for each way. It's a time-consuming job; another of those tasks which seem to invite mistakes.

As a starting point, assume that the payoffs for the way ticket are based on the casino's basic $1.00 or $2.00 rate—which is usually the case.

Make a photocopy of the appropriate chart (from the end of this chapter) and fill in the blanks in the payoff column with the basic rate payoffs for each possible catch. If the way ticket is priced at 50¢ per way, use 1/2 the $1.00 or 1/4 of the $2.00 payoffs listed in the casino's paybook.

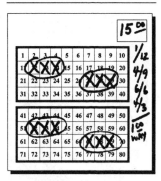

" INSTANT BANKRUPTCY "

ONE 12-SPOT WAY
FOUR 9-SPOT WAYS
SIX 6-SPOT WAYS
FOUR 3-SPOT WAYS

Next, multiply each payoff by the number in the "X" column, and total the extensions. Hopefully, all of the section totals will equal the "X-X-X-X" payoffs listed in the paybooks.

Some (or all) of the "X-X-X-X" payoff totals on your worksheet might not match what the casino lists in their paybooks.

You might have used the wrong payoff schedule, or erred in your math. Recheck your figures!

It's also a possibility that someone at the casino (or the casino's printer) might have made an error. It's very easy to make mistakes when preparing way ticket pay tables; even keno managers work on them so rarely that it's almost a new learning experience each time.

Or, perhaps the casino changed their regular rate payoffs and just forgot to change the way ticket payoffs accordingly.

And finally, the casino may have enhanced some of the payoffs.

If the casino has made any mistakes or enhanced any payoffs, you'll have to play with the numbers until you arrive at the same "X-X-X-X" payoffs as the ones listed in the paybooks.

Once you've determined the payoffs and reconstructed payoff schedules for each of the ways (including any enhancements),

HOW TO DISSECT WAY TICKET PAY TABLES

MARK 8 SPOTS

Catch	Play 1.00
8	50,000
7	1,500
6	100
5	5
House percentage 21.3850%	

MARK 6 SPOTS

Catch	Play 1.00
6	2,000
5	75
4	5
3	1
House percentage 23.7348%	

MARK 4 SPOTS

Catch	Play 1.00
4	150
3	3
2	1
House percentage 19.8112%	

MARK 2 SPOTS

Catch	Play 1.00
2	13
House percentage 21.8354%	

CATCH	PAYOFF	X	TOTAL
CATCH 2-2-1-0			
5 / 8	5	1	5
5 / 6	75	1	75
4 / 6	5	1	5
3 / 6	1	2	2
4 / 4	150	1	150
3 / 4	3	2	6
2 / 4	1	2	2
1 / 4	—	1	—
2 / 2	13	2	26
1 / 2	—	1	—
0 / 2	—	1	—
2-2-1-0 PAYOFF			271

MARK 4 GROUPS OF 2

Play $15.00 (1.00 a way)

CATCH	WIN
1-1-0-0	1.00
1-1-1-0	4.00
1-1-1-1	10.00
2-0-0-0	16.00
2-1-0-0	20.00
2-1-1-0	28.00
2-1-1-1	46.00
2-2-0-0	190.00
2-2-1-0	271.00
2-2-1-1	449.00
2-2-2-0	2,607.00
2-2-2-1	4,223.00
2-2-2-2	75,000.00

This is an enhanced payoff. Without the enhancement (i.e., using the 8-spot payoff schedule listed above), catching 2-2-2-2 would pay only $58,952.

When the bonus of $16,048 is added to the listed 8/8 payoff of $50,000 (total $66,048) the house percentage of the 8-spot way is reduced from 21.3850% to 14.4111%.

calculate the house percentages for each payoff schedule in the normal manner.

To find out the way ticket's house percentage, average the PCs of the ways.

In the next example I've used the numbers from the example illustrated on the preceding page.

When four groups of two numbers are marked, the ticket has four 2-spot ways, so multiply the PC for the 2-spot ways by 4; because there are six 4-spot ways, multiply the PC for the 4-spot ways by 6; multiply the PC for the 6-spot ways by 4, which is the number of ways to make 6-spots; and include the PC for the 8-spot way just once.

Total the products of the above calculations, then divide that sum by the total number of ways on the ticket—which, in this instance, is 15.

HOW TO DETERMINE THE HOUSE PERCENTAGE OF A WAY TICKET

SPOTS	NUMBER OF WAYS	X	HOUSE % OF WAYS	=
8	1		14.4111 ★	14.4111
6	4		23.7348	94.9392
4	6		19.8112	118.8672
2	4		21.8354	87.3416
TOTAL				315.5591
HOUSE PERCENTAGE OF WAY TICKET				21.0374
★ WITH ENHANCED PAYOFF				

WAY TICKETS
WITH THREE GROUPS OF TWO NUMBERS

CATCH	PAYOFF	X	TOTAL

CATCH 0-0-0		
0 / 6	1	
0 / 4	3	
0 / 2	3	
0-0-0 PAYOFF		

CATCH 1-0-0		
1 / 6	1	
1 / 4	2	
0 / 4	1	
1 / 2	1	
0 / 2	2	
1-0-0 PAYOFF		

CATCH 1-1-0		
2 / 6	1	
2 / 4	1	
1 / 4	2	
1 / 2	2	
0 / 2	1	
1-1-0 PAYOFF		

CATCH 1-1-1		
3 / 6	1	
2 / 4	3	
1 / 2	3	
1-1-1 PAYOFF		

CATCH	PAYOFF	X	TOTAL

CATCH 2-0-0		
2 / 6	1	
2 / 4	2	
0 / 4	1	
2 / 2	1	
0 / 2	2	
2-0-0 PAYOFF		

CATCH 2-1-0		
3 / 6	1	
3 / 4	1	
2 / 4	1	
1 / 4	1	
2 / 2	1	
1 / 2	1	
0 / 2	1	
2-1-0 PAYOFF		

CATCH 2-1-1		
4 / 6	1	
3 / 4	2	
2 / 4	1	
2 / 2	1	
1 / 2	2	
2-1-1 PAYOFF		

WAY TICKETS
WITH THREE GROUPS OF TWO NUMBERS (continued)

CATCH	PAYOFF	X	TOTAL

CATCH 2-2-0			
4 / 6		1	
4 / 4		1	
2 / 4		2	
2 / 2		2	
0 / 2		1	
2-2-0 PAYOFF			

CATCH 2-2-1			
5 / 6		1	
4 / 4		1	
3 / 4		2	
2 / 2		2	
1 / 2		1	
2-2-1 PAYOFF			

CATCH 2-2-2			
6 / 6		1	
4 / 4		3	
2 / 2		3	
2-2-2 PAYOFF			

WAY TICKETS
WITH FOUR GROUPS OF TWO NUMBERS

CATCH	PAYOFF	X	TOTAL

CATCH 0-0-0-0		
0 / 8	1	
0 / 6	4	
0 / 4	6	
0 / 2	4	
0-0-0-0 PAYOFF		

CATCH 1-0-0-0		
1 / 8	1	
1 / 6	3	
0 / 6	1	
1 / 4	3	
0 / 4	3	
1 / 2	1	
0 / 2	3	
1-0-0-0 PAYOFF		

CATCH 1-1-0-0		
2 / 8	1	
2 / 6	2	
1 / 6	2	
2 / 4	1	
1 / 4	4	
0 / 4	1	
1 / 2	2	
0 / 2	2	
1-1-0-0 PAYOFF		

CATCH 1-1-1-0		
3 / 8	1	
3 / 6	1	
2 / 6	3	
2 / 4	3	
1 / 4	3	
1 / 2	3	
0 / 2	1	
1-1-1-0 PAYOFF		

CATCH 1-1-1-1		
4 / 8	1	
3 / 6	4	
2 / 4	6	
1 / 2	4	
1-1-1-1 PAYOFF		

CATCH 2-0-0-0		
2 / 8	1	
2 / 6	3	
0 / 6	1	
2 / 4	3	
0 / 4	3	
2 / 2	1	
0 / 2	3	
2-0-0-0 PAYOFF		

WAY TICKETS
WITH FOUR GROUPS OF TWO NUMBERS (continued)

CATCH	PAYOFF	X	TOTAL

CATCH 2-1-0-0			
3 / 8		1	
3 / 6		2	
2 / 6		1	
1 / 6		1	
3 / 4		1	
2 / 4		2	
1 / 4		2	
0 / 4		1	
2 / 2		1	
1 / 2		1	
0 / 2		2	
2-1-0-0 PAYOFF			

CATCH 2-1-1-0			
4 / 8		1	
4 / 6		1	
3 / 6		2	
2 / 6		1	
3 / 4		2	
2 / 4		2	
1 / 4		2	
2 / 2		1	
1 / 2		2	
0 / 2		1	
2-1-1-0 PAYOFF			

CATCH	PAYOFF	X	TOTAL

CATCH 2-1-1-1			
5 / 8		1	
4 / 6		3	
3 / 6		1	
3 / 4		3	
2 / 4		3	
2 / 2		1	
1 / 2		3	
2-1-1-1 PAYOFF			

CATCH 2-2-0-0			
4 / 8		1	
4 / 6		2	
2 / 6		2	
4 / 4		1	
2 / 4		4	
0 / 4		1	
2 / 2		2	
0 / 2		2	
2-2-0-0 PAYOFF			

– 134 –

WAY TICKETS
WITH FOUR GROUPS OF TWO NUMBERS (continued)

CATCH	PAYOFF	X	TOTAL
CATCH 2-2-1-0			
5 / 8		1	
5 / 6		1	
4 / 6		1	
3 / 6		2	
4 / 4		1	
3 / 4		2	
2 / 4		2	
1 / 4		1	
2 / 2		2	
1 / 2		1	
0 / 2		1	
2-2-1-0 PAYOFF			

CATCH	PAYOFF	X	TOTAL
CATCH 2-2-1-1			
6 / 8		1	
5 / 6		2	
4 / 6		2	
4 / 4		1	
3 / 4		4	
2 / 4		1	
2 / 2		2	
1 / 2		2	
2-2-1-1 PAYOFF			

CATCH	PAYOFF	X	TOTAL
CATCH 2-2-2-0			
6 / 8		1	
6 / 6		1	
4 / 6		3	
4 / 4		3	
2 / 4		3	
2 / 2		3	
0 / 2		1	
2-2-2-0 PAYOFF			

CATCH	PAYOFF	X	TOTAL
CATCH 2-2-2-1			
7 / 8		1	
6 / 6		1	
5 / 6		3	
4 / 4		3	
3 / 4		3	
2 / 2		3	
1 / 2		1	
2-2-2-1 PAYOFF			

CATCH	PAYOFF	X	TOTAL
CATCH 2-2-2-2			
8 / 8		1	
6 / 6		4	
4 / 4		6	
2 / 2		4	
2-2-2-2 PAYOFF			

WAY TICKETS
WITH FOUR GROUPS OF THREE NUMBERS

CATCH	PAYOFF	X	TOTAL
CATCH 0-0-0-0			
0 / 12		1	
0 / 9		4	
0 / 6		6	
0 / 3		4	
0-0-0-0 PAYOFF			

CATCH	PAYOFF	X	TOTAL
CATCH 1-1-1-0			
3 / 12		1	
3 / 9		1	
2 / 9		3	
2 / 6		3	
1 / 6		3	
1 / 3		3	
0 / 3		1	
1-1-1-0 PAYOFF			

CATCH	PAYOFF	X	TOTAL
CATCH 1-0-0-0			
1 / 12		1	
1 / 9		3	
0 / 9		1	
1 / 6		3	
0 / 6		3	
1 / 3		1	
0 / 3		3	
1-0-0-0 PAYOFF			

CATCH	PAYOFF	X	TOTAL
CATCH 1-1-1-1			
4 / 12		1	
3 / 9		4	
2 / 6		6	
1 / 3		4	
1-1-1-1 PAYOFF			

CATCH	PAYOFF	X	TOTAL
CATCH 1-1-0-0			
2 / 12		1	
2 / 9		2	
1 / 9		2	
2 / 6		1	
1 / 6		4	
0 / 6		1	
1 / 3		2	
0 / 3		2	
1-1-0-0 PAYOFF			

CATCH	PAYOFF	X	TOTAL
CATCH 2-0-0-0			
2 / 12		1	
2 / 9		3	
0 / 9		1	
2 / 6		3	
0 / 6		3	
2 / 3		1	
0 / 3		3	
2-0-0-0 PAYOFF			

WAY TICKETS
WITH FOUR GROUPS OF THREE NUMBERS (continued)

CATCH	PAYOFF	X	TOTAL
CATCH 2-1-0-0			
3 / 12		1	
3 / 9		2	
2 / 9		1	
1 / 9		1	
3 / 6		1	
2 / 6		2	
1 / 6		2	
0 / 6		1	
2 / 3		1	
1 / 3		1	
0 / 3		2	
2-1-0-0 PAYOFF			

CATCH	PAYOFF	X	TOTAL
CATCH 2-1-1-1			
5 / 12		1	
4 / 9		3	
3 / 9		1	
3 / 6		3	
2 / 6		3	
2 / 3		1	
1 / 3		3	
2-1-1-1 PAYOFF			

CATCH	PAYOFF	X	TOTAL
CATCH 2-1-1-0			
4 / 12		1	
4 / 9		1	
3 / 9		2	
2 / 9		1	
3 / 6		2	
2 / 6		2	
1 / 6		2	
2 / 3		1	
1 / 3		2	
0 / 3		1	
2-1-1-0 PAYOFF			

CATCH	PAYOFF	X	TOTAL
CATCH 2-2-0-0			
4 / 12		1	
4 / 9		2	
2 / 9		2	
4 / 6		1	
2 / 6		4	
0 / 6		1	
2 / 3		2	
0 / 3		2	
2-2-0-0 PAYOFF			

WAY TICKETS
WITH FOUR GROUPS OF THREE NUMBERS (continued)

CATCH	PAYOFF	X	TOTAL
CATCH 2-2-1-0			
5 / 12		1	
5 / 9		1	
4 / 9		1	
3 / 9		2	
4 / 6		1	
3 / 6		2	
2 / 6		2	
1 / 6		1	
2 / 3		2	
1 / 3		1	
0 / 3		1	
2-2-1-0 PAYOFF			

CATCH	PAYOFF	X	TOTAL
CATCH 2-2-1-1			
6 / 12		1	
5 / 9		2	
4 / 9		2	
4 / 6		1	
3 / 6		4	
2 / 6		1	
2 / 3		2	
1 / 3		2	
2-2-1-1 PAYOFF			

CATCH	PAYOFF	X	TOTAL
CATCH 2-2-2-0			
6 / 12		1	
6 / 9		1	
4 / 9		3	
4 / 6		3	
2 / 6		3	
2 / 3		3	
0 / 3		1	
2-2-2-0 PAYOFF			

CATCH	PAYOFF	X	TOTAL
CATCH 2-2-2-1			
7 / 12		1	
6 / 9		1	
5 / 9		3	
4 / 6		3	
3 / 6		3	
2 / 3		3	
1 / 3		1	
2-2-2-1 PAYOFF			

CATCH	PAYOFF	X	TOTAL
CATCH 2-2-2-2			
8 / 12		1	
6 / 9		4	
4 / 6		6	
2 / 3		4	
2-2-2-2 PAYOFF			

WAY TICKETS
WITH FOUR GROUPS OF THREE NUMBERS (continued)

CATCH	PAYOFF	X	TOTAL

CATCH 3-0-0-0			
3 / 12		1	
3 / 9		3	
0 / 9		1	
3 / 6		3	
0 / 6		3	
3 / 3		1	
0 / 3		3	
3-0-0-0 PAYOFF			

CATCH 3-1-0-0			
4 / 12		1	
4 / 9		2	
3 / 9		1	
1 / 9		1	
4 / 6		1	
3 / 6		2	
1 / 6		2	
0 / 6		1	
3 / 3		1	
1 / 3		1	
0 / 3		2	
3-1-0-0 PAYOFF			

CATCH	PAYOFF	X	TOTAL

CATCH 3-1-1-0			
5 / 12		1	
5 / 9		1	
4 / 9		2	
2 / 9		1	
4 / 6		2	
3 / 6		1	
2 / 6		1	
1 / 6		2	
3 / 3		1	
1 / 3		2	
0 / 3		1	
3-1-1-0 PAYOFF			

CATCH 3-1-1-1			
6 / 12		1	
5 / 9		3	
3 / 9		1	
4 / 6		3	
2 / 6		3	
3 / 3		1	
1 / 3		3	
3-1-1-1 PAYOFF			

WAY TICKETS
WITH FOUR GROUPS OF THREE NUMBERS (continued)

CATCH	PAYOFF	X	TOTAL

CATCH 3-2-0-0			
5 / 12		1	
5 / 9		2	
3 / 9		1	
2 / 9		1	
5 / 6		1	
3 / 6		2	
2 / 6		2	
0 / 6		1	
3 / 3		1	
2 / 3		1	
0 / 3		2	
3-2-0-0 PAYOFF			

CATCH	PAYOFF	X	TOTAL

CATCH 3-2-1-1			
7 / 12		1	
6 / 9		2	
5 / 9		1	
4 / 9		1	
5 / 6		1	
4 / 6		2	
3 / 6		2	
2 / 6		1	
3 / 3		1	
2 / 3		1	
1 / 3		2	
3-2-1-1 PAYOFF			

CATCH 3-2-1-0			
6 / 12		1	
6 / 9		1	
5 / 9		1	
4 / 9		1	
3 / 9		1	
5 / 6		1	
4 / 6		1	
3 / 6		2	
2 / 6		1	
1 / 6		1	
3 / 3		1	
2 / 3		1	
1 / 3		1	
0 / 3		1	
3-2-1-0 PAYOFF			

CATCH 3-2-2-0			
7 / 12		1	
7 / 9		1	
5 / 9		2	
4 / 9		1	
5 / 6		2	
4 / 6		1	
3 / 6		1	
2 / 6		2	
3 / 3		1	
2 / 3		2	
0 / 3		1	
3-2-2-0 PAYOFF			

WAY TICKETS
WITH FOUR GROUPS OF THREE NUMBERS (continued)

CATCH	PAYOFF	X	TOTAL

CATCH 3-2-2-1			
8 / 12		1	
7 / 9		1	
6 / 9		2	
5 / 9		1	
5 / 6		2	
4 / 6		2	
3 / 6		2	
3 / 3		1	
2 / 3		2	
1 / 3		1	
3-2-2-1 PAYOFF			

CATCH 3-2-2-2			
9 / 12		1	
7 / 9		3	
6 / 9		1	
5 / 6		3	
4 / 6		3	
3 / 3		1	
2 / 3		3	
3-2-2-2 PAYOFF			

CATCH	PAYOFF	X	TOTAL

CATCH 3-3-0-0			
6 / 12		1	
6 / 9		2	
3 / 9		2	
6 / 6		1	
3 / 6		4	
0 / 6		1	
3 / 3		2	
0 / 3		2	
3-3-0-0 PAYOFF			

CATCH 3-3-1-0			
7 / 12		1	
7 / 9		1	
6 / 9		1	
4 / 9		2	
6 / 6		1	
4 / 6		2	
3 / 6		2	
1 / 6		1	
3 / 3		2	
1 / 3		1	
0 / 3		1	
3-3-1-0 PAYOFF			

WAY TICKETS
WITH FOUR GROUPS OF THREE NUMBERS (continued)

CATCH	PAYOFF	X	TOTAL
CATCH 3-3-1-1			
8 / 12		1	
7 / 9		2	
5 / 9		2	
6 / 6		1	
4 / 6		4	
2 / 6		1	
3 / 3		2	
1 / 3		2	
3-3-1-1 PAYOFF			

CATCH	PAYOFF	X	TOTAL
CATCH 3-3-2-0			
8 / 12		1	
8 / 9		1	
6 / 9		1	
5 / 9		2	
6 / 6		1	
5 / 6		2	
3 / 6		2	
2 / 6		1	
3 / 3		2	
2 / 3		1	
0 / 3		1	
3-3-2-0 PAYOFF			

CATCH	PAYOFF	X	TOTAL
CATCH 3-3-2-1			
9 / 12		1	
8 / 9		1	
7 / 9		1	
6 / 9		2	
6 / 6		1	
5 / 6		2	
4 / 6		2	
3 / 6		1	
3 / 3		2	
2 / 3		1	
1 / 3		1	
3-3-2-1 PAYOFF			

CATCH	PAYOFF	X	TOTAL
CATCH 3-3-2-2			
10 / 12		1	
8 / 9		2	
7 / 9		2	
6 / 6		1	
5 / 6		4	
4 / 6		1	
3 / 3		2	
2 / 3		2	
3-3-2-2 PAYOFF			

WAY TICKETS
WITH FOUR GROUPS OF THREE NUMBERS (continued)

CATCH	PAYOFF	X	TOTAL

CATCH 3-3-3-0			
9 / 12		1	
9 / 9		1	
6 / 9		3	
6 / 6		3	
3 / 6		3	
3 / 3		3	
0 / 3		1	
3-3-3-0 PAYOFF			

CATCH	PAYOFF	X	TOTAL

CATCH 3-3-3-2			
11 / 12		1	
9 / 9		1	
8 / 9		3	
6 / 6		3	
5 / 6		3	
3 / 3		3	
2 / 3		1	
3-3-3-2 PAYOFF			

CATCH 3-3-3-1			
10 / 12		1	
9 / 9		1	
7 / 9		3	
6 / 6		3	
4 / 6		3	
3 / 3		3	
1 / 3		1	
3-3-3-1 PAYOFF			

CATCH 3-3-3-3			
12 / 12		1	
9 / 9		4	
6 / 6		6	
3 / 3		4	
3-3-3-3 PAYOFF			

Chapter 28

MULTI-GAME KENO TICKETS

Are you tired of waiting in line before every keno game? While seated in the restaurant, do you worry about whether the keno runner will come to your table in time for your ticket to be entered in the next race?

These problems have been solved at casinos that have multi-game keno. With multi-game (also called multi-race) keno you can play one ticket for two to as many as a thousand games!

There are a few special rules for multi-game keno. Tickets must be for consecutive games, and you must play the same numbers and wager the same amount of money each game.

In Nevada, if you play twenty games or less, *by law* you must remain in a gaming area (casino, bars, restaurants) until all of the games on your ticket have been played.

In most instances, you must wait until after all of the games have been called before you can collect on winning tickets. However, most keno computer systems have "early out" or "quit race" capabilities; for acceptable reasons, a casino may agree to terminate multi-race tickets after any game.

And, most casinos require you to collect your winnings on 2–20 game multi-race tickets before the start of the draw that follows the last game on your ticket.

If you play 21 games or more, you don't have to stay on the premises. You can go home, or even travel around the world. Just telephone the keno desk to find out how much you've won; some casinos provide a toll-free 800 number, if you want to check on your ticket from out of state. And, you have up to a year after the last game is played to go back to the casino to collect your winnings. A few casinos allow you to redeem tickets for 21 games or more by mail.

There are a couple of reasons why some casinos limit multi-game tickets to twenty games.

First, the 21–1,000 game version of multi-game keno requires a greatly expanded (and costly) computer system, in order to track the tickets for 1,000 games, and to maintain the data in the computer for a full year.

Second, when multi-game keno exceeds twenty games, the Internal Revenue Service becomes involved. On multi-game tickets for 21 games or more the I.R.S. requires the casino to pay a Federal Wagering Tax of 1/4 percent on the amounts wagered. Further, casinos must be very careful to follow regulations precisely; if they don't, the I.R.S. might classify their keno game as a lottery ... and lotteries are illegal in Nevada!

You're probably familiar with the TV commercial for potato chips that proclaims, "No one can eat just one." The same philosophy applies to playing keno. Few if any keno players play just one game before moving on to something else. So, why not take advantage of multi-game keno, since it's a "given" that you're going to be playing more than one game?

More and more, keno players are playing multi-game keno for the convenience. At some casinos, there's another—even more important—reason to play multi-game keno. You can win more and lose less.

It takes the same amount of time for a casino to write a ticket for 500 or 1,000 games as it does to write a ticket for one game, and labor is a major expense of any keno department.

Smart casino management recognizes this fact and passes

some of their savings on to the players in the form of bonuses or special payoffs on multi-game tickets.

Depending upon the casino and the number of games played on a multi-game ticket, the bonuses increase the single-game payoffs by as much as 25%!

These bonuses cause the house percentages to drop, and to drop dramatically! In some instances, the PCs of multi-game tickets compute to just a few percent, making keno—for the very first time—competitive with the slots and table games.

The following example shows how playing a multi-game ticket with a low house percentage could make you a lot of money.

A Las Vegas casino has a 5-spot 80¢ rate with a house percentage of 18.0448%. But, when you play the same 5-spot 80¢ rate on a 501-game multi-game ticket, the casino increases all of the payoffs 15%, resulting in a 5.7515% PC.

The *average* loss for every 501 games (an investment of $400.80) is $23.05. Of course, you might do much better than that, or you might do much worse; as statistics go, 501 games is a very, very small sampling.

Here's a scenario of what you might expect if you were to play an extremely large number of 501-game multi-game tickets:

On approximately two out of three 501-game sessions you'll fail to catch all five of your numbers. Payoffs from catching three and four spots will total about $80, giving you a net loss on the ticket of $320.

But ... about a third of the time you'll catch all five numbers, for a payoff (including the 15% bonus) of $920. Add to that your expected payoffs from catching three and four spots, and the ticket will return about $1,000—for a profit of $600!

The odds of catching all five numbers are 1 in 1,551, but there's no rule that says you won't, on occasion, catch five spots several times in a 501-game series. If you're lucky, your $400.80 ticket might have payoffs totaling $2,000, or even more!

A $400.80 keno ticket isn't for everyone. But, for dedicated keno players, this perfect combination of an extremely low house percentage, a good top payoff, and a reasonable chance of catching the top payoff, may be your golden opportunity to win more and lose less at keno!

You don't always need a large bankroll in order to enjoy the advantages of multi-game keno; it's often possible to play multi-game tickets at a fractional rate. One casino lets you play multi-game tickets for 25¢ per game, when you play 50–199 games, and as low as 10¢ per game, when you play 200 games or more.

Another casino doesn't increase the payoffs or have bonuses on their multi-game tickets, but they achieve a similar result by selling twelve games for the price of ten; several of their "12 for 10" tickets compute to a PC of 5% or less, and your total investment can be as low as $10 for the twelve games.

When a casino offers special incentives for playing multi-game keno, it's often a good bargain ... and may well be the best bet in the entire casino, for on no other game can you win as much for so little!

But remember ... whether you play keno one game at a time or on a multi-game ticket, *always* learn the house percentage before placing your bet!

HOW PAYOFF BONUSES LOWER HOUSE PERCENTAGES					
SINGLE GAME	5% BONUS	10% BONUS	15% BONUS	20% BONUS	25% BONUS
30.000%	26.500%	23.000%	19.500%	16.000%	12.500%
27.500%	23.875%	20.250%	16.625%	13.000%	9.375%
25.000%	21.250%	17.500%	13.750%	10.000%	6.250%
24.000%	20.200%	16.400%	12.600%	8.800%	5.000%
23.000%	19.150%	15.300%	11.450%	7.600%	3.750%
22.000%	18.100%	14.200%	10.300%	6.400%	2.500%
21.000%	17.050%	13.100%	9.150%	5.200%	1.250%
20.000%	16.000%	12.000%	8.000%	4.000%	0.000%
19.000%	14.950%	10.900%	6.850%	2.800%	———
18.000%	13.900%	9.800%	5.700%	1.600%	———
17.000%	12.850%	8.700%	4.550%	.400%	———

When You Win Big on Multi-Game Keno ...

When you play multi-game keno you can't collect your winnings from any of the games until the last game on your ticket has been called (unless the casino agrees to terminate your ticket early).

If you've won a few hundred dollars, just smile and be patient. You're not in a hurry to leave, or else you wouldn't be playing multi-game keno.

But, let's say that you've won $40,000 or $50,000. A casino executive will have to verify that your winning ticket is legitimate and that no mistakes were made in calling the numbers. You'll also have to show your identification, and the casino will have to prepare a W2-G form for the I.R.S.

Don't wait until all of the games on your multi-game ticket have been called. Tell a keno writer—or, better yet, tell the keno manager—as soon as you realize that you're a big winner. (The keno department's computer system will alert the keno personnel that *someone* hit big, but they won't know who the lucky player is until you step up to the keno counter and identify yourself.)

It will save everyone a lot of time if the balls can be checked while they're still in the rabbit ears. Once they drop back into the blower or cage, in preparation for the next draw, it's too late. You may have to wait until a video tape of the game is reviewed—or, at some casinos, until film is developed—before you get paid. Now you know why there's a little camera pointed at the keno blower or wire cage!

And, while the rest of your multi-race games are being played (you might even get more winners!), the casino personnel can be checking your identification, preparing the I.R.S. forms, and—if you're smart—writing a casino check for you to take instead of cash.

Chapter 29

HIGH-ROLLER KENO

Some people think of keno as a game for people who live on a fixed income, gamblers for whom a $1.00 bet every five minutes or so borders on extravagance. Yes, keno is for retirees and others who love the casino action but don't have a lot of money to wager.

But, keno's a whole lot more. Keno's also for high-rollers, though many of them haven't discovered it yet.

Blackjack players think nothing of betting $10 or more a hand; $25 craps wagers are common; and a $100 bet on a football game never raises any eyebrows. Why, then, the reluctance to play keno for larger amounts?

The most you can win for a $100 blackjack bet is $250; roulette pays back—tops—36 times the amount of your wager. With keno, it's possible to win as much as a million dollars for a $25 bet ... and even if you don't catch all of your numbers, you can still take home enough to live in style for quite a while.

You can always play regular rate keno at a multiple of the regular ticket price—for instance, the $1.00 rate can be played for $50—but there is often a disadvantage in doing so. The casino's aggregate limit may put a cap on your potential top payoff, so any money wagered beyond a certain amount (which differs from ticket to ticket) is wasted. The rule here is never to play a multiple of the basic bet if it makes any payoff higher than the casino's aggregate limit. It's much better to choose from among the keno high-roller tickets now being offered by a handful of casinos; you're assured that all payoffs fall within the casino's aggregate limit.

What's even more important, the house percentages of high-roller tickets are often (but not always) much lower than the PCs on the casino's regular rate keno, and in some instances they're even comparable with the PCs on slots or table games. My usual recommendation applies: Never play any keno ticket if you don't know its house percentage.

There's a reason why high-roller tickets can have low house percentages but the lower priced keno tickets cannot. It costs the casino the same amount (for labor, materials, and overhead) to write a $1.00 ticket as it does to write a $100 ticket—about 25¢, at most casinos.

With a 30% house advantage, the casino has an average profit of 5¢ for every $1.00 keno ticket sold (30¢ less the 25¢ cost of writing the ticket). On a $25 ticket with an 8% house percentage, the casino has an average profit of $1.75 ($2.00 house edge less the 25¢ cost of writing the ticket). And, on a $100 ticket with a 3.5% house percentage, the casino has an average profit of $3.25 ($3.50 less 25¢).

Smart casino management encourages bigger keno bets by lowering the house percentages of their high-roller tickets. The casino makes more money per ticket sold, and the players get higher potential payoffs. It's a win-win situation all around.

You can sit in a keno lounge all day and evening, playing (at some casinos) for as little as 35¢ per game. Your bankroll can last a long time, and you'll probably become old friends with the keno writers and other players. With a little luck you'll take home more than enough money to finance another keno playing session.

Or, you can place your entire keno bankroll on a few choice high-roller tickets and be out of the casino within the hour—either tremendously wealthy, or with the time to enjoy some of the famous Las Vegas shows, play a few rounds of golf, take a scenic tour of Hoover Dam and the Grand Canyon, or go skiing at Mt. Charleston.

One More!

Wherever you go, you'll hear keno players exclaiming, "One more!" Perhaps that's what the game should have been called. Catching *one more* number will often change a losing ticket into a winner ... or a winning ticket into a *big* winner!

One more quarter bet on video keno can double your winnings. *One more* dollar wagered on some progressive keno games will increase a $25,000 win to as much as $250,000!

And, when you leave a casino, never look back at the keno flashboard as you walk to the door. You're liable to discover that if you'd played just *one more* game, you might have won enough money to retire!

Chapter 30

KENO "SPECIALS"

Once someone at the Dunes had a great idea for an advertising campaign. Soon, taxi signs and billboards all over Las Vegas boasted that the Dunes had "loosened the screws" on their slot machines, implying that they'd increased their slot payoffs.

Despite popular belief to the contrary, slot machines don't have any screws to be tightened or loosened; at least, not any that affect payoffs. If someone loosened screws on a slot machine, the most likely result would be that the machine would fall apart.

The Nevada Gaming Control Board takes appropriate action when they become aware of fraudulent advertising by casinos, and they brought the Dunes' promotion to a screeching halt.

I can't understand why the Board hasn't clamped down on the use—perhaps misuse is a better term—of the word *"special,"* as applied to alternate keno tickets.

If any department store, supermarket, or other retail establishment advertised the same merchandise at the same "special" price month after month, governmental agencies and consumer advocacy groups would quickly take action to halt the unsavory, deceptive practice. The rule is, whenever a "special" is kept too long, the deal is no longer special, it becomes the regular price of the product.

And, if a store posted signs stating "five pounds of detergent —special price $4.99, regularly $3.50" and "lemons, reg. 25¢ each, special—3 for $1.00," and, perhaps, "regularly $17.95, special price this week only, $24.95," the store would be laughed out of existence.

Yet, many casinos get away with calling some of their keno tickets "specials" year after year—even though the tickets may be anything *except* special. A majority of keno "specials" have higher house percentages than the same casino's regular tickets ... which means that on those tickets the casinos will win more, and the players less!

My dictionary defines the word "special" as "distinguished by some unusual quality ... being in some way superior."

It's true that the word "special" has other definitions, such as "readily distinguishable from others of the same category" and "designed for a particular purpose or occasion," but, to most people, the word "special" has just one meaning: *something better.*

Every day, thousands of trusting individuals play "special" keno tickets, in the mistaken belief that a casino wouldn't be allowed to advertise a ticket as "special" unless it really was a better deal. Are they ever wrong!

A few casinos do use the word "special" honestly, reserving it for tickets that, according to the law of probabilities, will ultimately pay more money to the players and hold less for the house.

Through experience I've learned that, at some casinos, the word "special" is a red flag that the tickets are rip-offs. Their so-called "special" keno tickets have higher house percentages— often, *much* higher—than the casino's regular rate keno.

At most casinos, however, the word "special" is used indiscriminately to promote any and every keno rate that's different from the casino's standard rate tickets. At such casinos the word "special" has no discernible meaning; the payoffs could be better or could be worse than their regular tickets.

The bottom line is this: If a casino calls a ticket "special," watch out! It may be "special" for the casino, and not for the players! Always remember, know the house percentages of the tickets you plan to play ... before you put your money on the line!

Why Go To A Psychiatrist?

My wife is firmly convinced that relaxing in front of a video keno machine is more therapeutic and less costly than psychoanalysis.

Now, if I can just find a way to get the expense covered by our medical insurance ...

Chapter 31

FREE PLAY

The keno paybooks of some casinos list "free play" for certain payoffs. *Free play* means that if you catch the required number of spots, you can play the same ticket again without paying for the second game. You haven't really won anything, but you haven't lost, either. It's a *push*, just as if you never played the first game.

In actual practice, most casinos that offer "free play" payoffs allow you to change your numbers on the second game, if you want to do so, and will even give you the amount of your original bet back if you're through playing for the day. If either of these options is your choice, don't hesitate to let a keno writer know.

When computing the house percentage of a keno ticket that has a "free play" payoff, treat that payoff as if it was a cash payoff equal to the original bet.

Chapter 32

STATE-OPERATED KENO

Some states have a stripped-down version of keno as an adjunct to their lottery games. In California, for instance, keno can be played in selected restaurants, bars, hotels, shopping malls, and at most regular lottery ticket retailers.

Every five minutes, from six in the morning until eleven at night, twenty numbers are drawn from a pool of eighty at lottery headquarters. The results of the draws are displayed on special lottery TV monitors at the locations where keno tickets are sold.

Here's a point-by-point comparison of California keno, to keno as it's played in Nevada:

Number of spots. From one to ten numbers can be marked in California keno. Most Nevada casinos let players mark from 1–15 spots, and many offer 16- through 19-spot, 20-spot, 32-number, and 40-number tickets.

Keno variations. California keno is keno at its simplest, a game that's called *straight* or *regular* keno. Straight keno is also the standard game in Nevada; but, in addition, most casinos offer one or more variations of keno, such as catch-all, catch-zero, high-end, pay-any-catch, top-and-bottom, hi-low, and progressive.

Way tickets. Most experienced keno players like to play way, combination, or king tickets, at least occasionally. California keno does not permit these methods of playing.

Ticket prices. California keno may be played at a minimum of $1.00 and a maximum of $20.00 per game. In Nevada casinos, the range is much greater.

Way tickets can be played at some casinos for as little as 5¢ per way. A number of casinos have multi-game tickets priced as low as 10¢ per game.

At the other end of the spectrum, some casinos have high-roller tickets with prices of as much as $100. And, any keno ticket can be played for any multiple of the basic price; the only practical limit to the amount of the bets is the amount that can be won, which is determined by each casino's maximum aggregate limit policy.

Multi-game keno. California keno may be played from one to a hundred games on a single ticket. However, the maximum wager is $100, so the full one hundred games can be played at the $1.00 per game rate only.

At most Nevada casinos you can now play from one to a thousand consecutive games on one keno ticket, and there is no limit to the total amount that may be wagered on the ticket.

Maximum payoffs/aggregate limit. Only one California keno ticket has an enticing top prize—the 10-spot $1.00, which pays $250,000 for matching ten numbers.

If the 10-spot ticket is played for the allowable maximum of $20.00, the potential top prize is $5 million. However, no more than ten million dollars will be paid for the 10-spot / 10-match prize in any one draw. Should the total wins exceed the $10 million limit, shares of the limit will be prorated among all of the winners based on the amount wagered. Another drawback ... the 10-spot California ticket has an extremely high 49.5758% house edge.

Nevada casinos differ in the maximum amount they will pay in any single game. As of this writing, two casinos in Las Vegas—Gold Coast and Barbary Coast—have top prizes of $1 million. Most other casinos have maximum aggregate limits of $100,000 or $250,000, although at some casinos the maximum is $50,000 or even $25,000 per game.

Payment procedures. Nevada casinos pay all keno prizes in full immediately after the last game on a ticket has been drawn. On multi-game tickets for 21 games or more players do not need to remain in the casino while the games are being played, and they can collect their winnings any time within a year, if they so choose.

California keno wins of $599 or less are paid immediately in cash. For all prizes of $600 or more per play the winner must mail a claim form, claim receipt, and original validated ticket to the lottery headquarters. Players are required to retain a photocopy of both the front and back of winning tickets. All prizes must be claimed within 180 days of the winning draw date.

In California, large keno wins are not paid immediately in full. Rather, they're paid in twenty equal annual payments ... after deduction of 28% for income taxes.

Reporting to the I.R.S. The California Lottery notifies the Internal Revenue Service of cumulative total prize winnings of $600 or more. In Nevada, casinos do not report keno winnings to the I.R.S. unless the player has a net win (after deducting cost of the ticket) of $1,500 or more.

Draw results. Nevada keno players are required to remain in a gaming area while playing individual games or multi-game tickets of twenty games or less.

Thus, they can find out what they have won by checking any keno flashboard or by inquiring at the keno desk. For results of 21–1,000 game multi-game tickets, they can phone the keno department at any time, using either a local phone number or a toll-free 800-prefix number.

California keno players may watch the Lottery Information System TV monitor at the store where they purchased their keno tickets while the games are being drawn. If they want to learn the result of any game or games at a later time, they may call a 900-prefix phone number. A charge of 50¢ *per minute* will be added to their phone bill automatically.

Comps. In California, you're on your own. You have to pay for your Slurpee or convenience-store sandwich.

Nevada casinos are very generous. Cocktail waitresses patrol keno lounges frequently, offering complimentary beverages of the player's choice. Premium keno players—as determined by the keno computer's player tracking system or observation of play by casino personnel—are offered free meals, rooms, shows, etc. The sky's the limit!

Payoffs / house percentages. If you were to decide whether to play keno in California or Nevada solely upon the above factors, Nevada would win hands down. But ... there's one more variable that tilts the scale even more in Nevada's favor ... the prizes.

For example, the usual 1-spot $1.00 ticket in Nevada pays $3.00 at most casinos, for a 25% house advantage. In California keno, the same ticket pays only $2.00, and has a whopping 50% house edge!

The other California keno tickets have PCs ranging from 44.4985% to 54.9975%. By comparison, the median house percentage of all Nevada keno tickets is about 27%, with very few tickets exceeding 33%. A few Nevada keno tickets have house percentages around 3%.

The Oregon Lottery's version of keno is similar to that of the California Lottery, with minor differences—e.g., the maximum prize per game on any one Oregon keno ticket is $100,000, and the house percentages aren't quite as high in Oregon (37.5609% to 50.0%) as they are in California.

To win more and lose less at keno, play tickets with low house percentages (which are a combination of the ticket price, the odds, and the payoffs). The lower the PCs, the longer your money will last. You'll be able to play more games for the same bankroll, so you'll increase your chances of catching a big prize.

CALIFORNIA LOTTERY KENO PAYOFFS $1.00 BET	
NUMBER OF SPOTS MATCHED	PAYOFF
10-SPOT TICKET	
10	$250,000
9	3,000
8	250
7	50
6	5
5	2
0	4
HOUSE PERCENTAGE	49.5758%
9-SPOT TICKET	
9	$25,000
8	2,500
7	100
6	10
5	4
4	1
HOUSE PERCENTAGE	53.9537%
8-SPOT TICKET	
8	$10,000
7	400
6	40
5	10
4	1
HOUSE PERCENTAGE	53.3163%
7-SPOT TICKET	
7	$2,500
6	100
5	10
4	2
3	1
HOUSE PERCENTAGE	50.0026%

TYPICAL LAS VEGAS KENO PAYOFFS $1.00 BET	
NUMBER OF SPOTS MATCHED	PAYOFF
10-SPOT TICKET	
10	$100,000
9	12,500
8	1,000
7	125
6	25
5	1
0	0
HOUSE PERCENTAGE	23.7046%
9-SPOT TICKET	
9	$50,000
8	5,000
7	250
6	25
5	5
4	1
HOUSE PERCENTAGE	23.2803%
8-SPOT TICKET	
8	$50,000
7	1,500
6	100
5	5
4	0
HOUSE PERCENTAGE	21.3850%
7-SPOT TICKET	
7	$7,500
6	500
5	20
4	1
3	0
HOUSE PERCENTAGE	22.5981%

CALIFORNIA LOTTERY KENO PAYOFFS $1.00 BET	
NUMBER OF SPOTS MATCHED	PAYOFF
6-SPOT TICKET	
6	$1,000
5	25
4	4
3	1
HOUSE PERCENTAGE	54.9653%
5-SPOT TICKET	
5	$250
4	10
3	2
HOUSE PERCENTAGE	54.9975%
4-SPOT TICKET	
4	$50
3	4
2	1
HOUSE PERCENTAGE	46.1203%
3-SPOT TICKET	
3	$20
2	2
HOUSE PERCENTAGE	44.4985%
2-SPOT TICKET	
2	$8
HOUSE PERCENTAGE	51.8987%
1-SPOT TICKET	
1	$2
HOUSE PERCENTAGE	50.0000%

TYPICAL LAS VEGAS KENO PAYOFFS $1.00 BET	
NUMBER OF SPOTS MATCHED	PAYOFF
6-SPOT TICKET	
6	$2,000
5	75
4	5
3	1
HOUSE PERCENTAGE	23.7348%
5-SPOT TICKET	
5	$600
4	25
3	1
HOUSE PERCENTAGE	22.6802%
4-SPOT TICKET	
4	$150
3	3
2	1
HOUSE PERCENTAGE	19.8112%
3-SPOT TICKET	
3	$45
2	1
HOUSE PERCENTAGE	23.6855%
2-SPOT TICKET	
2	$13
HOUSE PERCENTAGE	21.8354%
1-SPOT TICKET	
1	$3
HOUSE PERCENTAGE	25.0000%

Chapter 33

THE LAW OF PROBABILITIES

Probability is a concept which is not easily defined; mathematicians have struggled for centuries with the precise meaning to be ascribed to this term. For our purposes, think of the word **probability** as just another way of saying *"the chances that an event will happen."*

A good example to illustrate probability theory is something with which every schoolboy is familiar—flipping a coin.

There are just two possible results when a coin is flipped; half the time the coin will land head up, and half the time the coin will land tail up. No, I won't buy the argument that once in a great while a coin might land on its edge. If it does, we'll push it over.

Thus, the **odds** of a coin landing with a given side up are 1 in 2. The *probability* is expressed as a percentage; in this instance, it's 50%. Another way of stating this is that the **expected value** is 50 out of 100 flips.

The "expected" in expected value has a meaning slightly different from that which is normally given to it in everyday conversation. If we were to flip a coin 100 times, we would not really "expect" to observe exactly 50 heads since the probability of this occurring by chance is very small, about eight percent. Nonetheless, 50 is the expected value of the number of heads observed in 100 flips.

Suppose we do flip a coin 100 times. Suppose further that we observe 47 heads when we do this. If we repeat the experiment a second time we might observe a different number of heads, perhaps 51. If we repeat the experiment an extremely large number of times we would find that the average number of heads would be 50. This **long term average** is the expected value.

In a small sampling there will be times when it will seem like the law of probabilities isn't working the way that it should. Gamblers call this phenomenon a **run of luck**—either good or bad, depending on whether you're betting on "heads" or "tails!"

The odds of a coin landing head or tail up are always the same for every toss, no matter what may have happened on previous tosses—yet the coin may also land with the same side up several times in a row. The probability for this result can also be calculated.

On 25% of the tosses a coin will land head (or tail) up one time only; it will fall on the opposite side when next flipped. This event is a 25% probability, odds of 1 in 4.

Another 25% of the coins flipped will land the same side up (heads or tails) twice in a row. The sequence of two will occur 12.5% of the time. That's odds of 1 in 8.

Statistically, 18.75% of the coins will land the same way (heads or tails) three times in a row, or 6.25% of the time (1 in 16). 12.5% of the coins tossed will land with the same side up for four times in sequence, or 3.125% of the time (1 in 32); and so on.

There will be just five instances of coins landing the same way twenty times in a row (heads or tails) in ten million tosses! The odds of such an event are thus 1 in 2,000,000, a probability of .00005%.

If you're betting on the flipping of a coin, you have a 50% chance of winning. There are only two sides to the coin, and your wager covers half of the possibilities.

Keno, with twenty balls drawn from a pool of eighty, and from one to forty numbers played, gets a lot more complicated. The theory, however, remains the same.

Chapter 34

KENO ODDS

The odds of winning a keno game can be stated in numerous ways.

Your chance of winning is 1 in 4; you'll win 1/4 of the time; the odds against you are 3 to 1; you have a .25 expectancy of winning; you'll win 25% of the time. All of these statements express the identical thought.

Keno players seem to find the "1 in" figures most meaningful. For mathematical calculations, such as computing house percentages, figures in decimals or percentages are preferable.

The charts accompanying this chapter list the odds of standard keno games—that is, games with a pool of eighty balls, from which twenty are drawn per game.

A Note on Exponential Numbers ...

If there was enough space reserved in computer memory for each number to be the largest or smallest figure imaginable, there wouldn't be room left to hold any other data. Accordingly, computer manufacturers set a limit on the number of digits which may be entered or stored as one number.

The size of "legal" numbers differs from one brand or model of computer to another. My Wang 2200T computer provides for a maximum of thirteen digits per number. The digits may be to the right or left of the decimal point, or may straddle it. Arbitrarily restricting the size of numbers greatly reduces the amount of memory required, and the size of permitted numbers is amply sufficient for the vast majority of calculations.

When a computation results in a larger (or smaller) number than is allowed, computers change the format of that figure to an *exponential number*, which is merely a shorthand method of displaying the data.

You can readily recognize an exponential number. The fourth character from the right will be an *E;* or, in some instances, a *D.*

The last three characters of an exponential number are instructions on how to move the decimal point, in order to convert the exponential number to a conventional number.

If the third character from the right is a minus symbol (-), move the decimal point to the left. If it's a plus sign (+), move the decimal point to the right. In either instance, move the decimal point the number of spaces indicated by the last two digits of the exponential number.

Thus, the exponential number 1.60302707E-12 translates to .00000000000160302707, and the number 2.45988809E+18 becomes 2,459,888,090,000,000,000.

Because numbers as large (or small) as those in the above examples exceed the capacity of most computers and hand-held calculators, and cannot even be entered in their longhand form, it is impossible to make calculations which require them.

To overcome this problem, most computers (and some calculators) permit numbers to be entered in the exponential format.

KENO ODDS & PROBABILITIES
80 BALL GAME – 20 BALLS DRAWN

SPOTS CAUGHT	ODDS	PROBABILITIES PERCENTAGE
1 NUMBER MARKED		
1	1 in 4	25.0
0	1 in 1.333333333333	75.0
2 NUMBERS MARKED		
2	1 in 16.63157894737	6.012658227848
1	1 in 2.633333333334	37.9746835443
0	1 in 1.785310734463	56.01265822785
3 NUMBERS MARKED		
3	1 in 72.07017543859	1.387536514119
2	1 in 7.207017543859	13.87536514119
1	1 in 2.320903954802	43.08666017527
0	1 in 2.400935125657	41.65043816943
4 NUMBERS MARKED		
4	1 in 326.435500516	.3063392303899
3	1 in 23.12251461988	4.324789134916
2	1 in 4.702884329468	21.26354658
1	1 in 2.310900058445	43.27318251369
0	1 in 3.243368503082	30.832142541
5 NUMBERS MARKED		
5	1 in 1550.568627451	6.44924695E-02
4	1 in 82.69699346402	1.209233804171
3	1 in 11.91397363465	8.393505228948
2	1 in 3.697440093512	27.04573907106
1	1 in 2.464960062342	40.56860860658
0	1 in 4.401714397038	22.71842081969
6 NUMBERS MARKED		
6	1 in 7752.843137256	1.28984939E-02
5	1 in 323.0351307189	.3095638538677
4	1 in 35.04109892545	2.853791777842
3	1 in 7.703000194816	12.98195475411
2	1 in 3.243368503082	30.832142541
1	1 in 2.751071498149	36.3494733115
0	1 in 6.002337814144	16.66017526777

SPOTS CAUGHT	ODDS	PROBABILITIES PERCENTAGE
7 NUMBERS MARKED		
7	1 in 40979.31372548	2.44025560E-03
6	1 in 1365.977124183	7.32076681E-02
5	1 in 115.7607732359	.8638504841036
4	1 in 19.16040384593	5.219096674793
3	1 in 5.714506410192	17.49932414489
2	1 in 3.061342719745	32.66540507047
1	1 in 3.172664273191	31.51925050659
0	1 in 8.225425893456	12.1574251954
8 NUMBERS MARKED		
8	1 in 230114.6078431	4.34566066E-04
7	1 in 6232.270629084	1.60455163E-02
6	1 in 422.5268223109	.2366713655078
5	1 in 54.63708909193	1.830258559927
4	1 in 12.26938141011	8.150370149677
3	1 in 4.655792052945	21.47862251209
2	1 in 3.047427525564	32.81456217125
1	1 in 3.752850563889	26.64641138718
0	1 in 11.32936019287	8.826623772003
9 NUMBERS MARKED		
9	1 in 1380687.647059	7.24276777E-05
8	1 in 30681.94771242	3.25924549E-03
7	1 in 1690.107289243	5.91678413E-02
6	1 in 174.8386850941	.5719557999773
5	1 in 30.67345352528	3.260148059871
4	1 in 8.763843864366	11.41051820955
3	1 in 4.063236700752	24.61092162844
2	1 in 3.160295211697	31.64261352227
1	1 in 4.531744077149	22.06655943001
0	1 in 15.6868064209	6.374783835335

SPOTS CAUGHT	ODDS	PROBABILITIES PERCENTAGE
10 NUMBERS MARKED		
10	1 in 8911711.176467	1.12211895E-05
9	1 in 163381.3715686	6.12064882E-04
8	1 in 7384.468771462	1.35419355E-02
7	1 in 620.6773320841	.1611143098528
6	1 in 87.11260801181	1.147939457701
5	1 in 19.44477857407	5.1427687705
4	1 in 6.787995429493	14.73188970716
3	1 in 3.739682667173	26.74023677939
2	1 in 3.386882415554	29.52567811057
1	1 in 5.568816279422	17.95713756432
0	1 in 21.83849521341	4.579070078903
11 NUMBERS MARKED		
11	1 in 62381978.2353	1.60302707E-06
10	1 in 945181.4884133	1.05799786E-04
9	1 in 35244.05550016	2.83735791E-03
8	1 in 2430.624517253	.0411416898374
7	1 in 277.1764800376	.3607809724203
6	1 in 49.49580000671	2.020373445554
5	1 in 13.49885454729	7.40803596703
4	1 in 5.599524849246	17.8586581348
3	1 in 3.592148016497	27.83849650425
2	1 in 3.730307555593	26.80744107817
1	1 in 6.94861211336	14.39136310512
0	1 in 30.57389329877	3.270764342074
12 NUMBERS MARKED		
12	1 in 478261833.1373	2.09090487E-07
11	1 in 5978272.914216	1.67272390E-05
10	1 in 184230.2901145	5.42798906E-04
9	1 in 10482.06823065	9.54010199E-03
8	1 in 980.7783139794	.1019598400318
7	1 in 142.3004250193	.7027385897577
6	1 in 31.04736545876	3.220885203056
5	1 in 10.06164621349	9.938731483716
4	1 in 4.859964963494	20.57628002489
3	1 in 3.57487807411	27.97298199461
2	1 in 4.205738910717	23.77703469542
1	1 in 8.789994323401	11.3765716246
0	1 in 43.05303342074	2.322716706689

SPOTS CAUGHT	ODDS	PROBABILITIES PERCENTAGE
13 NUMBERS MARKED		
13	1 in 4065225581.666	2.45988809E-08
12	1 in 41694621.35043	2.39839088E-06
11	1 in 1060032.746197	9.43367083E-05
10	1 in 49844.79997794	2.00622733E-03
9	1 in 3847.668770226	2.59897631E-02
8	1 in 458.0558059793	.2183140104211
7	1 in 81.20080196909	1.23151493058
6	1 in 21.05205976976	4.750129017953
5	1 in 7.944173498018	12.58784189758
4	1 in 4.399849937366	22.72804787062
3	1 in 3.666541614471	27.27365744475
2	1 in 4.839834931101	20.66186170057
1	1 in 11.26002412542	8.880975643226
0	1 in 60.99179734599	1.639564734135
14 NUMBERS MARKED		
14	1 in 38910016281.65	2.57003233E-09
13	1 in 324250135.6804	3.08403880E-07
12	1 in 6764018.475734	1.47841110E-05
11	1 in 262397.2684552	3.81101528E-04
10	1 in 16739.85763669	5.97376645E-03
9	1 in 1644.093160747	6.08238038E-02
8	1 in 239.1408233813	.4181636518017
7	1 in 50.3745715919	1.985128544817
6	1 in 15.20741783907	6.575738304705
5	1 in 6.580132718828	15.19726185976
4	1 in 4.128710725538	24.220636089
3	1 in 3.860344528378	25.9044236246
2	1 in 5.672342980472	17.62939941119
1	1 in 14.59446579351	6.851912321756
0	1 in 86.94575366344	1.150142425438

SPOTS CAUGHT	ODDS	PROBABILITIES PERCENTAGE
15 NUMBERS MARKED		
15	1 in 428010179098.4	2.33639303E-10
14	1 in 2853401193.99	3.50458954E-08
13	1 in 48362732.10152	2.06770783E-06
12	1 in 1539397.308271	6.49604877E-05
11	1 in 81020.91096162	1.23424926E-02
10	1 in 6576.37264299	.0152059509746
9	1 in 789.1647171585	.1267162581217
8	1 in 136.3988400028	.7331440648467
7	1 in 33.45631924596	2.988971956683
6	1 in 11.58103358514	8.634807874862
5	1 in 5.67697724762	17.61500806471
4	1 in 3.9965S1982322	25.02131827375
3	1 in 4.159718185681	24.04009010616
2	1 in 6.759542051732	14.79390160379
1	1 in 19.12806580596	5.227920115626
0	1 in 124.7482552563	.8016144177293
16 NUMBERS MARKED		
16	1 in 5564132328279	1.79722540E-11
15	1 in 28979855876.46	3.45067278E-09
14	1 in 392947198.325	2.54487117E-07
13	1 in 10162427.54289	9.84016855E-06
12	1 in 438863.267709	2.27861403E-04
11	1 in 29388.16524837	3.40273028E-03
10	1 in 2914.528784962	3.43108637E-02
9	1 in 415.5902156335	.2406216417958
8	1 in 83.64079811491	1.195588782673
7	1 in 23.52397446982	4.250982338392
6	1 in 9.225088027381	10.8400049629
5	1 in 5.073798415058	19.70909993255
4	1 in 3.976201206903	25.14963272643
3	1 in 4.576773264195	21.84945467636
2	1 in 8.179764982813	12.22529011654
1	1 in 25.33948934894	3.946409441128
0	1 in 180.1919242591	.5549638276586

SPOTS CAUGHT	ODDS	PROBABILITIES PERCENTAGE
17 NUMBERS MARKED		
17	1 in 8.90261172E+13	1.12326588E-12
16	1 in 349122028440.9	2.86432799E-10
15	1 in 3698326572.469	2.70392562E-08
14	1 in 76517101.49936	1.30689738E-06
13	1 in 2684810.578924	3.72465755E-05
12	1 in 147517.0647761	6.77887674E-04
11	1 in 12069.57802713	8.28529380E-03
10	1 in 1422.340844948	7.03066359E-02
9	1 in 236.1622535008	.4234376938635
8	1 in 54.49898157713	1.834896673408
7	1 in 17.36487158095	5.758752636543
6	1 in 7.640543495617	13.08807417396
5	1 in 4.677883772826	21.37718781747
4	1 in 4.054165936448	24.66598594324
3	1 in 5.132401557842	19.48405612324
2	1 in 10.04165522187	9.958517574098
1	1 in 33.91847986053	2.948245334437
0	1 in 262.0973443768	.3815376315154
18 NUMBERS MARKED		
18	1 in 1.86954846E+15	5.34888514E-14
17	1 in 5193190173062	1.92559865E-11
16	1 in 41421257611.64	2.41421931E-09
15	1 in 669524638.1194	1.49359701E-07
14	1 in 18793674.05248	5.32093936E-06
13	1 in 839003.305914	1.19189041E-04
12	1 in 56324.69745997	1.77542010E-03
11	1 in 5476.012253053	1.82614638E-02
10	1 in 751.4253520486	.1330804180713
9	1 in 143.0598266399	.6990082565365
8	1 in 37.40126186665	2.673706581252
7	1 in 13.37095111733	7.478899527977
6	1 in 6.549037281957	15.26941986962
5	1 in 4.43424399299	22.55175857668
4	1 in 4.226683635872	23.65921100678
3	1 in 5.857632212756	17.07174441274
2	1 in 12.49628205388	8.00238019347
1	1 in 45.86703526596	2.18021503723
0	1 in 384.0030859475	.2604145738914

SPOTS CAUGHT	ODDS	PROBABILITIES PERCENTAGE
19 NUMBERS MARKED		
19	1 in 5.79560023E+16	1.72544682E-15
18	1 in 1.01677197E+14	9.83504688E-13
17	1 in 574447441088.3	1.74080329E-10
16	1 in 6991246747.52	1.43036004E-08
15	1 in 153316814.6387	6.52244179E-07
14	1 in 5475600.522811	1.82628370E-05
13	1 in 298669.119426	3.34818678E-04
12	1 in 23825.45682031	4.19719129E-03
11	1 in 2697.221526828	3.70751897E-02
10	1 in 424.3880024729	.2356334284129
9	1 in 91.53466719998	1.092482259006
8	1 in 26.85016904534	3.724371337519
7	1 in 10.68527135478	9.35867669428
6	1 in 5.787855317169	17.27755697406
5	1 in 4.310105023423	23.20129079374
4	1 in 4.497500894007	22.234570344
3	1 in 6.79622357317	14.71405390411
2	1 in 15.75488191961	6.34723893903
1	1 in 62.65313507566	1.59608932385
0	1 in 566.8616983035	.1764098726361
20 NUMBERS MARKED		
20	1 in 3.53531614E+18	2.82860134E-17
19	1 in 2.94609678E+15	3.39432161E-14
18	1 in 1.05123881E+13	9.51258632E-12
17	1 in 90624035964.73	1.10346001E-09
16	1 in 1496372110.873	6.68282971E-08
15	1 in 41751453.98641	2.39512616E-06
14	1 in 1821881.628498	5.48883080E-05
13	1 in 118084.9203656	8.46848180E-04
12	1 in 10968.70087576	9.11684994E-03
11	1 in 1423.821748296	7.02335107E-02
10	1 in 253.8006681455	.3940099950512
9	1 in 61.41976169118	1.628140475419
8	1 in 20.05543238896	4.986180205969
7	1 in 8.826479358683	11.32954555676
6	1 in 5.258328128576	19.01745147028
5	1 in 4.286680539599	23.32807380355
4	1 in 4.877289858388	20.5031898664
3	1 in 8.008731642469	12.48637168334
2	1 in 20.11495389271	4.971425762813
1	1 in 86.44640899126	1.156786050073
0	1 in 843.3795999147	.1185705701325

SPOTS CAUGHT	ODDS	PROBABILITIES PERCENTAGE
32 NUMBERS MARKED		
20	1 in 15657343883.08	6.38677931E-05
19	1 in 212026531.75	4.71639087E-07
18	1 in 6648088.341544	1.50419180E-05
17	1 in 361309.1489972	2.76771292E-04
16	1 in 30227.17063505	3.30828185E-03
15	1 in 3649.587363608	2.74003579E-02
14	1 in 611.0936980927	.1636410264287
13	1 in 138.2235745685	.7234655905273
12	1 in 41.49300549897	2.410044748445
11	1 in 16.33787091522	6.120748567478
10	1 in 8.378395341142	11.93545970658
9	1 in 5.578247424495	17.92677742491
8	1 in 4.824430204969	20.72783639755
7	1 in 5.444235474354	18.36805194615
6	1 in 8.088578419041	12.36311188683
5	1 in 16.05820715545	6.2273452467
4	1 in 43.60046548874	2.293553494878
3	1 in 167.9299178589	.5954865057697
2	1 in 975.0769424067	.102556009327
1	1 in 9572.005317959	1.04471316E-02
0	1 in 211244.2552929	4.73385654E-04
40 NUMBERS MARKED (top / bottom tickets)		
20	1 in 25646754.92720	3.89912877E-06
19	1 in 673227.3168391	1.48538238E-04
18	1 in 39975.71112135	2.50151897E-03
17	1 in 4032.637525399	2.47976663E-02
16	1 in 615.4740897271	.1624763766162
15	1 in 133.5664257220	.7486911434474
14	1 in 39.68830935740	2.5196336558326
13	1 in 15.75859342132	6.3457440220968
12	1 in 8.228263231645	12.1532329708908
11	1 in 5.592647665259	17.8806186238393
10	1 in 4.920217887325	20.3243031690973
9	1 in 5.592647665259	17.8806186238393
8	1 in 8.228263231645	12.1532329708908
7	1 in 15.75859342132	6.3457440220968
6	1 in 39.68830935740	2.5196336558326
5	1 in 133.5664257220	.7486911434474
4	1 in 615.4740897271	.1624763766162
3	1 in 4032.637525399	2.47976663E-02
2	1 in 39975.71112135	2.50151897E-03
1	1 in 673227.3168391	1.48538238E-04
0	1 in 25646754.92720	3.89912877E-06

Chapter 35

HOW TO COMPUTE KENO ODDS

The charts in the preceding chapter list the odds and probabilities percentages for every standard keno ticket: 1–20 spots, 32-numbers, and top/bottom keno (40 spots), all with twenty balls drawn from a total of eighty.

What about non-standard keno?

There are a few video "mini-keno" machines around. These machines draw ten numbers from a pool of forty. And, at one time, a few casinos in the Reno area had keno with 21 balls drawn, instead of the usual twenty. Who knows what bright ideas someone might come up with in the future?

Read on, and you'll learn how to figure the odds on virtually every type of keno imaginable.

I would not suggest that you attempt to figure keno odds by hand, unless you're a confirmed masochist. If you're working with pencil and paper, it's a cumbersome, time-consuming, tedious process. The more spots marked, the more difficult the task becomes—and, the more opportunities arise for errors to creep into your figures.

Because of the difficulty of figuring keno odds before electronic calculators and computers became available to the general public, it wasn't until 1960 that the odds for the standard

10-spot keno ticket were accurately determined and published.

Modern technology has changed the entire picture. There are still a lot of steps, but anyone with patience and time to spare can compute keno odds with the help of an electronic calculator.

For those who are privy to a computer, keno odds can be determined in an instant. More about that later; right now I'm going to step you through one of the easier calculations, a 4-spot ticket.

I'll assume that you're not an expert on statistics or algebra, and make the explanation as simple and non-technical as possible. All that you'll need to do is follow the steps outlined, using multiplication and long division.

---

4 SPOTS MARKED — 20 NUMBERS DRAWN FROM A POOL OF 80

Step 1 – 4 hits:

$$\frac{20 \times 19 \times 18 \times 17}{1 \times 2 \times 3 \times 4} = 4{,}845$$

Step 2a – 3 hits:

$$\frac{20 \times 19 \times 18}{1 \times 2 \times 3} \times \frac{60}{1} = 68{,}400$$

Step 2b – 2 hits:

$$\frac{20 \times 19}{1 \times 2} \times \frac{60 \times 59}{1 \times 2} = 336{,}300$$

Step 2c – 1 hit:

$$\frac{20}{1} \times \frac{60 \times 59 \times 58}{1 \times 2 \times 3} = 684{,}400$$

Step 3 – 0 hits:

$$\frac{60 \times 59 \times 58 \times 57}{1 \times 2 \times 3 \times 4} = 487{,}635$$

Step 4: Add the results of steps 1 through 3. If that answer is not equal to the answer obtained in the following control step, you have made a mistake which must be corrected before proceeding further.

Control step:

$$\frac{80 \times 79 \times 78 \times 77}{1 \times 2 \times 3 \times 4} = 1{,}581{,}580$$

To determine the probabilities percentages, divide each of the results of the steps 1 through 3 equations by the step 4 (or control step) answer, and multiply that number by 100.

The probabilities percentages for a 4 spot game are as follows:

4 hits	—	.3063392303899
3 hits	—	4.324789134916
2 hits	—	21.26354658
1 hit	—	43.27318251369
0 hits	—	30.832142541

To determine the odds, divide 100 by each of the probabilities percentages.

The odds for a 4 spot game are as follows:

4 hits	—	1 in	326.435500516
3 hits	—	1 in	23.12251461988
2 hits	—	1 in	4.702884329468
1 hit	—	1 in	2.310900058445
0 hits	—	1 in	3.243368503082

In the above example, the number 80 in the control step represents the total number of balls; the number 20 in steps 1–2 represents the number of balls drawn; and the number 60 in steps 2–3 represents the difference between the total number of balls and the numbers of balls drawn. By substituting other numbers, you can compute the odds for virtually any keno game.

The divisor in the control step and step 1 always starts with the number 1, and is incremented to and including the number of spots marked; in this example, 4.

In each equation, the dividend is decremented the same number of times that the divisor is incremented.

The following example shows how to compute the odds for keno with ten balls total, five spots marked, and three balls drawn.

---

5 SPOTS MARKED — 3 NUMBERS DRAWN FROM A POOL OF 10

Step 1 – 5 hits:

$$\frac{3 \times 2 \times 1 \times 0 \times \text{-}1}{1 \times 2 \times 3 \times 4 \times 5} = 0$$

Step 2a – 4 hits:

$$\frac{3 \times 2 \times 1 \times 0}{1 \times 2 \times 3 \times 4} \times \frac{7}{1} = 0$$

Step 2b – 3 hits:

$$\frac{3 \times 2 \times 1}{1 \times 2 \times 3} \times \frac{7 \times 6}{1 \times 2} = 21$$

Step 2c – 2 hits:

$$\frac{3 \times 2}{1 \times 2} \times \frac{7 \times 6 \times 5}{1 \times 2 \times 3} = 105$$

Step 2d – 1 hit:

$$\frac{3}{1} \times \frac{7 \times 6 \times 5 \times 4}{1 \times 2 \times 3 \times 4} = 105$$

Step 3 – 0 hits:

$$\frac{7 \times 6 \times 5 \times 4 \times 3}{1 \times 2 \times 3 \times 4 \times 5} = 21$$

Step 4: Add the results of steps 1 through 3. As the total is 252, which is equal to the answer obtained in the following control step, you know that no errors were made to this point.

Control step:

$$\frac{10 \times 9 \times 8 \times 7 \times 6}{1 \times 2 \times 3 \times 4 \times 5} = 252$$

The probability percentages and odds for this game are as follows:

5 hits	–	0.0	1 in	0.0
4 hits	–	0.0	1 in	0.0
3 hits	–	8.333333333333	1 in	12.0
2 hits	–	41.66666666667	1 in	2.4
1 hit	–	41.66666666667	1 in	2.4
0 hits	–	8.333333333333	1 in	12.0

It's necessary to use steps 1 and 3 (adapted for the actual variables) for every type of game. There will be one less intermediate step (in our examples, steps 2a–2c and 2a–2d) than the number of spots marked. Thus, in a 10-spot game, there will be nine intermediate steps, and in a 1-spot game, there will be no intermediate steps at all.

Each step is built upon the preceding step, by deleting the last pair of numbers (dividend and divisor) from the left portion of the equation, and by adding a pair of numbers to the right portion of the equation, as shown in the example.

If more spots are marked than balls drawn, some of the steps will result in an answer of "0"—because it's impossible to catch more spots than the number of balls that are drawn.

I've designed the *Keno Analyst,* a very elaborate suite of computer programs that calculates both odds and house percentages on all types of keno, including the keno exacta.

These programs are invaluable tools for casino management when they want to develop new keno tickets, and I use them on a daily basis for analyzing payoffs, prior to writing articles for *Keno Newsletter*.

Now, I've got a bonus for you; a bonus worth many times the price of this book. It's a simple, easy computer program that will figure the odds on nearly every type of keno!

This program is written in GW Basic, and will work on most computers with few or no modifications.

To save you a lot of time punching in code, I've stripped the program down to the bare essentials. It works great "as is" to compute keno odds, but feel free to add any fancy graphics of your own.

There are no traps in the program to check your input, so if you enter an impossible set of variables (such as drawing more balls than the total number of balls) the program will bomb. And, if you exceed your computer's memory, you'll get an overflow error.

```
10 REM ***** COMPUTE KENO ODDS *****
20 KEY OFF: CLS
30 DIM C(100), C1(100), D(100)
40 DIM D1(100), P(100), T(100)
50 INPUT "Total number of balls "; N
60 INPUT "Number of balls drawn "; B
70 INPUT "Number of spots marked"; S
80      FOR X=1 TO S+1
90          FOR Z=0 TO 100: C(Z)=0: D(Z)=0: NEXT Z
100         FOR X1=1 TO S
110             C(X1)=(B+1)-X1
120             D(X1)=X1
130         NEXT X1
140 C=1: D=1
150         FOR X1=1 TO (S+1)-X
160             C=C*C(X1)
170             D=D*D(X1)
180         NEXT X1
190 IF X < > 1 GOTO 220
200 T(X)=C/D
210 GOTO 360
220 FOR Z=0 TO 100: C1(Z)=0: D1(Z)=0: NEXT Z
230         FOR X1=1 TO X-1
240             C1(X1)=(N-B+1)-X1
250             D1(X1)=X1
260         NEXT X1
270 C1=1: D1=1
```

```
280          FOR X1=1 TO X-1
290             C1=C1*C1(X1)
300             D1=D1*D1(X1)
310          NEXT X1
320 IF X=S+1 GOTO 350
330 T(X)=(C/D)*(C1/D1)
340 GOTO 360
350 T(X)=(C1/D1)
360 T=T+T(X)
370 NEXT X
380 FOR Z=0 TO 100: P(Z)=0: NEXT Z: Q=1
390     FOR X=S+1 TO 1 STEP-1
400     IF (S+1)-X > B GOTO 430
410     P(Q)=T(X)/T*100: Q=Q+1
420     PRINT "Spots caught - "; S+1-X;
430     PRINT TAB(25); "1 in"; 1/(T(X)/T);
440     PRINT TAB(50); T(X)/T*100
450 NEXT X
```

Chapter 36

HOW TO CALCULATE HOUSE PERCENTAGES

It's easy to determine the house percentage of a keno ticket.

Let me modify the above statement. There's nothing tricky or mysterious about calculating the PC of a keno ticket—the algorithm is simple—but the chore of doing the mathematics by hand is a much more demanding task than most people care to tackle.

Not to worry! If you have a computer at your disposal, figuring PCs is a snap; and, you can even get acceptable results with minimal labor using a hand-held calculator, although the PCs will probably be less accurate, because the number of digits you can enter into most pocket calculators is limited.

To compute the house percentage of a keno ticket you need to know the ticket price, the payoffs for each possible catch, and the *probabilities percentage* for each possible catch.

The first two items are printed in every casino's keno paybook for each ticket offered by the casino, and the probabilities percentage chart for virtually every keno game is printed in this book (see chapter 34, "Keno odds").

The following example of the mathematics necessary to compute the house percentage of a 6-spot keno ticket should be self-explanatory. To make the job easier, I've rounded the probabilities percentages to eight digits to the right of the decimal point and the player percentages to five digits to the right of the decimal point; the resultant house percentage is sufficiently accurate for most purposes.

6-SPOT KENO TICKET HOUSE PERCENTAGE							
SPOTS CAUGHT			TICKET PRICE		PROBABILITIES PERCENTAGES		PLAYER PERCENTAGES
0	.00	+	2.00	X	16.66017527	=	00.00000
1	.00	+	2.00	X	36.34947331	=	00.00000
2	.00	+	2.00	X	30.83214254	=	00.00000
3	2.00	+	2.00	X	12.98195475	=	12.98195
4	10.00	+	2.00	X	2.85379178	=	14.26896
5	150.00	+	2.00	X	.30956385	=	23.21729
6	4,000.00	+	2.00	X	.01289849	=	25.79698
TOTAL PLAYER PERCENTAGE							76.26518
HOUSE PERCENTAGE (100 MINUS TOTAL PLAYER PERCENTAGE)							23.73482
TOTAL PLAYER PERCENTAGE AND HOUSE PERCENTAGE							100.00000

Use the above format to compute the house percentage of any keno ticket—just substitute the numbers of the ticket you want to analyze for those used in the example.

The next time you play keno take the probabilities percentages charts, your calculator, and a pad of paper with you to the casino. Computing house percentages will give you something to do while you're sitting in the keno lounge waiting for the next game to be called. Your efforts might result in discovering an especially good keno ticket and will most assuredly point out the ones you will choose not to play.

Always remember ... play only keno tickets with low house percentages.

KENO HOUSE PERCENTAGE GUIDE
25% OR LESS ..... LOCALS & FREQUENT KENO PLAYERS
26% - 32% .... TOURIST GAMES
33% & MORE ..... SUCKER BETS

Chapter 37

KENO COMPUTERS

Computers brought revolutionary changes to the game of keno ... and will undoubtedly result in many future innovations.

Only a few casinos have failed to jump on the bandwagon and make the switch from brush games to computer games. While those casinos may boast in their ads, "We still play keno the old-fashioned way," the slogan smacks of sour grapes. There are so many advantages to a computerized keno system for both the casinos and the players that the real reason why a particular casino hasn't modernized probably boils down to a matter of not wanting to make an outlay for the initial investment. Depending upon the number of writer stations and features desired, a multi-station keno computer system can easily run well in excess of $100,000.

A majority of the keno computer systems currently operating in Nevada were provided by Imagineering Systems, Inc., headquartered in Reno—though several other companies, from as far away as Australia, are making major inroads into Imagineering's market share, especially for keno games located in jurisdictions outside of Nevada.

A typical keno computer system consists of a PC-type computer interfaced with a number of standard or specially-designed peripherals, which are controlled by an elaborate suite of proprietary software programs.

The supervisor's station, which is usually positioned at the keno desk, includes the central processing unit (CPU) that drives the entire system; a CRT display screen, for use of the supervisor or shift boss; a standard dot-matrix type printer, for preparing management reports; and a hard disk drive, for storage of data.

Writers' stations—as many as the casino needs to run its keno game—have built-in intelligence to assist the writer in entering ticket information and to reduce the chances for mistakes or misunderstandings. Each writers' station has its own dot-matrix keno ticket printer.

The writers enter the numbers selected, price of the ticket, ways grouping, number of consecutive games to be played, and all other information needed on a keno ticket. The process is called *conditioning the ticket*. Displays on the writers' station terminals inform the keno writers how much to collect for tickets purchased and how much to pay on winning tickets.

A control station transmits the number draw to the central computer and controls the keno flashboard displays throughout the casino.

As soon as each draw is complete, a runners' printer provides each keno runner with a list of winning tickets and the amounts to be paid to the winners.

With computerized keno, players spend less time in line waiting for their turn with a keno writer, as keno tickets are prepared much more quickly with a computer than by hand. While it's still possible for a keno writer to make mistakes when entering details about a keno ticket (as with all computers, it's garbage-in, garbage-out), safeguards built into the software greatly reduce the possibility of writer error, so mismarked tickets are rare.

Some systems utilize Mark Sense keno blanks similar to those used in Lotto games. A scanner reads and records all of the data automatically.

All payoffs are accurately and automatically determined by

the computer—even complicated combination and way tickets. Players never have to wonder if they were paid correctly; the computer doesn't make mistakes.

Since less time is spent writing tickets, more games can be played each hour. Increasing the tempo makes keno more exciting. In a given period of time, more money can be wagered, more money can be won.

The versatility of computerized keno systems has made possible a number of innovations, including progressive keno jackpots and multi-race tickets for up to a thousand games.

A computerized keno system is an excellent investment for a casino. It lowers labor costs. It virtually eliminates the potential for employee or employee-player theft inherent in brush games. By accurately computing all payoffs and speeding up the games, it increases customer satisfaction. It provides accurate player tracking, so essential in determining which players to comp, and for how much. And, it spews out a plethora of reports to help management run the keno department more profitably.

Computerized keno is not without its shortcomings, however. If the system fails (which is rare, but does happen), with most systems, the entire keno department is shut down until a repairman can get to the casino and correct the problem. To date, most casinos have not seen the need to justify the extra cost of built-in hardware redundancy.

I once inadvertently closed the keno department at Gold Coast for over an hour and a half by playing a 190-way 8-spot ticket for two games and taking the Gold Coast's exacta add-on bet.

Gold Coast was one of the first casinos to install a keno computer. At the time I played the ticket, their system had a less powerful CPU than those in general use today. The number-crunching necessary for computing the payoffs on the complicated ticket was just too much for the computer's capacity, and everything locked up while the computer was "thinking." The keno supervisor panicked and called an Imagineering serviceman, but by the time he arrived at the casino the computations were completed and everything was on the way back to normal.

Random Number Generators

Most video poker players are quite aware of the fact that random number generators select the cards in video poker games. It's less well-known—especially by tourists—that the reels on slot machines are now just window-dressing. In the old days (not that many years ago) slot machine payoffs were determined by the positions where the reels landed when they stopped spinning. Today, a built-in computer in every electronic reel-type slot machine determines how much and when someone will win—before the reels even *start* spinning—and *causes* the reels to line up the appropriate symbols.

A random number generator (RNG) is incorporated in every video keno machine; it selects twenty numbers each game. Similarly, "live" keno games can eliminate their wire cage or blower and the Ping-Pong type keno balls, using instead a random number generator connected to the casino's keno computer system.

In theory, the RNG-selected numbers are drawn just as impartially as the would be by the traditional method, with the advantages of saving the casinos a considerable amount of costly labor, reducing the possibility of mistakes, and tightening security on their games. Indeed, in New Jersey, when keno was introduced in June, 1994, the Casino Control Commission mandated that casinos *must* use random number generators to pick keno numbers.

There's been only one thing stopping Nevada casinos from switching to random number generators *en masse*. Keno players just don't like them. Keno is, in many respects, a dog-and-pony show. A major part of the suspense and excitement of the game comes from watching the balls, one at a time, pop from the wire cage or blower into the rabbit ears.

A further deterrent is the fact that many players have an innate distrust of computers; they believe that it would be easy for casinos to program the computer to avoid picking the numbers that players had marked on their tickets. Of course the players are right. It would be possible to cheat them in this manner, but no casino management would ever risk losing their valuable gaming license by doing something that stupid.

Despite the public's dislike of random number generator keno games, they've been in Nevada for some time, with mixed results.

When a casino's restaurants are located too far from the keno lounge for runners to make the trek back and forth, the casino will often set up a separate keno operation just for their restaurant patrons. Although random number generators are rarely employed to select numbers for games played in Nevada keno lounges, a majority of "restaurant games" are now RNG games. Most players in restaurants aren't even the slightest bit aware that a random number generator is being used to select numbers. The keno substation is usually located out of sight of the players, so, even if the game was being played with keno balls, the players would not be able to see them being drawn.

Most people probably don't realize that when they play keno while dining they aren't participating in the same games that are being run in the keno lounge. Thus, having separate restaurant games poses a small problem for the player who buys a multi-game ticket in the keno lounge and then goes to dinner, expecting to be able to watch his numbers on the flashboard in the restaurant—only to discover that a different series of games is being played. To help avoid confusion, casinos distinguish between the two games, e.g., the "red" game and the "green" game.

The Gold Spike, a small downtown Las Vegas casino, has a random number generator in their minuscule keno department, where just one employee does it all—writes the tickets, operates the computer, calls the numbers, and pays the winners. It's like playing a video keno machine by proxy.

Then there was the RNG operation at O'Shea's Casino, a

sub-casino attached to and owned by the Flamingo Hilton on the Las Vegas Strip. Rumor had it that periodically O'Shea's random number generator would repeat a sequence of numbers. According to the story, a few players caught on to what was happening and made quite a bit of money before the casino became aware of the problem and pulled the plug.

The O'Shea's story may or may not be true—I was never able to pin it down. All of the people who could shed some light on the matter were extremely close-mouthed—especially employees of the company that manufactured the equipment. Perhaps it would have been better for all concerned if the alleged incidents at O'Shea's had been more widely publicized. The fiasco at Montreal Casino in Quebec might have been prevented—see chapter 45, "The big Canadian keno hit."

There's no logical reason for casinos to continue to draw keno numbers by the traditional means, except for players' superstitions and nostalgia. Remember, originally keno numbers were written on slips of paper, not printed on Ping-Pong balls.

Electronic keno display boards—such as those made by Mikohn Gaming Corporation or Current Technology Systems—have superb graphics capabilities that enable "drawn" numbers to be displayed in an exciting manner. Similarly, the number-drawing process can be simulated with animated graphics on large-screen television monitors.

Except for the die-hard keno purists, players of "live" keno should eventually adapt to the replacement of keno balls by electronic selection of numbers, just as they adapted to computerization of slot machines. It might not be long before the wire cage or blower and Ping-Pong balls become as obsolete as the brush and ink method that was, for centuries, the accepted way of writing keno tickets.

Chapter 38

KENO PAYBOOK MISTAKES

You should never play any game—particularly if you're wagering money on the outcome—unless you know and understand the game's rules. Keno is no exception.

The rules for most casino games are fairly well standardized, but those for keno differ, in varying degrees, from casino to casino. There is one way you can quickly learn the rules a casino applies to its keno games. Read the paybooks distributed throughout the keno lounge!

Read the keno paybooks to learn the casino's aggregate limit; special conditioning the casino may require written on some of the alternate tickets; whether the "original" tickets control payoffs and the "outside" tickets are a mere receipt for your wager, or whether the "outside" tickets control payoffs (which is usually the case with computer-printed tickets); whether you may leave the casino area when playing multi-game tickets; what happens if you don't redeem your winning tickets before the next draw starts; how the progressive jackpot is paid; and

EXAMPLE A

MARK 5 NUMBERS			
WINNING NUMBERS	$1.00 TICKET	$3.00 TICKET	$5.00 TICKET
3	1.00	3.00	15.00
4	20.00	60.00	100.00
5	605.00	1,815.00	3,025.00

everything else that a casino perceives may cause a conflict between the customer and the casino if not spelled out in advance.

Read keno paybooks with a high degree of skepticism; they may contain misleading advertising hype. At one casino, a number of tickets listed in the paybooks were highlighted with a star. According to the accompanying copy, the star "indicates player's best bets." In some instances the star did, indeed, point out the best bet for the number of spots marked. Other stars, however, did not.

At another casino the rate labeled "our highest payoffs" also had the highest house percentages of the three rates listed.

Don't assume that "special" means "better." Many keno "specials" are special for the casino but not for the players. If a casino requires you to mark your ticket with an "S" to play a "special" rate, be sure that the "S" doesn't stand for "sucker bet!" See chapter 30, "Keno 'specials'."

Keno paybooks (and any separate pay cards) list the payoffs for every possible winning catch on each ticket offered by the casino. Read the payoffs carefully.

EXAMPLE B

MARK 6 SPOTS		
CATCH	1.50	3.00
4	16.00	32.00
5	175.00	350.00
6	3,000.00	6,000.00

Make sure that you won't be shortchanged by the aggregate limit. Betting too much and getting shortchanged by the aggregate limit is one of the biggest, most foolish, and unnecessary mistakes a keno player can make—and one of the most common! It's like saying to the casino, "Take my money, I don't want it!" Reread chapter 10, "Watch that aggregate limit!"

I've encountered errors (and probable errors) in the pay tables of nearly half of the casinos—including some of the largest, most prestigious casinos in downtown Las Vegas and on the Las Vegas Strip.

Some of the errors were in the house's favor. At one large casino on the Strip the payoff was $370 for catching 6/7 on a $1.00

ticket. However, if you caught the same 6/7 spots on a $3.00 ticket, the payoff was—no, not three times $370, which comes to $1,110, but only $1,070. By tripling your bet, you would be shortchanged $40.

Sometimes paybook mistakes are in the players' favor, but are of little or no import because they're too small to change the house percentages materially.

At one famous downtown Las Vegas casino a catch of 11-out-of-12 on a 70¢ ticket

EXAMPLE C

MARK 10 SPOTS		
CATCH	1.50	3.00
5	1.50	3.00
6	30.00	60.00
7	200.00	400.00
8	3,400.00	6,800.00
9	15,000.00	30,000.00
10	50,000.00	50,000.00

paid $5,000, according to the paybook. If you bet ten times as much, however, their paybooks promised (for an 11/12 catch), not $50,000, but a full $100,000!

Despite the size of this mistake, it probably was of slight consequence, for not very many players buy 12-spot $7.00 tickets, and even fewer would be lucky enough to catch eleven spots on a 12-spot ticket (the odds of the catch are 1 in 5,978,273). Had someone done so, I guarantee that the casino would have put up quite a fight before handing over the extra $50,000. I pointed out the error in *Keno Newsletter*, and the paybooks were corrected on a subsequent printing.

Ahh ... but there have been a number of paybook errors substantially in the players' favor!

EXAMPLE D

	9 SPOTS MARKED			
CATCH	1.00 PAYS	2.00 PAYS	5.00 PAYS	10.00 PAYS
4	.50	1.00	1.50	5.00
5	3.00	6.00	15.00	30.00
6	39.00	78.00	195.00	390.00
7	270.00	540.00	1,350.00	2,700.00
8	3,800.00	7,600.00	19,000.00	38,000.00
9	25,000.00	50,000.00	50,000.00	50,000.00

Before reading further, please take the time to analyze the pay table examples scattered throughout this chapter. Look for possible errors, compute the house percentages, and make a note of which tickets you would (or would not) play. The exercise will, once again, point out why you need to determine the house percentages of keno tickets *before* you place your bet.

EXAMPLE E

	10 SPOTS MARKED			
CATCH	1.00 PAYS	2.00 PAYS	5.00 PAYS	10.00 PAYS
5	2.00	4.00	10.00	20.00
6	20.00	40.00	100.00	1,000.00
7	135.00	270.00	675.00	6,750.00
8	800.00	1,600.00	4,000.00	8,000.00
9	3,000.00	6,000.00	15,000.00	30,000.00
10	25,000.00	50,000.00	50,000.00	50,000.00

Example A is a pay table from the Marina, a casino that no longer exists. Part of the Marina property was incorporated into the MGM Grand Hotel and Theme Park mega-resort at the corner of Tropicana Avenue and the Las Vegas Strip.

There's nothing wrong with the $1.00 or $3.00 ticket payoffs, which show a house percentage of 28.4039%. However, the catch-3 payoff on the $5.00 ticket should have been five times the catch-3 payoff for the $1.00 ticket—i.e., $5.00, not $15. With the catch-3 payoff as listed, the $5.00 ticket has a house percentage of just 11.6169%.

Example B is also a pay table from the Marina. There's nothing obviously wrong with these payoffs, but when you compute the house percentages of the tickets you'll find that they're a very low 7.6468%.

Example C was from the same Marina paybook as example B, and again, nothing but the low house percentages tip you off to a possible mistake. I later learned that the catch-8 and catch-9 payoffs were exactly twice what the casino intended them to be!

The $1.50 ticket, as printed in the paybook, computes to a PC of 13.2268%; the $3.00 ticket has a slightly higher 13.4138% PC, due to the aggregate limit (note that the maximum payoff is the same whether the ticket is played for $1.50 or $3.00).

I couldn't wait to try these (examples B and C) tickets out.

I caught four spots on my first 6-spot $1.50 ticket, for a win, according to the paybook, of $16. But, when I went to the keno counter to collect, the writer handed me a mere $4.

"Would you like to play this ticket again?" he asked.

"Yes," I answered, "but first I'd like to receive the rest of what I've already won."

During the short discussion that ensued, I was told that their new keno folders had a lot of mistakes, and all the writer could pay me was what the computer indicated.

"I didn't bet according to what's in your computer, to which I don't have access, but according to the payoff folders which you have throughout the casino," I argued.

EXAMPLE F

$3.00 SUPER KENO SPECIALS		
PICK	CATCH	WIN
3	3	$ 150.00
4	3	$ 4.00
4	4	$ 600.00
6	4	$ 15.00
6	5	$ 800.00
6	6	$ 5,500.00

As my logic failed to convince the keno writer that I should be paid the amount promised in their keno folders, I asked to speak to the supervisor in charge.

The conversation with the supervisor also proved fruitless, so I requested to speak to the keno manager. The supervisor made a telephone call, and then told me that he would have an answer for me shortly.

While waiting for the decision, I went to dinner at one of the casino's restaurants. I looked forward to enjoying their special garlic cheese toast, which the menu proclaimed was served with every dinner.

Halfway through the meal, I reminded the waiter that he hadn't served the garlic cheese toast.

"Oh, we don't have that," he replied. "The machine kept breaking down and catching fire, so we just don't make the cheese toast anymore."

After dinner (sans the advertised garlic cheese toast), it was back to the keno lounge, to find out if the advertised keno payoff would be honored without further confrontation.

The supervisor had $12, the balance of my payoff, waiting for me.

I was going to continue playing, and thought I might try the 10-spot $1.50 ticket. When I asked if they would honor the payoffs on that ticket, as advertised in their keno paybooks, the supervisor questioned, "What paybooks?"

During the time I was in the restaurant every keno paybook in the casino had been removed. Later that evening they brought out an older version of their paybooks that didn't have the mistakes I had uncovered.

EXAMPLE G

PICK SEVEN NUMBERS		
CATCH $1.00	$5.00	$10.00
4 2.00	10.00	20.00
5 20.00	100.00	200.00
6 350.00	700.00	3,500.00
7 7,000.00	35,000.00	50,000.00

The casino didn't change the menus in the restaurant, however, which continued to tout the non-available garlic cheese toast.

Example D was from a paybook at the Landmark, another defunct casino. If the plethora of keno paybook mistakes I encountered at the Landmark over the years was indicative of how the entire casino was run, it's no wonder that they went belly-up.

The only mistake on this pay table (did you discover it?) is the payoff for catching four numbers on the $5.00 ticket. It should have been $2.50, which is five times the $1.00 ticket payoff—not $1.50. This minor error increased the house percentage more than three points! The PC computes to 32.0369% on the $1.00 and $2.00 tickets, 35.4054% on the $5.00 rate. The $10.00 ticket had a PC of 33.4854%, which, due to the maximum aggregate limit, is slightly higher than the PCs on the $1.00 and $2.00 rate tickets.

Example E was also from a Landmark paybook. There are

errors apparent in both the catch-6 and catch-7 payoffs for the $10.00 ticket. The payoffs should have been ten times as much as the $1.00 rate payoffs (or twice the $5.00 rate payoffs). Someone goofed, and made them ten times the payoff of the $5.00 ticket!

The house percentage for the $1.00 and $2.00 tickets was 32.0550%; the $5.00 ticket's PC was 32.2233%, a little higher due to the maximum aggregate limit. However, the percentage on the $10.00 ticket was a whopping 146.5575% *in the players' favor!* If you played this ticket for a thousand games, with a total of $10,000 wagered, the law of probabilities state that you would get a total payoff of $24,655.75!

I publicized the Landmark's mistake in *Keno Newsletter.* They promptly marked out the pay table in all of their paybooks, using a keno crayon; the Landmark's keno operation definitely lacked class.

EXAMPLE H

MARK 13 SPOTS				
CATCH	2.80 PAYS	5.60 PAYS	14.00 PAYS	28.00 PAYS
5	0.80	1.60	4.00	8.00
6	2.80	5.60	14.00	28.00
7	22.80	45.60	114.00	228.00
8	282.80	565.60	1,414.00	2,828.00
9	1,882.80	3,765.60	9,414.00	18,828.00
10	8,882.80	17,765.60	25,000.00	25,000.00
11	16,882.80	25,000.00	25,000.00	25,000.00
12	20,882.80	25,000.00	25,000.00	25,000.00
13	25,000.00	25,000.00	25,000.00	25,000.00

Example F shows the payoffs for three high-end tickets which were offered by the Continental. The 3-spot ticket had a house percentage of 30.6232%; the 4-spot had a PC of 32.9658%. Both PCs were four or five points higher than the PCs of comparable tickets at other southern Nevada casinos.

The 6-spot ticket turned out to be quite a bit more high-ended than Continental planned. Due to a mistake, the catch-5 payoff (which should have been $300) was listed in the paybooks as $800, resulting in a percentage 20.4666% *in the players' favor.*

I had a lot of fun writing a tongue-in-cheek article for a special edition of *Keno Newsletter*, which I'm reprinting below for your entertainment. And, until the newsletter was delivered, I had several days of very profitable play at the Continental.

Continental Offers Keno Ticket with 120% Payback!

Russ had spent the morning going from casino to casino, gathering up new keno paybooks.

It was now nearly 5:00 P.M., but Izzy wanted to finish analyzing all of the payoffs before he quit work for the day. He was hunched over his computer, diligently entering the data, and noting changes that the casinos had made since the last time they were monitored.

He had saved the Continental's paybooks for last, as they had made more changes than the other casinos. They had eliminated their 70¢, 80¢, and $1.10 rate tickets completely—some of which had quite low house percentages—and they had also lowered the PCs on most of their $1.00 rate tickets.

Izzy noted that the Continental had added some $3.00 "Super Keno Specials."

"Some specials these are," he thought, sarcastically. "The 3-spot ticket has a house percentage of 30.6232%, which is 2.7751 points higher than their $1.00 rate regular 3-spot ... and the 'special' 4-spot ticket's PC is 32.9658%, which is 5.4961 points higher than the $1.00 regular 4-spot."

Suddenly he let out a yelp. "Holy s—!" he exclaimed. He repeated the expletive several times, each time a little louder.

Thinking that something was wrong, Gerry, Betty, Steve, and I ran to Izzy's office. We found him staring intently into his computer terminal, transfixed as if in a trance.

"What's the matter?" Betty questioned, and broke the spell.

"I've just found a keno ticket with a house percentage that's 20% in the players' favor!" Izzy announced.

"Are you sure?" Steve asked, incredulously.

"Yes, I've rechecked all of the entries three times," Izzy replied.

"Exactly what does this mean?" Gerry questioned.

"It means that for every $10,000 of play that the casino gets on this ticket, they'll pay out, according to the law of probabilities, $12,046.66 to winners; thus, there's a payout of more than 120% on the ticket, giving the players a 20.4666% edge on the casino," Izzy explained.

Stuart, the night janitor, had joined the party. "Does this mean that for every $1.00 I bet, I'll get back $1.20?" he inquired.

"Of course not," Izzy answered, somewhat impatiently. "Let me educate you. Keno is a long shot game. It has a relatively small number of winners—some of whom win a whole lot of money—and a large number of losing tickets.

"The ticket which is being offered by the Continental is a $3.00 6-spot. You won't win anything at all, unless you catch four numbers or more. If you catch four numbers, you'll win $15. However, you've only got one chance in 35 of winning the $15, and, as it costs $3.00 per game to play, you'll invest $105 for every $15 that you win by catching four spots. So, you can see that playing just a few games won't do you much good, unless you're very, very lucky."

"Then, what's the point of playing it?" Betty inquired.

"Well, you might catch five out of your six numbers, and win $800," Izzy replied. "The odds of catching five numbers out of six are 1 in 323, so once every 323 games you should win $800—plus, what you win on the 4-out-of-6 catches."

"I still don't get it," Betty stated. "If I play 323 games at $3.00 apiece, I've wagered $969 to win $800, plus a few $15 hits. You call that winning?"

"Let's be a little more precise," Izzy corrected. "For every $1,000 you bet, you can expect to get back—on the average—$142.69 for the 4-spot catches, and $825.50 for the 5-spot catches. This totals $968.19, for a loss of about $32.

"Keep reinvesting what remains of your $1,000 starting

bankroll, because once every 7,753 games, according to the law of probabilities, you'll catch all six of your numbers and win $5,500!

"Let me emphasize that you can't play just a few games and realistically expect to come out a big winner! It's necessary to play keno with the same dedication you would apply to any endeavor and put the law of probabilities to work for you. That is, if you want to be a winner.

"If you play the Continental's 6-spot $3.00 special ticket 1,000 times, you might or might not wind up with the expected return of $3,614. On some days you would do better, and on some days you would do worse; sometimes, a lot better, and sometimes, a lot worse.

"But—and this is the important but—if you were to play 1,000 games a day, five days a week, fifty weeks a year (taking off weekends and a couple of weeks for a vacation), the law of probabilities would assure you a year-end profit of approximately $153,500!"

"And, if I bet twice as much, would I win twice as much?" Gerry asked.

"Not only would you win twice as much, but, assuming that you played twice as many games and didn't merely double the bet on each ticket, you would come even closer to achieving a precise 20.4666% return on your money," Izzy answered.

"Why would the Continental offer a ticket that pays out $120,000 for every $100,000 they take in? They can't make any money that way!" Steve observed.

"This might be the most brilliant marketing gimmick since sliced bread!" Izzy commented. "Think of it like a department store loss leader or doorbuster, where merchandise is sold at or below cost just to bring people into the store.

"By offering a ticket that has a 120% payout, with the right publicity, the Continental will attract myriads of players—players who will migrate to the video poker machines, the blackjack tables, or the slots. Perhaps they'll also play other keno tickets, ones where the casino has the advantage and not the players.

"Or ..." Izzy drifted off.

"Or, what?" Gerry queried.

"Or ..." Izzy went on, "or else, someone at the Continental made an incredibly stupid mistake. If that's the case, they'll drop the ticket like a hot potato, as soon as it's brought to management's attention—and then, heads will roll!"

"Well," I stated, "I might as well go on over to the Continental tonight, and find out what happens when I try to play their 6-spot $3.00 super keno special."

After dinner that evening, I drove the short distance from my house to Flamingo and Paradise. The Continental's parking lot was nearly full, but I eventually found a parking space and went inside.

I first looked around the keno lounge, to see if they had posted a disclaimer stating that their keno paybooks were in error. Not finding any, I wrote a keno ticket and stepped up to the keno cage.

Just as I reached the counter, I heard a horrendous yowl coming from the opposite side of the casino. I jumped a couple of feet into the air, and asked the keno writer, "What's going on? Did someone get hurt?"

"No," he replied. "That's Tiny Tim."

"Do you mean *the* Tiny Tim, the one who married Miss Vicki on the Carson show a few years back?"

"The one and only! Can you believe that they've got him booked into our lounge?"

I really couldn't, so I didn't respond to his question.

"What happened to your 70¢ rate tickets?" I asked, knowing full well the answer.

"We dropped them a month or so ago," the keno writer explained. "I preferred the 80¢ rate tickets, myself, but they've been dropped, also."

He went on to assure me, "You're playing a real good ticket. You can win $800 for catching 5-out-of-6, and if you get all six numbers, you'll win $5,500."

I thought to myself, "If the Continental is offering this ticket because someone made a mistake, the keno writers certainly aren't aware of it."

I played a few multi-race tickets and won $15 several times, but didn't have enough cash with me (or time to play) to go for the big bucks. But, I'll be back.

I hope that when I return the 6-spot $3.00 super keno special is still available.

Example G was taken from the same Continental paybook as

EXAMPLE I

	MARK 14 SPOTS			
CATCH	2.80 PAYS	5.60 PAYS	14.00 PAYS	28.00 PAYS
5	0.80	1.60	4.00	8.00
6	2.80	5.60	14.00	28.00
7	22.80	45.60	114.00	228.00
8	282.80	565.60	1,414.00	2,828.00
9	1,882.80	3,765.60	9,414.00	18,828.00
10	8,882.80	17,765.60	25,000.00	25,000.00
11	16,882.80	25,000.00	25,000.00	25,000.00
12	20,882.80	25,000.00	25,000.00	25,000.00
13	25,000.00	25,000.00	25,000.00	25,000.00
14	25,000.00	25,000.00	25,000.00	25,000.00

example F. The $1.00 ticket has a house percentage of 29.5803%. Our old bugbear the aggregate limit causes the $10 ticket to have a PC of 34.4608%.

If you computed the house percentage on the $5.00 ticket, you found that it's a whopping 44.9539%! The catch-6 payoff, which should have been five times the catch-6 payoff for the $1.00 rate ticket—$1,750—was listed as just $700. If you played this ticket and caught 6/7, the casino would have shortchanged you $1,050!

Example H is from another infamous Landmark paybook. If you couldn't find any errors on this pay table, it's because there aren't any. However, did you note that the $28 ticket has a PC more than five points higher than the PC on the $2.80 ticket?

The house percentages of the example H tickets are: $2.80

rate, 35.1478%; $5.60 rate, 35.3027%; $14 rate, 38.3440%; and $28 rate, 40.2217%.

The more you bet, the less you win.
The aggregate limit strikes again!

Example I was in the same Landmark paybook as example H, but in this instance, someone at the Landmark had made a huge mistake. The entire pay schedule was an unintentional duplication of the 13-spot payoffs (our example H), except for the catch-14 payoffs, which were set to the Landmark's aggregate limit of $25,000.

The resultant percentages are: $2.80 rate ticket, 31.5789%; $5.60 rate, 30.9637%; $14 rate, 21.5916%; and $28 rate, 15.9041% —*all in the players' favor!* That's right, these aren't *house* percentages, they're *player* percentages!

When the Landmark made the paybook error in example E, resulting in a player percentage of 146.5575%, I notified them, through publication in *Keno Newsletter*. It may have been embarrassing to the Landmark, but my article had the potential of saving them many thousands of dollars. They never bothered to pick up the phone to say "thank you."

This time, I decided to play keno first, and write an article later.

My wife and I and a few other friends started spending our evenings at the Landmark. I determined that each of us could sit down, relax with complimentary beverages, and go home after every session with an average net profit of more than 31%. Working just six days a week, six hours a day, each of us could have an income of nearly $300,000 per year!

On the very first test run we played ten different 14-spot $2.80 rate 20-game multi-race tickets, an investment of $560. Although we didn't make a big hit, we did catch 8-out-of-14 four times, which paid $282.80 each, as well as numerous smaller wins ($22.80, $2.80, and 80¢) for a total return of $1,297.60—a profit of

$737.60 for the 200 games.

Although I anticipated that the writers would attempt to pay us according to what the payoffs should have been, which is what happened to me at the Marina, we encountered absolutely no problems at all in collecting. The mistakes were not only in the paybooks, they were also entered into the casino's keno computer!

According to the law of probabilities, we should have made $176.84 profit on the first set of tickets, but—and this is most important to remember—two hundred games is a small sampling. We did much better than expected that time, but we could also have done much worse. It's necessary to play thousands of games in order to obtain a return close to that dictated by the law of probabilities.

On subsequent 20-game sets we also did well, though we never approached the bet-to-win ratio of our first test run. The keno writers were amazed at our phenomenal "luck," and we toked them generously on every winning ticket.

I'd like to point out that these events occurred just a few weeks before the Landmark closed its doors forever. Business throughout the casino was so bad that it would have been possible to roll a bowling ball down most of the aisles without striking anyone. Other than my group, there were never more than two players in the keno lounge whenever we were there.

Keno tickets costing $2.80 have never been popular, anywhere ... nor have 14-spot tickets ever received much play, anywhere. Yet, here were six people, most every player in the keno lounge, all buying multi-game 14-spot $2.80 tickets.

I couldn't believe it took the Landmark four nights to catch on, but it did. On the fifth night, as soon as we walked up to the keno counter, one of the writers (who had become quite friendly, thanks to our generous tokes) announced sadly that he could no longer accept wagers on the 14-spot ticket, as they had found a mistake in their paybooks.

"Oh, is that so?" I replied, feigning surprise.

Throughout this book I've constantly admonished you that

the way to win more and lose less at keno is to play tickets with low house percentages—exclusively! If you follow this advice, when you're lucky, you'll win more. When you have a bad streak, you'll lose less.

Now, I'm going to share with you the secret of how you can be virtually certain of winning at keno; you may have already guessed it from what you've already read in this chapter.

Play tickets with negative house percentages. They must also be in the player's favor. No, the two terms are not synonymous!

With rare exceptions, keno tickets with negative house percentages will fall into one of just two categories.

The first: When the jackpot on a progressive game gets high enough, some tickets may have a negative house percentage and be in the *players'* favor—that is, in the favor of *all* of the players collectively.

The negative house percentage of a high jackpot progressive game suggests a very favorable bet. Indeed, from the time a progressive keno game gets a negative house percentage until the time the jackpot is won, the expectation—according to the law of probabilities—is that the casino will pay out more money to the aggregate of players (including the jackpot) than they will take in on the tickets qualifying for the jackpot.

Here's the kicker. There's no assurance you'll win the jackpot before some other player does, no matter how much money you spend or how many tickets you buy. You can't play keno one-on-one with the house, and you can't get a monopoly on all keno tickets sold. Each and every player has an equal chance to win a progressive game.

Many times, when a jackpot gets large enough, a group of players will pool their money and play as a team, thereby increasing each individual's chances of winning a portion of the jackpot. Of course, there's still a chance that the winner of a huge jackpot will be a grandmotherly type, in a casino for the first time in her life, and who has bought just one keno ticket.

The second: Paybook mistakes, similar to those I wrote about above.

A few truisms: Casinos love to have lots of winners; winners are good for business, because they spread the word and they keep coming back. Casinos know that in the long run they'll always take in more on keno than they'll have to pay out—the house percentages guarantee it. Casinos never deliberately set themselves up to lose at keno, or for that matter, to lose on any game in the house. They want to stay in business.

But ... casinos are run by human beings, and "to err is human."

When the payoffs of a non-progressive keno ticket compute to a negative house percentage, the ticket is in the *player's* (singular) favor, for each and every keno player can (theoretically) win the prizes, over and over again. When you find such a situation, you'll know, without a doubt, that someone has made a big mistake.

Mistakes creep into keno paybooks in numerous ways. The casino employee who's assigned to devise the new pay schedules can easily blunder, particularly if he or she attempts to compute the house percentages by hand. Inexperience and carelessness also take their toll.

More often, though, keno paybook mistakes are simply typographical errors. Typos on charts with lots of numbers are particularly hard to detect. Proofreading by the typographer or printer is ofttimes ineffective, because he doesn't understand how keno payoffs are devised—and, proofreading by the person who prepared the schedules is next to useless, because that person "reads" the numbers as they should be printed, not as they actually are. Just ask any secretary; it's virtually impossible to find errors in copy a person has personally typed.

It's easy to understand how paybook errors also get into a casino's keno computer. For security reasons, keno computer system programs have several levels of access. Revising payoffs in the computer requires a high-level access code in addition to knowledge of the system, so major changes in keno pay schedules are usually installed by a programmer from the company that services the casino's keno computer system.

It's common practice for a casino to give the programmer a copy of their newly-printed paybooks to work from, rather than the source document. Thus, any errors which may be printed in the paybooks get replicated into the computer's data base, and are seldom uncovered thereafter unless someone makes a big hit.

Computers never make mistakes. They always correctly compute payoffs *based on the data entered in the computer*—but, computer programmers can and do err! A programmer might make additional mistakes (not related to paybook errors) by keying in wrong numbers. Programmer errors can rarely be employed to a player's advantage, however, because players don't become aware of them until such time as they have a winning ticket and are paid short or overpaid.

If you're ever in doubt about whether your payoff is correct, ask the keno writer, supervisor, or manager to explain how the payoff was determined. Never settle for an amount that's less than that which you believe you're entitled to receive, until you fully understand *and agree* that the proffered payoff is right.

Above all, don't become intimidated just because the keno department is busy, or because there's a long line of people behind you waiting to be served. After all, it's *your* money, and you're entitled to be paid accurately!

When a mistake in the preparation or printing of a casino's keno paybooks promises a higher payoff than was contemplated by the casino, what happens?

Well, if the same erroneous payoffs were programmed into the keno computer, chances are you'll be paid the amount printed in the paybooks without any hesitation. Keno writers are busy and work by rote. Seldom will a writer try to re-think what the computer indicates is the correct amount due the customer, but, if a payoff is large enough to require approval by a supervisor, manager, or pit boss, it's possible for a paybook error to be caught.

If the computer figures differ from the paybook numbers, the keno manager or someone with even more authority will have to decide which amount to pay. I interviewed the keno managers at a number of casinos, in order to get a cross-section of casino policies. Here are some of their comments:

Casino A: "We would definitely pay what is advertised in the paybooks. The customer has no idea that there is an error, and plays according to the printed material. We have never had this situation happen to us. I double and triple check our paybooks and cards, and we dread going to new booklets because of the possibility of a typographical error. It doesn't matter the amount of the mistake, we would pay."

Casino B: "If the amount was small, we would explain to the customer that there was an error in the paybook; if the customer complained or caused a scene we would pay the printed amount. If the mistake was substantial, we would pay only the amount in our computer. If the customer complained, we would call the Gaming Control Board and go on their advice."

Casino C: "We recently had this situation happen to us. We paid the customer the $1,000, even though it was a printer's mistake. Many times keno paybooks contain errors that aren't discovered until a customer wins. We would pay the amount printed in the paybooks and then post a notice at the cage that the booklets contain an error. We would not take that bet again, unless the customer was aware of the correct payoff."

Casino D: "We would pay the amount printed in our keno paybooks. We once had a $900 error, which we paid immediately. We would stand behind our printed material, even if it contained errors. Of course, once we discovered an error, we would pull all booklets ASAP, and pray that there are no errors in our new booklets."

Casino E: "We have never had this happen to us. I would make sure that both the booklets and the computer had the correct payoffs. If it was a matter of a few dollars, we would pay the difference. I'm confident we would never have a large error in our keno paybooks, as we proofread them thoroughly."

Casino F· "If the difference was small, we would pay the

customer, and pull the keno paybooks. If it was a large amount, it would be up to the casino manager."

Casino G: "If the amount was small, we would pay the amount printed in our booklets, and immediately remove them from circulation. If the difference between the correct payoff and what was printed is large, I would have to get permission from management, but strongly believe that they would pay the printed amount. Casinos should stand behind their printed material. All keno managers dread making changes in their keno booklets, as it's very easy for an error to creep in."

Casino H: "We would *not* pay the amount printed in our booklets, if it was in error. We would pay only the amount in our computer. If the customer complained, we would refer him to the Nevada Gaming Control Board. Once we discovered an error, we would immediately remove the booklets from the casino floor."

Casino I: "We have never had a mistake in our paybooks. Our booklets are checked and rechecked by many different people before they are put into use. I cannot comment on what we would do if a mistake did slip through." I didn't have the heart to enlighten the keno manager; Casino I's paybooks in use at the time had three obvious (although inconsequential) errors.

Summing it up: A few casinos will honor all advertised payoffs immediately, even though incorrect, regardless of amount. Other keno managers will pay the amount printed in the keno paybooks, provided that there isn't a large difference between the payoff shown in their computer ... but if the discrepancy between the intended payoff and what was printed in the paybooks is substantial, they will ask the Nevada Gaming Control Board for a decision. In any instance, as soon as a mistake is discovered the casino will post a disclaimer in the keno cage or remove the paybooks from the casino floor, and limit future losses by refusing to accept further bets on that proposition.

Most casinos now permit a keno ticket to be played for up to a thousand consecutive games. During a long multi-game series a player might win a misprinted payoff numerous times, and it's quite likely that the error will not be discovered until after all games have been played and the player attempts to cash in his ticket. I have not heard of any instances of this happening yet, but when it does occur it will be a most interesting situation.

O.K. You've been playing keno for days. Up to this point you've lost more than $5,000, but at long last ... *you've hit the big one!*

You step up to the keno cage. According to the casino's keno paybook, you've just won $85,000!

The keno writer tells you, "Sorry, there's a mistake in our paybooks. You've only won $15,000."

What do you do? Be content with your $10,000 profit, or demand that the casino pays you the amount promised in their keno paybooks?

I don't for a moment believe that any casino ever wants to cheat its players. After all, the only way they get repeat customers and new customers is to have winners, and lots of them ... and good publicity, not bad publicity.

However, some casinos may be reluctant to stand behind their mistakes, particularly when thousands or tens of thousands of dollars are involved. If a casino does refuse to honor the payoffs in their keno paybooks there are a number of steps you can and should take.

First of all, don't get upset with the keno writer. He or she has authority to pay you only the amount that's shown by the casino's computer. Start by discussing the problem with the keno manager—although most keno managers cannot approve payment of a discrepancy as large as the one in our hypothetical example.

Your next step is to explain your problem to the casino manager. He may decide to pay you in full, to promote customer goodwill and to avoid adverse publicity. If a large amount of money is involved, however, there's a strong possibility that he'll refer you to the Nevada Gaming Control Board.

I spoke with E. J. Vogel, an agent at the Nevada Gaming Control Board. He stated that the Board is very concerned about printed material that may mislead the public, either intentionally or negligently. As a result, casinos are held to a high standard.

Vogel informed me that the Gaming Control Board examines all of the facts before issuing a ruling, but, in general, casinos are accountable for promises made in their printed material, *including those made in error*. Therefore, in most instances, casinos must honor the payoffs listed in their keno paybooks. An exception would be when the casino is aware of a mistake and has prominently posted a disclaimer in their keno department.

I've given the subject of paybook mistakes extensive treatment in this chapter because playing tickets which have percentages in the player's favor virtually guarantees that you will win. You must, however, play enough games for the results of your play to average out to the expected results predicted by the law of probabilities.

At times, the casino may cancel a game after you've turned in just one winning ticket. On other occasions you'll be able to buy player's-advantage tickets for days or even weeks before someone becomes aware that you're winning because of a paybook mistake. And, if and when the casino finally catches on, in most instances they'll have to pay you everything you've won on the tickets you've already purchased.

It would therefore stand to reason that when you find a rare player's-advantage opportunity—always be very certain that your analysis of the payoff schedule is correct—the best strategy is to play multi-race tickets for as many games as you can afford.

Saying a couple of prayers won't do any harm, either.

Chapter 39

VIDEO KENO

Video keno is a favorite of the local players. And no wonder! You can win as much as $2,500 for a wager of just 25¢, $10,000 for just four quarters!

Regular (live) keno moves relatively slowly—about twelve games per hour. It can't be played faster, because of the time it takes to write up tickets and the time needed for all of the keno runners to complete their rounds. With video keno you can set your own pace, up to eight games per minute! And, of course, the more games you play, the more chances you have of winning.

Video keno machines have colorful TV-type display screens, with great graphics and sound effects—chirps, beeps, clicks, etc.

Most video keno machines have two screens. The upper screen shows what you can win for the number of coins played and the number of spots selected. The more numbers you mark, the higher the potential payoff; but, more catches are required in order to win. With each additional coin played, the amount you can win increases proportionately.

The lower screen is laid out much like a paper keno ticket, with ten columns and eight rows displaying numbers 1 through 80. The numbers you select and the numbers picked by the machine are indicated on this screen.

PLAYER'S EDGE PLUS DUAL-SCREEN VIDEO KENO
manufactured by International Game Technology

Some versions of video keno have only one screen. The CRT display is similar in appearance to the lower screen of the two-screen models. A printed pay scale tells you how much you can win, according to the number of coins played, spots marked, and numbers caught.

Playing video keno is very easy. First, drop in one to four quarters. (Some video keno machines accept nickels or dollars, but the vast majority of them are designed for quarter play.)

Before selecting the numbers you want to play, press the *erase* button to clear the screen. Then, using the light pen attached to the machine, touch the screen display to mark the numbers you hope will make you a winner. (Instead of a light pen, some video keno machines have a keyboard.) You can change the numbers as often as you wish; just erase and start over again.

Push the *start* button and the machine's computer selects twenty numbers at random, at the rate of about three per second. When a number is selected it changes color on the screen. Most keno machines "beep" whenever one of the numbers you've marked is matched. With a little luck, the computer will pick as many of your numbers as you need to make you a winner of as much as $10,000!

Earlier models of video keno machines dispense the coins automatically every time you have a winner. Your winnings appear on the screen as *credits* on newer machines. You can play these credits just like coins, one to four at a time. At any time, you can push the *collect winnings* button and what you've won will be dispensed into a tray—one coin for each credit.

When you win approximately $300 (or more)—the exact figure varies from casino to casino—the change light flashes, a bell rings, and an attendant quickly brings your winnings in cash!

Video keno machines can be located anywhere in the casino, but there'll usually be a bank of them close to the keno lounge, for the convenience of those also playing live keno.

With live keno you have the possibility of winning as much as the casino's aggregate limit; at some places, this is a million dollars. Except for the progressive machines, the most you can win per game on video keno is $10,000 (for four quarters). To compensate for the smaller maximum payoff, the house percentages for most video keno machines are considerably lower than the PCs on most live keno tickets.

In fact, the house percentages on video keno machines are about the same as the PCs on video poker and reel-type slot machines, but the top payoff on video keno is usually greater.

By way of comparison: To equal the top pay on video keno (per coin wagered), video poker would have to pay $12,500 for a royal flush instead of the usual $1,000. And, the top jackpot on a $1.00 3-coin multiplier slot machine would have to be $30,000! Few $1.00 slots have payoffs this high, except for the progressives and Megabucks machines.

There's also a down side to video keno; the smaller payoffs won't come as often as they do on video poker or the slots. If you're looking a for a lot of action, video keno may not be your game. But, if you want a realistic chance to be a really big winner for a minimum cost, you'll have to look a long time to find a better game to play.

The house percentages on video keno vary from casino to casino, just as they do with live keno. Naturally, you'll want to play where the PCs are lowest. The lower the PC, the longer you can play before you exhaust your keno budget for the day. And, the longer you play, the more chances you have of becoming a big winner!

Before you start playing you'll want to determine which pay schedule the casino has programmed into their video keno machines. It won't cost you anything to find this out if the machine has a printed payoff schedule—just compare the posted payoffs with the following pay charts.

However, on two-screen video keno machines you'll need to drop in a quarter, erase any numbers that have been selected, and then mark one number at a time. Each time you add an additional number the payoffs for the number of spots selected will be displayed on the upper screen.

There are not nearly as many different pay schedules for video keno as there are for live keno. The manufacturers of the machines give the casinos a limited number of payoff options, unless a casino is willing to pay for specially designed software and computer chips. Most machines have one of the following pay schedules, but casinos have a proclivity for making payoff changes, and making them often. If you encounter a machine that doesn't utilize one of the following pay schedules, you'll have to figure out the house percentages for yourself.

Please note: The following pay charts list the number of *coins* paid for a *one coin bet*. If the payoffs displayed on the machine are in dollars, you'll have to convert the charts to dollars, or convert the machine's pay schedules into coins.

Schedule A. When you see a lot of locals playing video keno, chances are that the machines they're playing have the payoff schedule I call Schedule A. You won't find many regulars playing keno machines if they have higher house percentages. Most casinos have their 25¢ video keno machines set to schedule A.

25¢ VIDEO KENO – SCHEDULE A

SPOTS SELECTED	• • • • • • • • • • • • • • SPOTS CAUGHT • • • • • • • • • • • • • •										HOUSE PERCENTAGE
	1	2	3	4	5	6	7	8	9	10	
1	3	-	-	-	-	-	-	-	-	-	25.0000
2	0	15	-	-	-	-	-	-	-	-	9.8101
3	0	2	46	-	-	-	-	-	-	-	8.4226
4	0	2	5	91	-	-	-	-	-	-	7.9721
5	0	0	3	12	810	-	-	-	-	-	8.0698
6	0	0	3	4	70	1600	-	-	-	-	7.3319
7	0	0	1	2	21	400	7000	-	-	-	7.5568
8	0	0	0	2	12	98	1652	10000	-	-	7.6895
9	0	0	0	1	6	44	335	4700	10000	-	7.9986
10	0	0	0	0	5	24	142	1000	4500	10000	7.4489

Schedule B. The house percentages are very close to those of Schedule A, but the payoffs are somewhat different. For example, catching 8-out-of-8 pays 10,000 coins on a Schedule A machine, but only 8,000 coins on a Schedule B machine. Catching 6-out-of-8 pays 122 coins on Schedule B, but only 98 coins on Schedule A.

25¢ VIDEO KENO – SCHEDULE B

SPOTS SELECTED	SPOTS CAUGHT										HOUSE PERCENTAGE
	1	2	3	4	5	6	7	8	9	10	
2	0	15	-	-	-	-	-	-	-	-	9.8101
3	0	3	37	-	-	-	-	-	-	-	7.0351
4	0	2	4	105	-	-	-	-	-	-	8.0081
5	0	0	3	12	810	-	-	-	-	-	8.0698
6	0	0	3	5	76	1200	-	-	-	-	7.7801
7	0	0	1	3	18	360	7000	-	-	-	7.8575
8	0	0	0	1	15	122	1500	8000	-	-	7.9770
9	0	0	0	1	3	58	350	5000	9000	-	7.9788
10	0	0	0	0	3	29	140	1300	5000	10000	7.9484

Schedule C. Notice how much higher the house percentages are on Schedule C! Further, the maximum payoff for a 25¢ bet on a Schedule C machine is only $625; most everywhere else, it's $2,500!

25¢ VIDEO KENO – SCHEDULE C

SPOTS SELECTED	SPOTS CAUGHT										HOUSE PERCENTAGE
2	0	14	-	-	-	-	-	-	-	-	15.8228
3	0	3	30	-	-	-	-	-	-	-	16.7478
4	0	2	4	70	-	-	-	-	-	-	18.7300
5	0	0	4	20	400	-	-	-	-	-	16.4443
6	0	0	2	8	60	1000	-	-	-	-	19.7334
7	0	0	2	4	15	120	2500	-	-	-	16.2816
8	0	0	1	3	7	60	500	2500	-	-	17.9490
9	0	0	0	2	8	25	230	1500	2500	-	18.1203
10	0	0	0	2	3	13	80	500	2000	2500	19.2724

Schedule D. This is another payoff schedule with PCs that are much too high.

25¢ VIDEO KENO – SCHEDULE D

SPOTS SELECTED	SPOTS CAUGHT										HOUSE PERCENTAGE
	1	2	3	4	5	6	7	8	9	10	
2	0	14	-	-	-	-	-	-	-	-	15.8228
3	0	2	40	-	-	-	-	-	-	-	16.7478
4	0	2	3	100	-	-	-	-	-	-	13.8646
5	0	0	2	14	800	-	-	-	-	-	14.6897
6	0	0	2	4	92	1500	-	-	-	-	14.7933
7	0	0	1	2	15	348	7760	-	-	-	14.6921
8	0	0	0	1	12	112	1500	8000	-	-	15.8345
9	0	0	0	1	3	47	352	4700	9000	-	15.1297
10	0	0	0	0	3	28	140	1000	4800	10000	13.2813

Schedule E. You won't find many locals *or* tourists playing video keno on machines with this pay schedule. Even the most naive player quickly discovers that machines set to the Schedule E payoffs don't give you a fair shake. Steer clear of Schedule E machines and save your money.

25¢ VIDEO KENO – SCHEDULE E

SPOTS SELECTED	••••••••••••• SPOTS CAUGHT •••••••••••••										HOUSE PERCENTAGE
	1	2	3	4	5	6	7	8	9	10	
1	3	-	-	-	-	-	-	-	-	-	25.0000
2	0	14	-	-	-	-	-	-	-	-	15.8228
3	0	2	40	-	-	-	-	-	-	-	16.7478
4	0	2	4	80	-	-	-	-	-	-	15.6666
5	0	0	3	16	600	-	-	-	-	-	16.7763
6	0	0	2	6	80	1000	-	-	-	-	19.2497
7	0	0	1	3	16	360	3000	-	-	-	19.3463
8	0	0	0	2	16	25	800	6000	-	-	33.0545
9	0	0	0	1	5	44	300	3000	8000	-	19.0152
10	0	0	0	0	3	24	140	1100	2000	10000	18.2327

Schedule F. The house percentages are slightly lower on machines with Schedule F payoffs than on Schedule A machines when you play 4, 5, or 8 spots; they're slightly lower on the Schedule A machines when you play 6, 7, 9, or 10 numbers.

In the long run, you'll win more and lose less if you choose the machine that has the lowest PC for the number of spots you play. But, the tale doesn't always end with house percentages.

The Schedule F video keno machines are the electronic equivalent of low-end live keno tickets. Schedule F machines pay one coin (for each coin bet) for catching 2-out-of-5, 3-out-of-8, 3-out-of-9, and 4-out-of-10.

These catches don't pay at all on Schedule A machines, so, if you play 5, 8, 9, or 10 spots, you'll win more often on Schedule F machines. These little one-coin wins cost you through the nose.

Except for the catch-8 and catch-9 pays on the 10-spot, the big payoffs are considerably higher on Schedule A machines.

Catching 5-out-of-5 pays 810 coins (per coin bet) on Schedule A, but only 260 coins on Schedule F. Catching 7-out-of-8 pays 1,652 coins on Schedule A, 500 on Schedule F. Catching 7-out-of-9 pays 335 on Schedule A, 181 on Schedule F.

The above catches are fairly common, so the higher payoffs on Schedule A machines can make the difference between going home a winner or a loser.

Catching 8-out-of-8 pays 8,000 coins, 9-out-of-9 pays 9,000 coins, and 10-out-of-10 pays 10,000 coins on Schedule F machines. On Schedule A machines, all of these catches pay 10,000 coins.

Despite the fact that the house percentages are similar, I would not recommend playing a machine with Schedule F payoffs. Bear in mind that you're playing keno because it's a long-shot game and you want to make a big score for a small wager. You're not playing just to win back the amount of your bet—that's like eating soup with a fork!

25¢ VIDEO KENO – SCHEDULE F

SPOTS SELECTED	************** SPOTS CAUGHT ***************										HOUSE PERCENTAGE
2	0	15	-	-	-	-	-	-	-	-	9.8101
3	0	2	46	-	-	-	-	-	-	-	8.4226
4	0	2	6	77	-	-	-	-	-	-	7.9361
5	0	1	3	19	260	-	-	-	-	-	8.0303
6	0	0	2	10	71	1200	-	-	-	-	8.0409
7	0	0	1	3	19	350	7000	-	-	-	7.7258
8	0	0	1	3	13	47	500	8000	-	-	7.6541
9	0	0	1	2	4	21	181	2400	9000	-	8.3330
10	0	0	0	1	3	17	135	1300	5000	10000	7.7973

Schedule G. Schedule G machines yield house percentages about two points higher than the PCs that are the accepted standard at most casinos (Schedule A). Players of Schedule G machines will ultimately win less and lose more.

25¢ VIDEO KENO – SCHEDULE G

SPOTS SELECTED	************* SPOTS CAUGHT ***************										HOUSE PERCENTAGE
	1	2	3	4	5	6	7	8	9	10	
2	0	15	-	-	-	-	-	-	-	-	9.8101
3	0	2	45	-	-	-	-	-	-	-	9.8101
4	0	2	3	112	-	-	-	-	-	-	10.1885
5	0	0	2	18	800	-	-	-	-	-	9.8528
6	0	0	2	4	105	1500	-	-	-	-	10.7690
7	0	0	1	2	15	416	7760	-	-	-	9.7140
8	0	0	0	1	13	130	1500	8000	-	-	9.7442
9	0	0	0	1	3	50	403	4700	9000	-	10.3963
10	0	0	0	0	3	30	147	1000	4800	10000	9.8576

5¢ video keno. The following payoff schedule is typical for 5¢ video keno. As you can see, the house percentages are nearly double those of Schedule A.

Nickel machines often have a progressive jackpot, which you can win for catching 10/10 spots with four coins in. When the progressive reaches $20,000 the house percentage for the 10-spot drops to 12.5577%. At $100,000, it's down to 8.06919%, and at $243,820.60, the house percentage is actually in the players' favor! Before you get too excited about this, let me remind you that the odds of catching 10-out-of-10 are 1 in 8,911,711. This means that for every $1,782,342.20 played you can expect to hit the progressive jackpot once.

At 5¢ per play the nickel video keno machines can be a lot of fun—sort of like an adult version of Pac-Man. Don't expect to make any money on them, however. If you're willing to play the nickel machines four coins at a time, add another 5¢ and play a quarter machine instead. The PCs are lower, and you could win as much as $2,500!

5¢ VIDEO KENO											
SPOTS SELECTED	************* SPOTS CAUGHT *************										HOUSE PERCENTAGE
	0	1	2	3	4	5	6	7	8	9	10	
2	1	0	5	-	-	-	-	-	-	-	-	13.9241
3	1	0	2	11	-	-	-	-	-	-	-	15.3359
4	1	0	1	5	40	-	-	-	-	-	-	14.0268
5	1	0	0	3	10	400	-	-	-	-	-	14.2117
6	1	0	0	2	5	49	1000	-	-	-	-	15.0398
7	1	0	0	2	2	22	250	3000	-	-	-	15.2777
8	1	0	0	1	2	10	40	500	5000	-	-	15.4290
9	1	0	0	0	1	5	40	400	1000	7500	-	15.5661
10	1	0	0	0	0	5	25	120	500	2000	10000	13.5676

25¢ progressive games. There are a few video keno machines around that have the Schedule A payoffs *plus* pay a progressive jackpot if you hit 8/8, 9/9, or 10/10 with four coins in. If you're going to play four quarters at a time anyway, you might want to try the 8-spot when the jackpot gets high enough. (The odds of catching 8/8 are 1 in 230,115.)

Number of spots. Note that some video keno machines let you play one number, while others start with two spots. No matter.

I don't recommend playing *any* 1-spot keno, whether live or video. The percentages are too much against you, the potential winnings much too small.

A *Keno Newsletter* reader brought to my attention a poorly-written and shoddily-printed paper from an outfit in Kingman, Arizona, which espoused the theory that certain patterns be played, in order to have more winning video keno games.

This theory is a bunch of hokum, hogwash, balderdash, nonsense, gibberish, and old-fashioned bunkum. It just ain't so.

The random number generators in computers select *one number at a time*—not groups of numbers. Consequently, the patterns formed by random numbers also occur randomly.

Over a period of time, every conceivable pattern will show up. Simple patterns with fewer numbers will "repeat" more often than complicated patterns with more numbers, for the same reason that it's easier to catch four numbers out of four than eight numbers out of eight.

Sometimes a pattern will *appear* to repeat, but it's because some patterns are more noticeable. If a particular pattern appears once it isn't a sign that it will or won't appear again in the near future. If it does, it's only by chance.

Further, each draw stands on its own, and you can *never* predict which numbers or which patterns will show up next.

From the standpoint of winning, it doesn't make any difference at all which numbers you pick, and whether they form a pattern or not.

Do I play patterns? Always! When numbers are scattered around the screen I find it difficult to know when I've got a hit, particularly if the "beep" isn't working on the machine I'm playing. The only reason I play patterns is because it's easier on my eyes!

I wrote a program for my office computer that accurately duplicates the action of the video keno machines, and I can play it automatically for hundreds of thousands of games at a time.

Everything that you experience on a video keno machine I

see on my computer. There are winning streaks, there are losing streaks, and patterns appear to repeat. When I change my numbers, it seems that, a few plays later, all of my previously selected numbers come up—and it's just as frustrating on my computer as it is on the video keno machines!

Sure, variations from randomness can be built into a computer program, but they are *not* built into mine, and yet they happen. If they *were* to be built into a video keno machine, the Nevada Gaming Control Board would close up any casino using it.

The casinos *never* have to resort to "fixing" the computer programs of video keno machines. They know that over a period of time they'll make their house percentage.

At maximum play of about eight games per minute, with one coin played, each video keno machine will process $120 per hour. At a PC of 7.5% each machine will hold an average of $9.00 per hour.

If a machine is played just twelve hours a day, this amounts to a profit for the casino (after paying all winners) of $39,420 per machine per year.

Some people may play slower, some people will play more than one coin at a time, and some machines receive more than twelve hours of play per day, but using the $39,420 figure as a benchmark, you can readily see that the casinos don't have to resort to cheating in order to make a darn good profit on video keno.

Another point ... machine-hopping doesn't help you win more, nor does it cause you to win any less. There's no such thing as a "hot" or a "cold" machine. Just because a machine has had a big payoff doesn't mean that it will (or will not) hit another one in the immediate future. The odds of winning are exactly the same each and every play!

Chapter 40

HOW TO WIN AT VIDEO KENO AND VIDEO POKER?

I have the distinct pleasure of knowing a very classy lady. This lady shops almost exclusively at Neiman Marcus and Saks; when she goes to any other store she refers to it as "slumming." She won't even set foot inside of K-Mart, as she's afraid that one of her friends might see her there.

She's also extremely intelligent. She has a Master's degree in Business Administration, and is an adjunct professor at Southern Nevada Community College.

She is a gourmet cook, and she enjoys dining in fine restaurants. Some of her favorites in Las Vegas are Michael's (in the Barbary Coast), The Tillerman, Rafters, and Piero's.

This lady also likes to "drop a few quarters" in the video poker and keno machines. She claims that it's a lot cheaper, more fun, and more therapeutic than going to a psychiatrist.

All gamblers have superstitions about the things that will help them win, and this lady is no exception. She believes that when she finds a coin, preferably head up, it is a sure sign that she will get a royal flush or a big keno hit in the very immediate future.

Her eyes are as sharp as those of an eagle, and she can spot a coin from twenty or thirty feet away. It's uncanny, but even at a distance she can differentiate between a product of the U.S. Mint and a wadded up chewing-gum wrapper. I certainly can't.

Few people stoop over to pick up small change these days; it's no wonder that so many of today's teenagers consider pennies and other small coins worthless and throw them away. Not this lady. She never fails to pick up money that she discovers lying on the ground.

She never spends this "found money," and keeps it in a large jar for luck. Over the years she's accumulated more than a gallon of the lesser coins of the realm.

This lady has made a discovery—a discovery that is of invaluable assistance when she has the urge to sit on a casino stool and exercise a few quarters, but hasn't found any "lucky" money.

She's discovered that the cracks in the driveways of McDonald's drive-throughs are veritable gold mines, a bonanza of lost coins waiting for her to pluck them up. And so, this lady of distinction and class, this connoisseur of the finer things in life, can occasionally be seen entering McDonald's, but always by way of the entrance nearest to the drive-through order window.

Of course, there's absolutely not a shred of truth in her superstition. It's total nonsense. The odds of winning are exactly the same whenever you play a machine, whether you have found a few coins or not.

There must be some other reason why, over the last several months, my wife has hit twelve royal flushes and I've only gotten two.

Chapter 41

TOURNAMENTS AND CONTESTS

Scenario 1. You and your spouse/friend/traveling companion decide to come to Las Vegas to try your lucky numbers. You have a bankroll of $500 and agree to buy exactly $500 worth of keno tickets, taking home whatever you win after running the money through just once.

If you play tickets with a 28% house advantage—which is about par for Las Vegas keno—the law of probabilities says that the average return for your $500 investment will be $360. Of course, you might hit it really big—or, you could play the entire $500 and wind up with nothing but pocket change. It all depends on what tickets you choose and how lucky those numbers really were. For now, let's agree that your cost of keno play is going to be the statistical average of $140.

Las Vegas is the best vacation bargain in the world, but even so, a good room in a top hotel for two nights will cost about $120, and food for your stay another hundred or so. Total cost of your trip, about $360 (not including transportation).

Scenario 2. You and your s/f/tc decide to enter a keno tournament. The buy-in is $500, for which you receive a full $500 worth of keno play—and, you get to keep all of your winnings.

You'll quickly learn that when you enter a keno tournament the casino treats you like royalty. They'll provide a deluxe hotel room for you and your guest, at no charge, for the length of the tournament.

The tournament starts with a get-acquainted party, complete with a lavish buffet. You'll get a surfeit of free cocktails throughout the several-day event. Each tournament contestant is given a lovely gift, compliments of the casino, as a memento of his or her stay.

As part of the tournament package you'll receive enough vouchers for both of you to dine free during your entire visit.

There'll be friendly competition among the entrants for the cash prizes which will be awarded to the players who win the most money during the course of the tournament.

And, after the tournament ends, there'll be a gala awards party, where cash prizes, trophies, and plaques will be presented.

If your luck was the same as in Scenario 1, the total cost of your Las Vegas trip will be the $140 lost on keno (assuming that you'll lose the statistical average ... of course, your goal is to be a winner). By entering the tournament you've saved at least $220. However ... if your total keno winnings put you among the top twenty entrants, in addition to the money you won you'll get a cash prize of up to $5,000!

Keno tournaments are an increasingly popular way to play keno. A well-run keno tournament can be a lot of fun, a mini-vacation at a minimum cost. Participation in a tournament can also be very profitable, if you have a fair amount of luck.

There are two distinct types of keno tournaments; the type of tournament can usually be determined by the term used on the registration form. Some require payment of an "entry fee." At others, there is no entry fee, but you must make a specified "buy-in."

At buy-in type tournaments you'll be given special scrip in the amount of your buy-in. You'll use the scrip to purchase your keno tickets, but everything you win will be paid in cash, for you get to keep all the money won on the games played during the tournament.

With a little luck you'll be able to win back the cost of your buy-in, and perhaps a good deal more! The players winning the most *money* in buy-in type tournaments are awarded the tournament prizes.

You also play with scrip at entry fee type tournaments, but you may receive several dollars in scrip for each dollar of the entry fee. This is an illusory benefit, however, for whatever you "win" on the tournament games counts only as "points," which are of no value other than to establish the tournament winners.

That's right, you *don't* get to keep what you win on the entry fee type tournament games. At the end of the event, the cash prizes are awarded to the players who have accumulated the most *points*. Everyone else leaves with just their memories.

The total prizes awarded in a keno tournament can range from a few thousand dollars to more than $100,000, depending upon the buy-in or entry fee, tournament type, and the number of players.

The buy-in or entry fee, rules, and amenities vary from casino to casino and tournament to tournament, so be sure to find out all of the particulars before signing up as an entrant.

There's one minor downside to playing in a keno tournament —you're stuck with the keno house percentages at the casino where the tournament is being held. You can still play that casino's lowest house percentage rates, and should always do so to increase your chances of winning more money or points.

The buy-in type keno tournament described in scenario 2 (above) is based on the Stardust's extremely successful twice-yearly tournaments, which are hosted by keno manager Anita Houchin, a very special, lovely, personable, and knowledgeable lady. Anita is unique, definitely one-of-a-kind ... and has forty years of experience in keno.

Anita's advice on tournament strategy? Here's what she's observed at the Stardust:

"Everybody plays keno differently, but what usually wins is a straight ticket that pays about $7,000. One year, we had four winners of more than $7,000." (A catch of 6/6 or 7/8 on a Stardust $5.00 ticket pays $7,000.)

Some casinos have keno "tournaments" with no entry fee. If there's a buy-in at all, it will be for a minimum number of games. I prefer to call them "contests," for they differ markedly from the regular tournaments.

You won't get the free hotel room, dining allowance, cocktail parties, entrant gifts, or other amenities. Unless there's a buy-in, you'll be competing with all of the casino's other keno players.

Contest rules and prizes differ tremendously.

The contest winners might be determined by the largest accumulation of winnings during the period of the contest, which can be from a few hours to several months; or, perhaps the winners will be established by the largest amount won on any single ticket played during the contest.

Some contests permit you to play any keno ticket offered by the casino; others require you to play a specific type of ticket, such as a 20-spot or catch-all.

Keno contests offer a wide variety of prizes; you might win a cash prize of several hundred to several thousand dollars; free dinners, complimentary rooms, tickets to the casino's showroom, vacation certificates, and other hotel services. Occasionally, merchandise awards are featured; perhaps you'll win a big-screen television set, VCR, stereo, cruise, or even a new car!

Call the keno department or tournament office at your favorite casinos (most have a toll-free 800 prefix phone number) to find out about their current tournaments and contests, and to get on their mailing lists so that you'll be notified about future events.

Chapter 42

WHAT IS LUCK?

The very first time I played video keno, I dropped four quarters in the machine, selected ten numbers, and watched while eight of my ten numbers came up—for a win of $1,000!

Now, the odds of hitting 8-out-of-10 are 1 in 7,384—yet I did it on the first try! That was luck.

Luck—good or bad—can be described as *temporary deviations from the results that can be expected by chance.* Some people seem to be born losers; others win, and win consistently.

Why is this so? Do the winners have some magic formula? Do they practice positive thinking? Do they have ESP? Were they born under a lucky star?

The explanation is very simple. Anyone can have a "lucky streak." It's merely a matter of being in the right place at the right time, *and making the right decisions.*

I'll never forget my first craps game. It was at the Holiday Casino, many years ago.

It was my turn to throw the dice. I was playing the "don't pass" line, for someone had told me that "don't pass" was a good bet to make.

I kept catching "7" or "11" on the first roll. If another number came up, it repeated a short time later. I lost my wager with virtually every roll of the dice.

The table filled with black ($100) chips. Other players were yelling excitedly, goading me on to success. I continued losing.

Shortly, the pit boss and several other casino executives began scrutinizing me very, very carefully. I knew that something unusual was going on, but at the time I had no concept of what it might be.

I broke out in a cold sweat. I wanted to stop betting or pass the dice to another player, but didn't know whether I was allowed to do so or not.

I held the dice for 45 minutes. Even with my minimum bets, I lost nearly $200.

In the meantime, my wife had migrated to the opposite end of the craps table. The man next to her confided, "Look at that fool over there! I've never seen such a long winning streak, and he's betting against himself!" She never admitted that she was married to "that fool," but quickly learned the right way to play, and more than made up for my losses.

It should become apparent that luck bears no relationship whatsoever to the status of being a winner or a loser. I lost money on a once-in-a-lifetime lucky streak playing craps because I didn't know what I was doing.

Consistent winners utilize techniques that maximize their chances for winning and minimize their chances for losing; these are the foundations of the playing strategies and money management systems that gamblers have developed over the years.

Most keno players are full of myths and superstitions about "luck" and how to pick winning numbers, and are always more than willing to share their misinformation with you. Pay no attention to them. If you want to win more and lose less playing keno, make your own luck! Concentrate on fact and reality, which can be summarized very succinctly.

1. It doesn't make any difference which numbers you mark. *Over a period of time, all numbers are called equally.*

2. In the long haul, the casino will always win, and the aggregate of players will lose. *Players would not lose as much as*

they do now if they avoided tickets that have high house percentages.

3. Some people will win a whole lot of money playing keno, but most keno players will lose most of the time. *Winning more and losing less is not a matter of luck ... it's playing smart.* To paraphrase an old saying, "The smarter I play, the luckier I become."

4. Playing smart means playing tickets with low house percentages. *The lower the house percentage, the more you'll win when you win, and the less you'll lose when you lose.*

5. Never try to guess which keno tickets are the best bets. *It's impossible to determine which rate tickets have low PCs just by reading the casino's keno paybooks.*

One Way To Change Your Luck

I was talking with a keno player who was really crying the blues. His luck had never been the best, he told me, but of late he just couldn't seem to win anything.

"I'd sell my soul to the Devil for one good win," he exclaimed jokingly.

Just then the next game started. As each number appeared on the keno flashboard his eyes got larger and larger. Seven of his eight numbers were called, for a win of $4,000. It was a very shaken man, indeed, who went up to collect his money.

Chapter 43

HONESTY IS THE ONLY POLICY

When Bill Cosby performs in Las Vegas he often comments about the game of keno in his comedy monologue.

"To play keno," he explains, "all you have to do is mark the numbers you want to win on a piece of paper, and give the paper and your money to The Man.

"Now remember, you're telling him which numbers you want him to pick, and if he picks them, he's going to have to pay you a whole lot of money."

Then, with a sly grin, Cosby asks, to no one in particular, "Tell me, do you *really* think he's going to pick your numbers?"

The question always brings a huge laugh from the audience.

Despite Bill Cosby's humorous story, the truth is that keno games are scrupulously honest. There's absolutely no reason for them to be otherwise, for the casinos have a healthy house percentage built into virtually every keno ticket they sell. Even more important, no casino would ever risk losing its valuable gaming license by rigging a keno game to save a few dollars, or even hundreds of thousands of dollars. The potential consequences would far outweigh any possible benefit.

On the other hand, dishonest employees and players, often in cahoots with each other, have always been a source of concern for the casinos.

Let me explain how the game worked in the days B.C. (before computers), when keno tickets were written by brush.

The keno blank marked by the customer was copied by a keno writer. The copy, called an "outside" ticket, was given to the customer as a receipt for his bet. The customer-prepared copy, called an "inside" ticket, was retained by the keno writer until just before the start of the draw.

In an effort to eliminate liability for writer errors, casinos printed a rule in their keno paybooks stating that all payoffs were determined according to the "original" (inside) ticket. Casinos went to great length to establish their position that any game's "original" tickets were those submitted for that game only, regardless of whether they were hand-written by the customer or replayed tickets.

When a game was "closed out" just before the draw began, all of the inside tickets were handed up to the supervisor in charge, who sat at the "keno desk." The keno desk was located in an elevated position behind the keno writers, in order to provide the supervisor or shift boss a good view of everything that went on in the keno lounge.

After the game had been called the winners lined up to collect on their tickets. All larger pays had to be approved by the supervisor, who would verify the matched numbers on the original inside ticket, compute the amount of the win, and announce it to the keno writer. However, to speed up the game, if a player had won less than $10 or so the keno writer would pay the customer without any approval, and without verificatation of the numbers marked on the inside ticket.

Outside tickets probably caused keno personnel more headaches "in the days B.C." than anything else. Even the best writers would mismark a ticket periodically, and only too frequently, wanting to have their cake and eat it too, players demanded payment on a mismarked outside ticket when it worked to their advantage.

But, when it was in their favor to do so, players would argue that the only "original" ticket was the one they wrote for the first game played, perhaps 25 games previously. Many times a keno manager, rather than lose a regular customer, would back down from the established policy and make the payoff anyway.

It was sometimes possible for players to cheat the system by writing an inside ticket after the game had been called and the winning numbers known, and somehow get the scam ticket placed among the inside tickets from the already-called game. To do so required a conspiracy between the player, the keno writer, and the supervisor. It didn't happen often, but it did happen.

Strange as it may seem, there was a time when some casinos allowed—even encouraged—keno writers to accept, spot, and condition tickets for a game after the ball draw started, right up to the last number called.

This practice was eventually halted, but not before at least one player at a downtown Las Vegas casino waited for the draw to begin, X'd out the first six numbers called, and submitted his ticket to be written. You can imagine the stir such a "catch" created. Collusion? Possibly. Was the player paid for his winning 6-out-of-6 ticket? Some old-timers recollect that he was not, but others believe he was.

One keno writer found an opportunity for minor embezzlement, good for $40 or $50 per day. The writer, being groomed for promotion, worked the keno desk while the shift boss or second man were on lunch break. During his time on the desk the writer removed the staple from each "book" of tickets he had written at his writer's station previously, pocketed a number of the tickets, and restapled those remaining. Later, he surreptitiously took the matching dollar value of the tickets from his cash drawer.

The writer accidently flawed his "perfect crime" by removing the inside ticket of an $1,100 winner. The following morning the keno auditor looked in vain for the ticket originally submitted by the customer. Upon further investigation, the auditor discovered the second stapling.

A somewhat similar theft occurred at another casino, where

the writers were not trusted, but desk personnel were. There, it was the policy for writers to hand up to the desk all $20s, $50s, and $100s, as they received them from players. A certain desk person removed tickets from all of the writers' "books," dropped them crumpled up into his wastebasket, and at his convenience, pocketed many dollars from the stash of bills at hand.

As Ripley would say, believe it or not, this practice had apparently gone unnoticed for months before someone's idle curiosity prompted an inspection of the rumpled tickets.

Keno computers have completely eliminated these opportunities, but thieves will always find a way.

A casino in the northern part of Nevada discovered that their keno manager had set up a top-and-bottom ticket with a player edge of about 80%. The ticket got a lot of action; it's said that friends and relatives of the keno manager "won" several hundred thousand dollars before casino management caught on. Of course, the manager could have made an honest mistake when devising the pay table. Sure.

The casinos won't cheat the players, but the players can still get cheated. They can cheat themselves.

If an 8-spot $1.00 ticket pays $50,000, and the casino's aggregate limit is $50,000, it's folly to play the ticket for more than $1.00. If you play the ticket for $2, $5, $10, or any other amount, and all of your numbers come in, all the casino will pay you is $50,000. If you win $32,000 and your spouse wins $48,000 in the same $50,000 aggregate limit game, all you'll be paid is $20,000; your better half will get only $30,000.

Many keno paybooks state: "Federal regulations require that all winning tickets must be presented for payment immediately after each keno game is played and before the start of the next game." However, any federal rule concerning when keno tickets must be submitted for payment—if, in fact, there is one—has long ago fallen into disuse.

So, what happens if nature calls—suddenly—and you're not able to get back to the keno lounge to collect your $100,000 winning ticket until after the next draw has started? Whether or not you'll be paid is entirely up to the casino.

The keno computer systems in use throughout Nevada have a "late pay" feature to provide for this contingency, and the casino's policy is programmed into the computer. Submit your tickets within the number of games subsequent to yours that are specified in the programming and you'll be paid.

The late pay policy differs greatly from casino to casino. Some casinos are very strict, and will refuse to pay any winning keno tickets submitted after the next game begins (unless the customer raises enough commotion). Others have a more liberal policy, and will not question a ticket brought to the keno counter five or even ten games late. A few casinos will pay until the ticket data has been purged from the computer, which is usually about two days after a game has been played.

So, despite what may be printed in the paybooks, if you've been distracted, perhaps by playing video poker or some other game, and you've temporarily forgotten about your keno tickets, don't assume that all is lost and throw the tickets away. There's a good chance that you will be paid, provided that you turn in the tickets within what the casino considers to be a reasonable time.

The very worst way to cheat yourself is to play a keno ticket with a high house percentage. Don't ever tell me that someone at the casino reached into your pocket or purse, took money from your wallet, and forced you at gunpoint to play any particular ticket.

To avoid cheating yourself, know the games you're playing as thoroughly as you know the stats of a ball team you've wagered on ... and, in keno, this means know the house percentage of every ticket you play. In addition, study the keno paybooks; they're furnished free by the casino, they don't cost you a cent. Make sure that you completely understand all of the rules the casino applies to their keno games.

Chapter 44

LIGHTNING STRIKES AGAIN!

Every keno player's fantasy is to hit a really big jackpot—just once! A big keno prize could pay off the mortgage on the house, buy a new car, and pay for Junior's college education. It could finance a cruise in the Caribbean, or an extended jaunt through Europe. It could mean an early retirement from the job, and an immediate retirement of all of the credit card bills.

But, if you're going to hit it really big in keno, why settle for just once? Make it twice, or even more!

Winston and Alice Hagen did. In January, 1989, playing an 8-spot $2.00 ticket, they beat odds of 1 in 230,115 to win the Gold Coast's progressive keno jackpot of $226,518.07.

A year later, "lightning" struck again for the Hagens. The Las Vegas couple won the Gold Coast's progressive jackpot for the second time, making them another $170,703.84 richer!

The next story sounds like it might have been written for the National Enquirer or one of the other tabloids. It may be hard to believe, but it's a factual account that proves that sometimes truth is, indeed, stranger than fiction.

The odds of catching all numbers on a 9-spot keno game are 1 in 1,380,688, so it's not often that someone hits all nine spots. Most casinos have a 9-out-of-9 hit about once a year. However, the

Winston and Alice Hagen, pictured holding their $170,703.84 winning progressive keno ticket, point to their previous $226,518.07 winning ticket displayed in the Gold Coast keno lounge.

Wanda Louise Smartt (C), with son Lloyd Daniels (L) and husband William Thompson (R). Smartt won $250,000 on a 9-spot Peppermill (Reno) keno ticket ... and then repeated with another $250,000 keno win three weeks later!

Peppermill Casino in Reno had two 9/9 winners in one month. What's more, the same person won both times!

On September 3, 1990, Wanda Louise Smartt, a home health care center owner, won $250,000 on a 9-spot $5.00 ticket.

She credited the win to her father, who had passed away in 1975. Smartt says that she was upset over financial problems, when her father came to her in a vision and said, "everything will be all right, don't worry." The message prompted Smartt to review her father's obituary, which contained the numbers she played on her winning ticket.

Then, on September 25—barely three weeks after the first win—Smartt looked up her father's name, Cornelius, in the book "Three Wise Men," and marked another 9-spot ticket with combinations from the numbers that, according to the book, symbolized his name. When all nine of Smartt's numbers were called, for another $250,000 win, she remarked, "My father's still taking care of me."

Michael LoMonaco, a shift manager of a baccarat pit at a major Strip resort, has won the Gold Coast's progressive keno jackpot three times. His most recent hit was for $402,819.01—one of the highest payouts in the history of keno!

Chapter 45

THE BIG CANADIAN KENO HIT

Early one morning in April, 1994, I began receiving a series of telephone calls from reporters for La Presse Canadienne (the Canadian equivalent of Associated Press) and on-the-air newscasters at several radio stations in Montreal, Quebec—all wanting to know the odds of catching 19-out-of-20 on three consecutive keno games.

I explained, patiently, that the odds of catching 12-out-of-12 in keno are 1 in 478,261,833. I told them it was possible that somewhere, sometime, a player might have actually caught 12/12, but, in my years of keno experience, I had never talked with anyone—a casino executive, keno manager, keno writer, or player—who'd heard even a rumor of anyone ever doing so.

What about catching 19/20, three times in a row? Ridiculous, I stated flatly. The odds of catching 19/20 just once are 1 in 2,946,096,780,000,000—making a single 19/20 catch approximately six million times more difficult than 12/12. It was not absolutely impossible, mind you, but as close to impossible as one can conceive. According to the law of probabilities, if a person played keno one game per second, 24 hours a day, 365 days a year, a 19/20 catch would be expected just once every 93,420,116 years.

As for catching 19-out-of-20 three times in a row? The

mind-boggling odds of that extremely unlikely event happening are 1 in 25,570,606,400,000,000,000,000,000,000,000,000,000, 000,000,000.

I was gleefully informed that Daniel Corriveau, a self-proclaimed computer whiz, had caught 19/20 at Montreal Casino in Quebec—not merely once, but (using different numbers on each ticket) on three consecutive keno games.

In a public announcement made immediately after his big hit, Corriveau bragged to the press that he had used the "chaos theory" featured in Spielberg's movie *Jurassic Park* to detect a flaw in the random number generator (RNG) system Montreal Casino used to select winning keno numbers, and he was therefore able to forecast the numbers that would be drawn in subsequent games. Corriveau reiterated an oft-repeated example of the chaos theory, saying that all events, no matter how trivial, are somehow related, and that the flapping of a butterfly's wings in Beijing affects the weather, albeit to a very minor degree, in New York City.

The Canadian media ran with the story. Instantly, Corriveau became a national folk hero. He was hailed as a common man who had beaten the system. He received more than his Andy Warhol-allocated fifteen minutes of fame.

Michel Crete, chairman of the board for Societe Des Casinos and president of Loto Quebec (the government organization that runs Montreal Casino), held a press conference to dispel a widely-circulated rumor that Corriveau had been banned from the casino. In response to a question posed by one of the reporters present, Crete offered, only half-jokingly, to hire Corriveau as a consultant for Loto Quebec.

Corriveau was swamped with other job offers as well. Writers vied for the rights to prepare a book about his stunning accomplishment. But, there were those—many of them—who had doubts about the honesty of Corriveau's win. Catching 19/20 once would have been a miracle. Three times in a row, a virtual impossibility. Eyebrows arched. Suspicions abounded. Montreal Casino pulled the plug on their RNG keno game and withheld payment of the prize money.

When it was disclosed that several backup computer chips for the casino's random number generator had been missing for a period of time, it was speculated that Corriveau might have managed to gain access to them and performed a little "reverse engineering." A criminal investigation was instigated by the Quebec provincial police, Surete du Quebec.

The supposedly missing backup chips turned out to be a red herring that clouded the real issue for a period of time. It's now believed that Imagineering Systems, Inc., the Reno-based vendor of the computer system, may have merely neglected to send the spare parts to the casino when the rest of the equipment was shipped; or, if the chips had been received, they were subsequently mislaid somewhere in the casino.

As part of the police inquiry, Corriveau took a polygraph test. He passed it with flying colors. Not long thereafter, Robert Poeti and Pierre LeMarbre, spokesmen for Surete du Quebec, stated that there was absolutely no evidence linking Corriveau with either the casino or the manufacturer of the keno computer equipment. Corriveau was completely exonerated of any criminal wrongdoing, the case was officially closed, and Louise Sansregret, Director of Public Affairs for Loto Quebec, announced that Corriveau was paid in full—$200,000 for each of the three hits, a total of $600,000.

It took me over three weeks of investigation (which involved making an extensive number of long distance phone calls to Montreal, Quebec; Reno and Laughlin, Nevada; and Bullhead City, Arizona; and required numerous meetings and phone conversations with many people in Las Vegas) before I was able to separate fact from fiction, rumor, and speculation, and arrive at the conclusion I reported in *Keno Newsletter* and my keno column in *Sports Form's Gaming Today*.

Along the way, the saga of Corriveau's win became curiouser and curiouser. While searching for the truth of the matter and attempting to unravel the mystery, I encountered evasiveness, intransigence, and stonewalling reminiscent of what Woodward and Bernstein must have faced when they tried to arouse interest in the minor burglary and break-in incident we now call Watergate. The air reeked with the unmistakable foul stench of coverup.

One might think that the Imagineering people and the Nevada Gaming Control Board would want to find out what happened at Montreal Casino as quickly as possible, before someone else learned Corriveau's secret and made a similar hit at a casino in Nevada. But, that did not appear to be the case. Rather, it seemed that everyone who might be able to shed some light on the Canadian incident wanted to bury the event under a rug. Perhaps they felt that anything they said might imbue them with liability.

It had been determined that Corriveau won honestly—that is, without gaining access to the inner workings of the RNG, either through theft or with the help of an accomplice working for the casino or the equipment manufacturer. But, everyone knew that something had to be wrong, someone had to be at fault. The triple 19/20 hit couldn't just happen, and nobody put any real credence in Corriveau's chaos theory explanation of how he was able to outsmart the computer.

Montreal Casino had purchased their keno computer system from Imagineering on a turnkey basis. Neither the Quebec Gaming Board nor the casino had inspected the random number generator before it was put into operation.

Additional facts soon came out. Almost from the day the keno operation was put on line, around the beginning of 1994, some Montreal Casino employees had noticed a repetition of number sequences in the RNG keno draws. Nothing was done to investigate the situation. Finally, on April 1st, one employee took it upon himself to write a memo to alert management to the problem. Inexplicably, the memo was pigeonholed somewhere within the casino for nine days and no action was taken until after Corriveau hit the casino for the $600,000.

As the casino is run by the government, the $600,000 award was, in effect, paid for by Canadian taxpayers—and they wanted to know why the game wasn't shut down at the first indication that something was amiss. Perversely, the fickle public lauded Corriveau for his accomplishment at the same time they soundly criticized the casino management.

Which brings us to the crux of the matter: Who was responsible for the fact that Daniel Corriveau was able to hit the casino for $600,000? Was it because Imagineering furnished faulty equipment to the casino? Or, were the casino executives to blame, because they knew (or should have known) that the supposedly random number sequences were repeating, yet did nothing? Perhaps, both parties have culpability. As of this writing, the issue has not been resolved.

When Imagineering executives were notified of the problem, they became noticeably and understandably nervous. Informed that a rumor was circulating that Loto Quebec was going to sue the company for recovery of the money paid to Corriveau, on the assumption that the RNG Imagineering supplied was defective, Carl Conti, vice president of Imagineering, blurted out in what appeared to be a show of bravado, "Let 'em try"—not exactly a remark to inspire confidence in Imagineering's other customers and potential customers.

Even the Nevada Gaming Control Board employees seemed anxious, for the Board had approved Imagineering's RNG for use in Nevada, where sixteen of the systems were operational— primarily for satellite keno games in large, spread-out casinos, where providing keno runner service between the main game and restaurants is impractical because of the distance involved.

It turned out that the random number generator supplied by Imagineering to Montreal Casino did not have a necessary clock chip. According to Ed Allen, Chief of Electronic Services for the Nevada Gaming Control Board, without the clock chip, an algorithm in the software was shortened. Moreover, the RNG failed to continuously scan the random number list between interrupts for the draws.

Allen further stated that the random number generator was certified in Nevada for continuous use with an uninterrupted power supply (UPS). In other words, once installed, the equipment should never be turned off, and there should be an emergency backup power supply in case of a power outage. Was that information provided by Imagineering to those in charge of Montreal Casino? If not, why not? And, if Montreal Casino was properly instructed in the use of the equipment, were the instructions ignored? Those questions have not yet been answered.

By itself, the absent clock chip might not have caused a problem. Some (but not all) of the RNG systems that had been operating in Nevada were also lacking a clock chip, according to Allen, but apparently there had been no repetition of number sequences—at least, not that anyone was aware of.

There was another, even more critical factor at Montreal Casino. In Nevada, keno games are run twenty-four hours a day; in Montreal, they were not. Each night, the RNG was turned off. Each morning, when it was turned on, the RNG selected numbers in basically the same sequence as the day before. Thus, it was the combination of two separate problems—the missing clock chip and turning the machine off each night (with the RNG starting over again each morning at the same point in the random number list)—that caused the number sequences to repeat noticeably in Montreal.

According to Ed Allen, the number sequence repetition at Montreal Casino was so patently obvious that "even your grandmother could have found it." So much for the chaos theory.

It's a wonder that someone didn't catch on to the fiasco at Montreal Casino long before Daniel Corriveau did. Indeed, any of the many keno players who routinely track and log keno draws could have spotted the repeating number sequences easily by simple observation.

Perhaps some of them did. Keno managers at other casinos, when discussing Corriveau's win, invariably volunteered that a smart player could have milked the game for years with smaller, yet very profitable, wins of 6/6, 7/7, and an occasional 8/8, and probably no one at the casino would have ever discovered what they were doing. It was clear that the thrill and notoriety of the huge triple win was as important to Corriveau as the prize money itself. In order to prove a point—that he could beat the casino—he made his big hit so obvious that no one could avoid taking notice. Were other players also aware that there was a flaw in the system, and using their knowledge to win, but on a lesser scale? That question may never be answered.

There is a very definite possibility that the Nevada casinos that were running RNG keno games without the clock chips could have been scammed also. Any employee who knew about the equipment's shortcomings could have turned the RNG off momentarily and back on again, and stood by smiling while an outside accomplice played a keno ticket marked with what both knew would be the winning numbers.

If you have any thoughts of duplicating Corriveau's feat, forget them. The RNG game was shut down at Montreal Casino. According to Bill Williams, president of Imagineering, all of their company's random number generators used in Nevada keno games have been inspected. Presumably, any missing clock chips have been replaced. Ed Allen stated that the Nevada Gaming Control Board is satisfied that all RNG games in Nevada are now operating satisfactorily.

Chapter 46

MONEY MANAGEMENT

There are probably as many different money management systems as there are gamblers. Two of the most popular systems are:

When you lose, increase your bets. The theory behind this system is that you'll eventually have a winning game, and with the one win recoup all of your losses. A lot of people have gone broke by chasing their losses this way.

When you're winning, increase your bets. Advocates of this method theorize that when you get a little bit ahead you're playing on the "casino's money," therefore, you don't have to be as careful with it as if it were your own. Followers of this system don't seem to realize that once you've won the money, it's yours, not the casino's—you really can take it home if you want to!

Casinos love players who subscribe to either of these "money management" systems. Note that in either instance, you're constantly increasing your bets!

While these systems may have some value when playing blackjack, roulette, or craps, they are of no use at all when playing keno. Keno is a very different type of game. Playing keno is like always picking the long shot at the horse races, but carried to the ultimate extreme.

The only money management system I know of that works in keno is the self-discipline system. Here's how to use it:

Before you ever enter a casino, determine how much money you're going to play. Note that I said *play*, not *lose*. It's time you started thinking positively.

Separate your "play money" from all other money you may be carrying; put it into a different pocket or section of your purse.

Never mix the money you win with your betting money. *Never* replay your winnings. When you're out of "play money," get something to eat or go home.

Follow this method, and if you've been lucky you'll take your winnings home instead of giving them back to the casino. If you've had only fair luck, you'll still go home with something. And, if you've had no luck at all, you've limited your loss to the amount you played.

One Man's Money Management System

It was after 3:00 a.m. A gray-haired gentleman had been sitting at the same video keno machine since the previous afternoon. He hadn't hit a jackpot large enough to make the bell ring, but had won smaller sums fairly often throughout the long evening.

"I'm really tired," he remarked to me. "I'd like to go home and get some sleep."

"Why don't you?" I countered.

"Oh, I can't go yet," he answered. "I never leave until either I run out of money or the casino runs out of money—whichever comes first!"

Chapter 47

WHEN YOU WIN BIG ...

What a great feeling! You've finally won BIG! There are few sights prettier than a stack of $100 bills being counted out to *you!*

If you were playing live keno you probably created quite a stir when you spontaneously yelled, "I've got it! I hit the big one!" The keno writers and other players were quick to congratulate you on your good fortune.

When you win big on video keno, a loud bell starts clanging, the change girls and passers-by cluster around, and a supervisor soon arrives with your payoff.

What happens next?

Be on your guard. You may have been spotted by a thief or mugger. Can you think of a better place to find someone who's carrying a lot of cash than a casino?

As soon as you've been paid off, go directly to the cashier's cage and deposit your winnings for safekeeping. Don't just put the cash in your wallet or purse and continue playing; you could become the victim of a pickpocket or purse snatcher.

If you've won at night, you might want to return to the casino during daylight hours to get your money from the cashier's cage. Even better, exchange your cash for a casino check.

If you really want to take the cash with you (so you can

shower it on your spouse when you get home), ask a security guard to escort you to your car. Lock your doors and start the motor before he leaves.

Drive carefully, and don't stop until you arrive at your destination. If you do get involved in a fender-bender, *don't* get out of your car until the police arrive. You could have been followed from the casino, and the "accident" not an accident at all, but a deliberate effort to get you into a vulnerable position.

And finally, don't think that you have to give all of your winnings back to the casino in the next few days or weeks. Forget the old adage, "I'm playing on *their* money." Once you win it, it's *yours!*

Chapter 48

REPORTING WINNINGS TO THE I.R.S.

Casinos are required, by law, to report net keno winnings of $1,500 or more to the Internal Revenue Service.

For example: If you win $1,501 on a $1.00 ticket, your net win is $1,500; the casino must prepare a W2-G form and submit it to the I.R.S.

However, if you win $1,510 on a $15.00 keno ticket, no form is required, because your *net* win is $1,495.

Before paying you a reportable amount, the casino must be satisfied that you are the person you claim to be. For this reason, you'll be asked to present identification, such as a driver's license and social security card. Along with your payoff, the casino will present you with a copy of the W2-G form for your use; it must be submitted with your income tax return.

The I.R.S. considers a multi-game keno ticket to be one game. Casinos will deduct the *total* wager from the *total* winnings of the ticket to determine if form W2-G is required.

What happens if you play several different tickets at one time, and your total net winnings are $1,500 or more—for instance, net wins of $800, $400, and $700?

It depends. If you cash in the $400 and $800 tickets, and your wife cashes in the $700 ticket, the casino probably won't make out the W2-G form.

If you cash in all three tickets yourself, some casinos will insist on writing up the W2-G. Other casinos are more lax, and will treat the payoffs as three separate wins.

Both players and casinos want to avoid the inconvenience of the W2-G form. However, remember this: Regardless of whether the casino is required to fill out the W2-G form or not, *all* gambling winnings must be reported on your income tax return.

You may deduct your losses from what you have won, *provided* that they are documented to the satisfaction of Internal Revenue.

In order to substantiate the amounts you made or lost on keno throughout the year, maintain a log of your keno bets and wins. It must be fully detailed, and written contemporaneously to your play and not after-the-fact. Retain cancelled checks made out to the casino. Keep your losing keno tickets, and have the keno writers make an "off-line" copy of the winning tickets for you. And, keep a file of anything else you can think of that can help verify your position.

If your records are accurate and complete, they will be accepted by the I.R.S. If not, you may be required to pay tax on your gross winnings—a most unpleasant circumstance!

In accordance with United States tax laws, if a keno winner is a non-resident alien, the casino will withhold 30% of net winnings of $1,500 or more, unless U.S. treaties or conventions specify otherwise.

Chapter 49

JUICE, COMPS, AND TOKES

Juice

In Nevada, *juice* isn't something that's been squeezed. Rather, it's the ability to "squeeze" favors from a person in authority to grant them. Having juice is having an inside edge, being able to exert influence.

If your checking account is in the mid six figures, you've got juice with the bank. If your brother-in-law owns the restaurant, you'll never need reservations ... provided that you keep on good terms with him. That's juice. And, if you're a high-roller in the casinos, your wish will be the casino's demand.

Comps

A *comp* is a freebie, a truncated version of the word "complimentary."

If you've got a lot of juice in the casinos, you'll get a lot of comps. They'll send a private jet to bring you to Las Vegas. You'll be met at the airport with a chauffeured limousine. Your deluxe suite will be comped, as will your meals, drinks, and shows. *All* of your needs will be taken care of while you're in town, and I won't elaborate on this further.

Even if you're not a high-roller, the policy at Nevada casinos is to make every player feel like a welcome guest, and, within limits, you'll get comps.

Play keno, the slots, or any of the table games, and before long a cocktail waitress will offer to bring you a beverage of your choice ... coffee, soft drinks, or the hard stuff. You're being comped.

If you're making fairly decent size wagers, someone in the casino will probably take notice. Sooner or later you'll be offered a comp for a meal in one of their restaurants—whether you've been winning or losing. If you're hungry and no one has taken the initiative to invite you to dine, seek out the department or casino manager and ask for a comp. Chances are you'll get it.

Bear in mind that comps never include gratuities. Don't be a cheapskate. When you're being comped, always tip according to the tab. If you err, make it on the generous side.

Tokes

In Las Vegas, a tip is called a **toke**. The word is probably a shortening of the phrase, "token of appreciation," and may be used as a noun or a verb.

Think about it. Toke makes a lot more sense than the word tip, which is an acronym for "to insure promptness." Today, most gratuities are given *after* a service has been performed ... too late to affect the quality or celerity of the accommodation rendered.

In medieval England, where the custom originated, you probably wouldn't be able to get a tavern wench's attention unless you tipped her in advance. If the tip was inadequate, any food or drink needed to be inspected thoroughly before it was ingested.

If it sometimes seems like everyone connected with a casino has his or her hand out, there's a valid reason. When tokes constitute a major part of a person's income, salaries are minimal. Your tokes are needed in order for them to survive. You might as well get used to it, tokes are a part of the cost of being in Las Vegas.

On the other hand, if you've received sullen or indifferent attention to your needs, toke accordingly ... and let the person's supervisor know why.

Now, for the subject of how much to toke. Figures vary dramatically, depending upon whether one is a big winner or loser, wants to impress his girlfriend, has had a few too many cocktails, and so on. The following seems to be the range at most casinos:

Parking attendant: $1.00, paid when your car is returned to you; more, if you drive a Rolls Royce or other luxury or exotic car.

Cocktail waitress: 50¢ to $1.00 per drink, if drinks are complimentary. If not, toke 15–20% of the tab.

Restaurants: 15% of the bill; more, if service was exceptional.

Change persons: Most people don't toke change personnel unless they win an amount that must be hand-paid (not paid in coins). Then, they toke the one who makes the cash payoff, who might or might not be the same person who supplied change. If one or two supervisors are involved in the payoff, they should receive part of the toke. Tokes for slots average 2% to 5% of the jackpot.

Keno writers and runners: If you've been given attentive service or special assistance, give the keno writer or keno runner a couple of bucks, even if you don't have any winners. When you win, a toke of 2% to 5% of the payoff is customary.

Remember ... you're never under an obligation to toke anything at all, and you can always toke more than these guidelines if you wish to do so.

Chapter 50

NICE PEOPLE

Each casino attracts a decidedly different clientele, partly as a result of varied marketing strategies and partly because people congregate where they feel most comfortable—and that means where they can find other people like themselves.

Some casinos seem to be filled with young professionals ... doctors, lawyers, accountants. Others have a lot of customers from countries in the Far East, South America, Europe, or the Middle East. At some places visitors from Hawaii or New York are highly visible. Certain casinos have a large local following. At others, the parking lots are always full of campers and RVs. Convention attendees, families with kids, Mr. and Mrs. Middle America ... every possible regional, ethnic, or social group can find a casino where they will feel right at home.

Similarly, inside the casinos, each game draws a different type of player. Baccarat players tend to be very intense, perhaps due to the high stakes. Craps shooters are exuberant, the noisiest players in the entire casino. Poker players are, truly, "poker-faced" —that is, expressionless. Roulette, blackjack, and slot players all have different types of personalities, at least while they're playing the game.

Which brings me to the "typical" keno player.

Keno is the slowest-paced game in the casino, and the relaxed atmosphere in the keno lounges rubs off on (or perhaps attracts) relaxed players. Look around a keno lounge and you'll find that the median age of keno players is somewhat higher than that of the average casino gambler. You'll see a lot of husbands and wives together, and groups of people who obviously know each other.

Keno players are down-to-earth, never pretentious. They're the folks-next-door from back home. In short, they're nice people.

The appellation "nice people" also applies to keno writers, runners, and keno managers.

A lot of casino employees probably regard their occupation as merely the source of income that enables them to pay their bills. I don't mean to imply that they don't like their jobs or their employers; most of them probably do.

But, there's something quite special about those who work in the keno department. I've never met a keno manager or writer who doesn't truly love the game. You can tell of the genuine affinity for keno by their attitude, the sincere way they discuss the game, and by the many anecdotes they love to tell. Another tip-off: The majority of those who work in keno play the game themselves.

More than a few of these wonderful, interesting people have been in the keno department of one casino or another for most of their careers. In these days of corporate management, I wonder how many CEO's and casino managers recognize the deep dedication of their keno department employees to the game of keno.

It's hard to conceive of true friendships being formed between players or between players and dealers at the blackjack, baccarat, or craps tables, but it's a common occurrence in the keno lounges. It would be strange if it were otherwise; nice people with a common interest, playing and relaxing in casual surroundings, practically guarantees that strangers will become acquaintances and acquaintances will become friends.

It isn't always all work and no play for those employed in the keno lounges. Jim Bopp, one of the "nice people" and keno manager at Binion's Horseshoe in downtown Las Vegas, relates a tale about a trick played time and again by veteran keno crews on naive break-ins, eager to learn the all-not-that-simple keno game —the punch-sharpener prank. Here's the story, as Bopp tells it:

In the old days, the man on the punch worked a heavy wrought-iron instrument with a round, honed punch for making draws, auxiliary tickets showing the winning numbers called or drawn. A keno vet, feigning irritation with the punch, would grab the new hireling and direct him to go to some neighboring casino for a punch sharpener.

The new man, of course, never suspected that punch sharpeners were in the same genre as left-handed screwdrivers and left-handed monkey-wrenches. Soon he would return with the message, "Their punch sharpener is in the shop for repair."

So, off to another keno game he'd be sent, and to another, until he sensed the deception or the old-timers had had their snickering kicks for the shift with a final, unpitying guffaw over their humiliated prey.

Perhaps this is the place to tell you about Ralph Schoup and Michael Gaughan.

Before computers were invented, figuring the odds and house percentages of keno games was a tedious task, prone to error, and beyond the capabilities of many who worked in the game. More than one keno payoff schedule was prepared "by guess and by golly." Conservative keno managers, hesitant to take the risk of creating tickets that might—heaven forbid!—wind up being in the players' favor, simply copied pay schedules from other casinos, hoping and praying that the person who devised them had come up with the right figures.

Ralph Schoup had a natural talent for numbers. He also had a lot of time to work on them, for he spent his days in bed in Mexico, ill with coal-miners' disease, a result of his many years in the mines.

His constant companion was a hand-crank Comptometer, a mechanical device with many keys, gears, wheels, cams, and levers. The Comptometer was a crude contraption, looking somewhat like one of Rube Goldberg's brainstorms, but it did have the capacity to multiply and divide very large or very small numbers. Lying in bed, Schoup laboriously and painstakingly calculated keno odds and house percentages, using a No. 2 pencil (with a well-worn eraser) to methodically record the results of his efforts in ledger books.

Fortunate indeed was the casino owner or keno manager who was able to latch on to one of Schoup's invaluable notebooks, for it gave the possessor a major competitive edge over the poor souls who had to figure the percentages from scratch.

Michael Gaughan is one of the down-to-earth, truly nice people I've been telling you about who've been captivated by the game of keno. Despite his busy schedule as CEO of the Barbary Coast and Gold Coast casinos in Las Vegas, he personally prepares the keno payoff schedules for both casinos. For him, it's a labor of love, not a burdensome chore.

Gaughan's always working on ideas that will make the game better for the players, and, at the same time, allow his keno departments to show a fair profit. His philosophy of giving customers more for their money is undoubtedly a prime reason for the success of his casinos and the large number of locals who frequent the Gold Coast and Barbary Coast.

Gaughan had one of Schoup's notebooks; it was one of his most prized possessions. But, one day when he wanted to revise some keno payoffs, the book was nowhere to be found.

Had it been misplaced amidst the normal clutter of a busy desk, then inadvertently thrown out? Did a corporate spy hired by a competitor surreptitiously remove it from his office? No matter, Gaughan needed Schoup's book and wanted it back. It was impossible to replace the book with another, for Schoup had long since succumbed to his illness.

Gaughan announced that he would pay a reward of $1,000 to anyone who located the notebook, no questions asked. His efforts to recover it proved to be futile, however ... the book was gone forever.

In the long run, Michael Gaughan's loss proved to be seren-dipitous for both him and for me. Jim Abraham, General Manager of the Gold Coast, was aware that I had developed the "Keno Analyst," a computer program that computes the odds and house percentages on virtually every type of keno game. With a little prompting from Abraham, Gaughan visited my office, and, after a short demonstration, was ecstatic. Not only could my program provide every answer that was in Schoup's notebook, it could do much more, instantly, and with greater precision.

These days, whenever Gaughan wants to change his casino's keno payoffs or to analyze keno tickets being offered by other casinos, he merely turns his chair around to the computer sitting on the credenza behind his desk, where the "Keno Analyst" awaits his request for information.

Nice people, yes; but, the game has had its ration of char-acters. Jim Bopp shared with me a couple of humorous tales from many years ago, and I'll pass them on to you:

During my first months as a keno writer, I was introduced—from a distance, fortunately for me—to an elderly gentleman, quite impressive with his silky white hair and perfectly tailored brown suit. But what a scourge he was to any keno game!

Over the years he duly acquired the sobriquet "Burma Road." His tickets were nickel-a-way ten-way-tens, using five groups of five numbers. The groups could not be lined off as groups of five should be, but had to be circled; for one group might be an outlandish 3, 8, 12, 23, and 51. And, the other groups were similarly interwoven among the eighty numbers on the ticket. They were very, very difficult to reproduce with the Chinese writing pen and black ink without making a mistake, especially when the error was really the player's, like marking six numbers instead of five in an intricate grouping. Then, Burma Road would positively excoriate the hapless writer calling him an inept so-and-so and threatening to have him fired.

None of this was good fun, either. A most unaccommodating, almost sinister curmudgeon he was. Nothing so completely spoiled our day than hearing someone say, "Oh, oh, here comes Burma Road!"

Then there was "Wild Bill," another of our notorious keno characters. I'll never forget the time when Wild Bill strode up to my station and handed me 646 14-spot tickets, all to be played the next game on the 70¢ rate. I shared them as equally as I could with the other four or five writers to spot in and condition with their frenzied brushes; for time lost is money lost. As they returned handfuls to me, I "clocked" the tickets on my Simplex. We had to look like a three-ring circus. We must have spent at least forty minutes preparing Wild Bill's tickets, much to the irritation of the other players in the lounge, all of whom were most anxious to get on with the game.

Wild Bill had promised each of us $30 apiece if we called him a good winner. Well, he did win something like $1,400 that game. The promised $30 was tucked in each of our shirt pockets, and also into the pocket of the casino owner, who just happened to walk by at the time.

"Play them again!" shouted the gleeful Wild Bill. So, we wrote and clocked and wrote and clocked them again.

Meanwhile, Wild Bill played craps, losing more, however, than he realized; because when all the tickets were ready, he had barely enough money left to pay for ten or twenty of them. There was nothing left to do but void out the remaining six hundred plus. What a night! We didn't run many games that memorable shift, having twice written 646 tickets and once voided over six hundred of them.

Quite a few months passed before we saw Wild Bill again. Because of some mishap, we were secretly informed, he had spent the time "working for the State up north."

I could fill a book with interesting tales from the keno lounges, as told to me by keno managers, writers, and players. Perhaps that will be my next effort.

Chapter 51

THE FUTURE OF KENO

In this book I've chronicled the game of keno, from its origin more than two thousand years ago in China to the present. In the United States, keno has grown hand-in-hand with legalized gambling, and it has realized a high level of popularity in the casinos of Nevada.

What does the future hold for keno?

For one thing, several companies in Nevada are working on a multi-casino progressive keno jackpot system to compete directly with state lotteries—probably to be called Megakeno. If the concept ever gets beyond the planning stage, all participating casinos in the state will be linked together by computer and share a common progressive jackpot, similar to the highly successful state-wide Megabucks, Fabulous Fifties, Quartermania, and Nevada Nickels slot machines. A fraction of each bet placed in the system will be added to the jackpot, which is likely to be in excess of several million dollars each time it's won.

Look also for more promotional activity in keno departments. Tournaments, contests, and merchandise giveaways are presently luring players to those casinos offering "something extra," and other casinos will be forced to follow suit in the future in order to remain competitive.

And, look for lower house percentages. The efficiency of computer-prepared tickets and multi-race games lowers the casino's cost of operations, and smart casino management will pass some of the savings on to the players. Raising the payoffs will bring keno PCs more in line with the percentages of other casino games.

Advanced technology may open the door to drastic changes in the way we play keno. Prototypes of self-service keno ticket vending machines—which may be operated by inserting coins or by charging the cost of tickets to a credit card—have already been displayed at gaming industry trade shows. Interactive television may even enable you to play keno in the comfort of your home in the not-too-distant future!

You'll be able to play keno in an increasing number of venues outside of Nevada. Legalized gambling is spreading at an explosive pace throughout the United States, and, for that matter, the entire world. You can be certain that wherever gambling is legal, keno will eventually be introduced.

The California and Oregon State Lotteries have added a version of keno to their other lottery offerings. Nebraska has had a number of keno games for some time. Keno went on line in Atlantic City casinos on June 15, 1994. Casinos in other states, Indian reservations, riverboats, and cruise ships, all have keno games now or in the planning stages.

No matter what the future holds for keno—improved computer systems, different types of tickets, new playing locations—the basics will remain the same. Just remember to follow the guide-lines set forth in this book and you'll always win more and lose less at keno!

GLOSSARY OF KENO TERMS

AGGREGATE LIMIT: The maximum amount that a casino will pay in any single game to all winners combined.

ALL-OR-NOTHING TICKET: A ticket that pays when no marked numbers are drawn or when all marked numbers are drawn.

AUTHORIZED GAME TICKET: See *outside ticket*.

BALL GAME: A keno game where the numbers are selected by drawing numbered Ping Pong type balls from a blower or cage.

BALLS: See *keno balls*.

BANK: The game's operating funds.

BANKROLL: Total amount of money available (or set aside) for wagering.

BET: See *wager*.

BINGO: A game that is often confused with keno, primarily because both games are played with Ping-Pong type balls. Adding to the confusion, the original name of *bingo* was *keno*.

BLANK: An unmarked keno ticket.

BLOWER: A mechanical device for mixing and dispensing keno balls.

BRUSH GAME: A game where the outside tickets are prepared by hand using a sable brush and Chinese writing ink. Now almost completely obsolete.

BUY-IN TOURNAMENT: A keno tournament that requires entrants to play a specified amount of money. Whatever players win during tournament play is paid in cash. In addition, entrants compete for cash prizes. Compare with *entry fee tournament*.

CAGE, KENO: See *keno cage*.

CAGE, WIRE: See *wire cage*.

CALL: To announce the numbers of drawn balls.

CALLER: A keno department employee who announces the numbers as they are drawn.

CATCH: A match of a number marked on a keno ticket with a number drawn by the casino. The term is said to have originated from the ancient Chinese concept of the game: "If there are twenty monkeys in eighty mountains, how many of them can ten soldiers catch?"

CATCH-ALL TICKET: A ticket that pays only when all marked numbers are drawn.

CATCH-ZERO TICKET: A ticket that pays only when no marked numbers are drawn.

CHASE THE NUMBERS: To change the numbers played each game.

CIRCLE: A line drawn around a group of numbers.

CLOSE: The time (immediately prior to a draw until after the draw is completed) when no tickets will be written.

COMBINATION TICKET: A way ticket played with a combination of wager amounts on the different arrangements.

COMP: Complimentary. Any beverage, meal, room, entertainment, or other merchandise or service furnished gratuitously by a casino to a player.

COMPUTER-GENERATED TICKET: An outside ticket that was printed by a keno computer.

COMPUTER, KENO: See *keno computer.*

CONDITIONING: Instructions written in the margin of a keno blank to specify the details of the wager.

CONTEST: An event sponsored by a casino wherein contestants compete for prizes. See *tournament.*

COUNTER, KENO: See *keno counter.*

CRAYON, KENO: See *keno crayon.*

DESK, KENO: See *keno desk.*

DEUCE: A group of two spots.

DRAW: Selection of twenty numbers from a pool of eighty. A single keno game.

DRAW SHEET: A keno blank that has punched-out holes to indicate the numbers selected in a given draw.

DUPLICATE TICKET: See *outside ticket.*

EARLY OUT: See *quit race.*

EDGE TICKET: A ticket with all 32 numbers on the perimeter of the grid marked.

ENHANCED PAYOFF: A payoff on a way ticket that is greater than the same ways would pay if written as separate tickets.

ENTRY FEE TOURNAMENT: A keno tournament in which players pay a fee to enter. Entrants do not win from tournament play, but compete only for the cash prizes offered. Compare with *buy-in tournament.*

EXACTA TICKET: A ticket with special payoffs when played for two consecutive games and (usually) the same number of spots is caught each game.

EXPECTED VALUE: The number of times a particular result is likely to occur (according to probability theory) compared with the total number of events.

FIELD: An uncircled group of spots.

FLASHBOARD: An illuminated sign that displays the results of the keno draws.

FRACTIONAL RATE TICKET: A ticket played for less than the rate indicated in the paybooks. Fractional rate tickets are usually way or multi-game tickets.

FREE PLAY: A win that entitles a player to repeat the wager without betting any additional money. A push.

GAME: See *keno game.*

GAMING AREA: An area where gambling activities are conducted; e.g., casino, keno lounge, restaurants, bars.

GOOSE: See *blower.* (The term *goose* is virtually obsolete.)

GROUP: Two or more spots circled or otherwise separated from the other marked numbers on a ticket.

HANDLE: The total monetary value of all wagers taken over a given period of time.

HIGH-END TICKET: A ticket that has higher payoffs than the casino's regular rate when most or all of the marked numbers are caught, but pays less than the regular rate (or not at all) when the minimum number of spots required for a payoff on the regular rate tickets is caught.

HIGH-LOW TICKET: A way ticket (marked with three groups of four numbers) that has a special payoff schedule based on the number of spots caught in each group. Now virtually obsolete.

HIGH-ROLLER TICKET: A ticket played at a rate that has a high minimum ticket price, e.g., $25.

HI-LO TICKET: See *high-low ticket.*

HIT: (a) A catch. (b) A win, especially a large win.

HOLD: The total of all wagers less all payoffs for a specified period.

HOUSE: The casino.

HOUSE EDGE: See *house percentage.*

HOUSE PERCENTAGE: The average percentage of the bets placed on a keno ticket that a casino expects to win. Computed according to probability theory.

INSIDE TICKET: A keno blank that has been filled out by the player and has been used to place a wager.

JACKPOT: (a) The amount of money paid to the winner of a progressive game. (b) Any large prize or payoff.

JACKPOT METER: An illuminated sign (usually incorporated into the flashboard) that displays the current progressive jackpot amount.

KENO: A game that developed from the centuries-old Chinese lottery. The player's goal is to match as many marked numbers as possible with the twenty numbers (out of eighty) drawn by the casino.

KENO BALLS: Ping-Pong balls numbered from 1 to 80 inclusive.

KENO CAGE: An enclosed area where the keno writers work.

KENO COMPUTER: A PC-type computer interfaced with a number of standard or specially-designed peripherals, controlled by proprietary software programs. Used for entering wagers, printing keno tickets, determining payoffs for winners, and preparing management reports.

KENO COUNTER: A counter at the front of the keno cage. Writers stand on one side of the counter (inside the cage) and players on the other (outside the cage). Similar in appearance to the teller windows in a bank.

KENO CRAYON: The black crayon used by players to mark their keno blanks.

KENO DESK: The area in the keno cage where the keno supervisor sits. It is usually in an elevated position behind the keno writers, so the supervisor will have a good view of everything that goes on in the keno cage and the lounge.

KENO GAME: The term *keno game* has three distinct meanings: (a) A single draw. (b) The casino's keno department. (c) A keno business run independently of a casino.

KENO LOUNGE: The casino area where keno is played. Typically, it consists of a keno cage and a seating area for players.

KENO MANAGER: The person in charge of all shifts of a keno department. He or she usually reports to the casino manager.

KENO PUNCH: A device used to punch the holes in draw sheets.

KING: An individually circled number.

KING TICKET: A way ticket that contains one or more kings.

LEFT / RIGHT TICKET: See *top / bottom ticket.*

LIMIT: See *aggregate limit.*

LIVE KENO: Keno played with keno tickets.

LOUNGE: See *keno lounge.*

LUCK: Temporary deviations from the results that can be expected by chance.

MARK: To prepare a keno blank by placing an *X* over the spots to be played.

MULTI-GAME KENO: A single keno ticket played for two or more consecutive draws.

MULTI-RACE KENO: See *multi-game keno.*

NET WIN: The amount of a payoff less the cost of the ticket. Often, the net win is actually a loss.

NEVADA GAMING COMMISSION: Nevada licensing authority.

NEVADA GAMING CONTROL BOARD: Nevada regulatory agency.

ODDS: The chance of winning a specified proposition. Expressed as a ratio.

OPEN: The time between draws during which tickets are written.

ORIGINAL TICKET: See *inside ticket.*

OUTSIDE TICKET: A ticket prepared by a keno writer and handed to the player as evidence of his bet.

PATTERN: (a) The design of the drawn numbers displayed on the flashboard. (b)

The design of the marked spots on a ticket.

PAY-ANY-CATCH TICKET: A ticket that has a payoff regardless of the number of spots caught.

PAYBOOK: A pamphlet supplied by the casino that lists the pay tables for the keno games offered, house rules, playing instructions, etc.

PAYOFF: Any return of money to a player. A payoff may be more than, less than, or equal to the cost of the ticket.

PAYOFF FOLDER: See *paybook*.

PAY TABLE: A chart that lists the payoffs for a given rate.

PC: House percentage.

PERCENTAGE: See *house percentage*.

PRIZE: A payoff. The amount of money won.

PROBABILITY: The chance that an event will happen. Always a number of one or less, expressed as a decimal or percentage.

PROGRESSIVE GAME: A game where the top prize increases each game (or time period) by a fixed amount or a set formula, such as a percentage of the total wagers placed on the tickets written in the preceding game.

PROGRESSIVE TICKET: A keno ticket for a rate that features a progressive jackpot.

PUNCH, KENO: See *keno punch*.

PUSH: A winning ticket with a payoff equal to the amount of the wager.

QUICK-PICK TICKET: A ticket with the numbers chosen randomly by the casino's keno computer.

QUIT RACE: To cash in a multi-game ticket before all of the games have been played.

RABBIT EARS: Tubes attached to the wire cage or blower, made of clear plastic or other material. After thorough mixing, keno balls are dispensed from a cage or blower into the rabbit ears.

RACE: A keno game. Even though the name "race horse keno" is all but dead, the term *race* lingers on.

RACE HORSE KENO: The name originally given to keno when the game was brought to Nevada. Now obsolete.

RACK: A tray where keno balls are stored when not in use.

RANDOM NUMBER GENERATOR: A computerized device used in some keno games to select winning numbers.

RATE: The ticket price for a single game or way using a specified pay table.

REGULAR TICKET: The simplest type of ticket, with one bet made on one group of numbers. Usually, a casino's regular tickets are the ones featured most prominently in their paybooks.

REPLAYED TICKET: An outside ticket used as an inside ticket on a subsequent game.

RNG: See *random number generator.*

RNG GAME: A game where the numbers are selected by a random number generator in the keno computer system.

ROAD MAP: A ticket marked with odd-shaped groups.

RUNNER: An agent of the player (though on the casino's payroll) who picks up bets in restaurants and lounge areas, places the bets with a writer at the keno cage, and returns the outside tickets to the players. The keno runner also collects on winning tickets and takes the money to the players.

SHIFT BOSS: A supervisor for a given shift. He or she reports to the keno manager.

SLEEPER: A winning ticket that is not cashed in.

SPECIAL: Any rate other than the casino's regular rate. A virtually meaningless term, which may explain why it is used by casinos *ad nauseam.*

SPLIT RATE TICKET: See *combination ticket.*

SPOT: Each number marked on a keno ticket.

STRAIGHT TICKET: Same as *regular ticket.*

TICKET: A piece of paper, usually newsprint, printed with an 80-square grid. See *inside ticket* and *outside ticket.*

TICKET PRICE: The total amount of money wagered on a single ticket for one or more draws.

TOKE: A gratuity given by a player to an employee. A tip.

TOP / BOTTOM TICKET: A ticket on which players have wagered that a winning number of spots will be drawn on one half of the ticket.

TOURNAMENT: An event sponsored by a casino, usually scheduled over a period of several days. Entrants compete against each other for prizes. See *entry fee tournament* and *buy-in tournament.*

VIDEO KENO: Keno played on a slot machine.

WAGER: The amount of money played on a ticket.

WAY: A bet.

WAY TICKET: A ticket with two or more groups of numbers circled or separated with lines to provide two or more wagers on one piece of paper.

WIN: (a) A catch of a sufficient number of spots to entitle a player to a payoff. (b) From the casino's standpoint, the hold.

WINNING NUMBERS: The twenty numbers drawn each game.

WINNING TICKET: A ticket that has a payoff of any size.

WIRE CAGE: A mechanical device for mixing and dispensing keno balls.

WRITE: To enter the ticket information in the keno computer. (Old definition: To make a duplicate of an inside ticket.)

WRITER: An employee who take bets, prepares outside tickets, and pays winners.

Pro-Master II Lotto/Lottery Strategies

- Prof. Jones' Ultimate Winning Strategy For Non-Computer Users -

Finally, after years of research into winning lotto tickets, Prof Jones has developed the ultimate in **winning jackpot strategies** for non-computer users! This **new power-house** gives you the **latest** in winning lotto strategies!

EASY TO USE - MINUTES A DAY TO WINNING JACKPOTS!

These **scientific winning systems** can be used successfully by anyone! Spend only **several minutes a day** inputting past winning numbers into the master templates and this **amazing system** quickly and **scientifically** generates the numbers that have the **best chances** of making you rich.

THE MASTER LOTTO/LOTTERY STRATEGIES AND MORE!

All the goodies of the Master Lotto/Lottery strategies - the winning systems, instruction guides, clear working template and bonus templates - are included in this **powerful winning strategy**, plus such **extra** features as the 3-Ball, 4-Ball and 6-Ball Sum Total charts. You also receive...

100 WHEELING SYSTEMS

That's right, **100** advanced Dimitrov Wheeling Systems - **double** the systems of the excellent Master Lotto/Lottery package! You'll be using the **most powerful** lotto and lottery winning systems ever designed.

BONUS

Included **free** with this **super strategy** are 15 Positional Analysis templates, 10 each 3-Ball, 4-Ball and 6-Ball Sum Total Templates and 15 Best Number templates!

EXTRA BONUS

Order now and you'll receive, **absolutely free** with your order, the extra bonus, 7 Insider Winning Tips - a conside guide to **extra winning strategies!**

$50.00 Off! This $99.95 strategy is now only $49.95 with this coupon!

To order, send $99.95 $49.95 plus postage and handling by check or money order to:
Cardoza Publishing, P.O. Box 1500, Cooper Station, New York, NY 10276

AVERY CARDOZA'S 100 SLOTS

THE ULTIMATE SIMULATION FOR SLOTS FANATICS!
For CD-ROM Windows 3.1 & 95 - Requires 486 or better, 8MB RAM

---

100 SLOT MACHINES - 27 VARIETIES!

GET READY FOR FUN! Enter Avery Cardoza's incredible 3D slots world where *you're really part of the action.* The ultimate in realistic slots simulations, play Las Vegas style slots at **100 incredible machines** (actually 101!) - so many that you'll be trying new machines for months!

WIN 5 MILLION DOLLARS! If you play big, you can win big - if you're lucky. Our **monster jackpot** payout gives you the chance to beat the game for all it's worth.

PLAY MACHINES OF EVERY STYLE! Play traditional slots with standard machines and "new" slots with our latest designs. Three reel slots with 1-3-5 payout lines, four reel slots with 1-3 lines, plus multiplier, wild symbol, bonus, progresssives, rocket-reels, wild Road Rally, and 25X payout pick-your zodiacs! Choose from $1, $5, $10, $50, $100, $500, and $1,000 machines, and 5¢, 10¢, and 25¢ ones too.

FREE BONUS BOOK! ($15.00 VALUE)! Receive the *Slots Strategy Guide* by gambling guru **Avery Cardoza**. This 160 page $15.00 strategy guide shows you how to win money at slots, and is included **free** for you!

STATE-OF-THE-ART GRAPHICS! Individually hand-enhanced **3D animation** frames, **full casino sound** with tunes written specifically for **winning** pulls on every machine, 3D artwork, and **complete realism** put you right at the helm of victory.

SUPER FEATURES - In addition to the strategy guide, there is a **complete player record** that tracks every conceivable stat for every machine in every denomination.

GRI MASTER KENO STRATEGY
David Cowles Professional Winning Strategy

Finally! David Cowles, the *world's foremost expert on keno*, and publisher of the *Keno Newsletter*, has released his **powerhouse strategy** on winning money at keno **exclusively** to Cardoza Publishing. It is now available for the **first time** and is only through us!!!

TIRED OF LOSING? LEARN HOW TO WIN!
Learn how to bet the tickets that provide the **highest payoffs** and push the percentages in your favor, how to increase winning tickets **tenfold** using way, combination and king tickets, how to set goals and plot a winning course, how to parlay small bankrolls into large fortunes by **playing smart** instead of betting haphazardly, and how to stretch your bankroll so you have **more winners** and chances for **big jackpots!**

WIN MORE PLAYING KENO! - Cowles reveals, for the first time, the magic *wager-to-win ratio* - a quick way to determine if a keno ticket is playable; also how to find the most **profitable** tickets, the *real scoop* on how to **pick winning numbers**, tips from the pros on how to **win keno tournaments** and contest prizes.

THE SECRET TO THE MOST PROFITABLE BETS
Many keno tickets are blatant ripoffs. Learn to avoid the sucker bets and how to **slash the casino edge** to the bone. You can't change the odds, but you can get the best deals once you learn the *secrets* revealed here.

FREE ROOM, FOOD & DRINKS? - You bet! They're yours for the taking. You just have to know *who, how* and *when* to ask - and then *how much*.

DOUBLE BONUS! - With your order, **absolutely free**, receive two insider bonus essays: *12 Winning Tips From the Pros* - the 12 master jewels that can increase winnings drastically; and *The 10 "Don'ts" of Keno*, mistakes made by both novice and experienced players. You'll never make these mistakes again. Be a winner!

To order, send $50 by check or money order to <u>Cardoza Publishing</u>